IMAGES
of America

THE CIVILIAN CONSERVATION CORPS IN ARIZONA

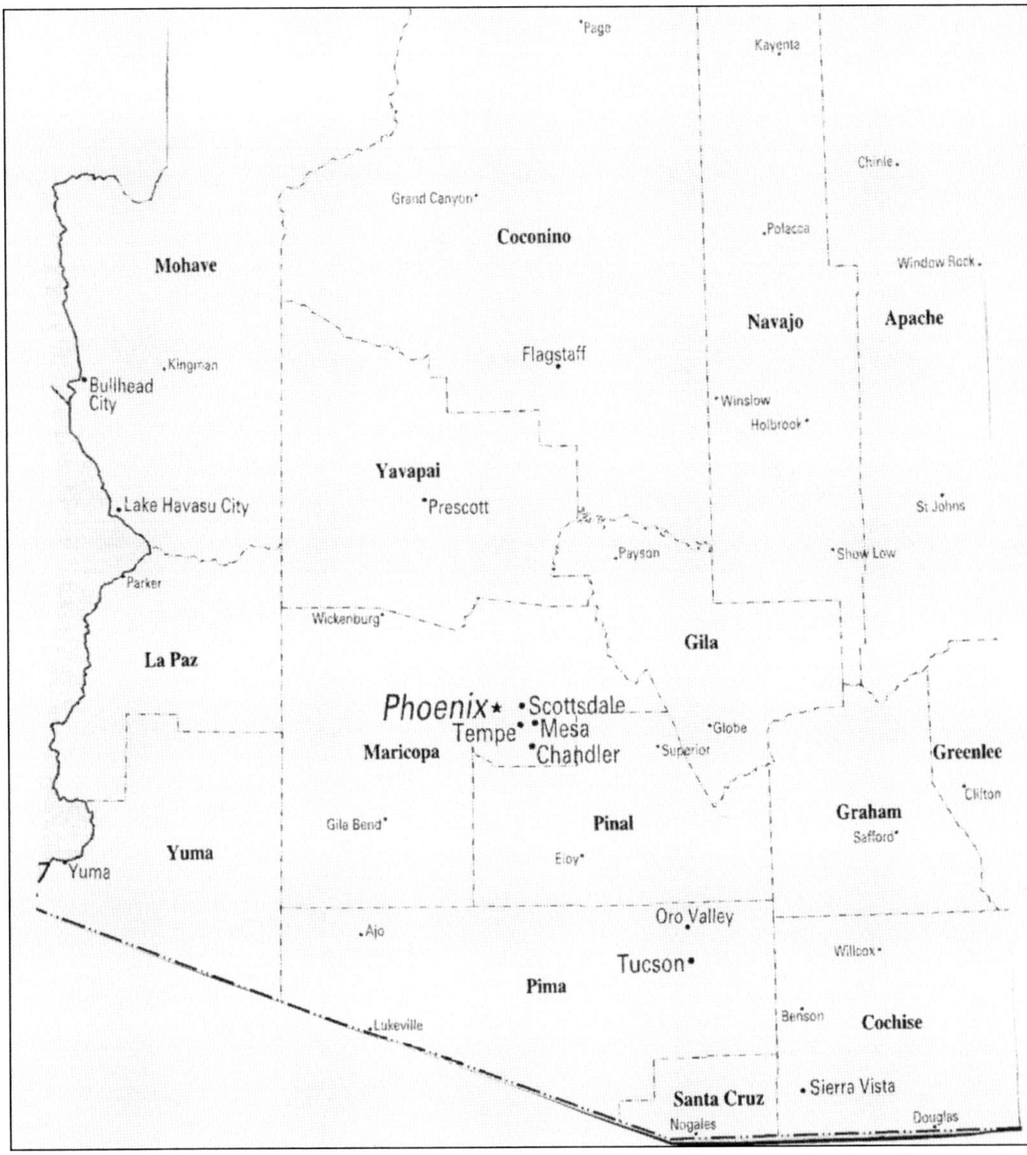

This map shows Arizona's major cities and 15 counties. The state during the Civilian Conservation Corps era had 14 counties. La Paz County was carved out of the northern part of Yuma County in 1983. Phoenix in Maricopa County is the state capital. Other major cities are Flagstaff, Tucson, and Yuma. Much of the state is composed of small communities, ranches, farmland, Native American reservations, and federal and state land. (US Department of the Interior, *The National Atlas of the United States*, nationalatlas.gov.)

On the Cover: Pictured around 1934, enrollees from Company 818, Camp NP-1, Grand Canyon, are cutting aspen logs for the North Rim boundary fence. The North Rim's high altitude necessitates closing it during the winter. CCC boys worked there every summer between 1933–1942. (Courtesy of Grand Canyon National Park Museum Collection.)

IMAGES
of America

The Civilian Conservation Corps in Arizona

Robert W. Audretsch and Sharon E. Hunt

ARCADIA
PUBLISHING

ISBN 978-1-4671-3097-4

Published by Arcadia Publishing
Charleston, South Carolina

Printed in the United States of America

Library of Congress Control Number: 2013941935

For all general information, please contact Arcadia Publishing:
Telephone 843-853-2070
Fax 843-853-0044
E-mail sales@arcadiapublishing.com
For customer service and orders:
Toll-Free 1-888-313-2665

Visit us on the Internet at www.arcadiapublishing.com

To the CCC boys, whose enduring work ensured that generations of Americans could enjoy this country's natural wonders

Contents

Foreword

The Civilian Conservation Corps is a story of people, places, and accomplishment. For me, it's always exciting when a new work on Civilian Conservation Corps history hits the bookshelves. When the new work in question is authored by researchers who have an established track record working with CCC history and, perhaps more importantly, interacting with the men who labored in the CCC, my excitement is multiplied. Naturally, I'm thrilled to see the release of *The Civilian Conservation Corps in Arizona* by Sharon E. Hunt and Robert Audretsch. Sharon and Bob know their subject, and they know where to find images and stories about the CCC that you'll not find in print anywhere else.

It seems there are two primary reasons to be interested in the story of the CCC: people and places. The people of the CCC were our people, whether we know it today or not, and the places they worked are the places that continue to hold our hearts. They are the places we go to find quiet beauty or perhaps recreational fun—even today, more than 70 years after the closure of the last CCC camp.

By most estimates, some three million young men worked in the CCC between 1933 and 1942, so it should come as no surprise that every one of us has a connection, even if somewhat remote, to the CCC. I'm the grandson of a US Forest Service foreman who worked almost exclusively in CCC camps during the lifespan of the program, which represented nine years of useful employment he might not otherwise have had if not for the New Deal. Furthermore, I'm the son of a CCC enrollee who served a short stint in a CCC camp in Idaho Springs, Colorado, from 1940 to 1941. It means something to me when someone I meet says, "My uncle was in the CCC," or "My husband's brother worked in the Cs." I suspect that for every person who knows their family's connection to the CCC, there are a couple others who have no idea that someone in their family was a soil soldier in Roosevelt's forest army.

If our individual connectedness to the CCC is not obvious through the people in our lives, then the story of the CCC is surely woven into our collective consciousness through the astounding range of places where the CCC and its enrollees worked. Visit any national park or forest whose history dates back to the 1930s or before, and you'll likely be treading ground where the CCC had an impact in the form of recreational improvements, tree planting, and firefighting. Travel through the vast stretches of the Midwest and throughout the area once referred to as the Dust Bowl region, and you'll pass through areas where CCC enrollees worked on erosion control and irrigation projects. By design, much of this work may go unnoticed, perhaps like the individuals among us whom we never knew were CCC enrollees.

So then, if the story of the Civilian Conservation Corps is a story of people and of places, this book is a story of the people and places that made the CCC a success in Arizona. Yet, what you have here is so much more than that. Sharon and Bob have really created a photo album that chronicles the people and places of the CCC in Arizona in a way never before seen in my recollection. The images and text here represent what the photo album of a CCC enrollee would have looked like had he worked in camps across the state, chronicling what might have been the biggest adventure of a young man's life if a world war hadn't intervened so abruptly and so violently in 1942.

Sadly, many of the people in this story are gone, which makes this book all the more special as a record of the work done by the CCC in Arizona. On the bright side, the places where the CCC worked largely remain, and the improvements they made there still exist for us to see and enjoy today. This brings up a third aspect of the CCC that makes it appealing today: accomplishment. What the CCC accomplished is astounding and somewhat incomprehensible for me on some levels—even after more than two decades of study of the subject. In Arizona, enrollees labored at the bottom of Grand Canyon, on the shoulders of Bill Williams Mountain, in the forests outside Payson, in the deserts around Phoenix and Tucson, and in a thousand other Arizona places. On the reservations, the boys of the CCC built tourist amenities, installed irrigation improvements, performed soil conservation work, assisted in archeological digs, fought fires, and searched for lost hikers. The range of work is staggering, and in the pages that follow, you will get a glimpse of what was accomplished by a peacetime army of young men during the Great Depression. The images and text here offer a lesson in what cooperation between government agencies can produce when coupled with a young workforce that is eager for an opportunity, even as it stands in the shadow of a gigantic national economic depression during a time that seems to offer little or nothing in the way of a fighting chance at success. In the process, that young workforce learned a thing or two about how to work and get along with others and what it means to create something that is of lasting value both personally and to the nation. That young workforce was also being prepared for an even bigger struggle, a struggle that few of them saw coming.

The Civilian Conservation Corps very likely saved my mother's family during the Great Depression, so it isn't an exaggeration to say that I am occasionally brought to tears by the story of the CCC. However, there is a deeper reason that any one of us might become emotional at the thought of those CCC boys working so hard in the 1930s and 1940s. The images in this book show young men on the cusp of military service in a worldwide war on fascism. After their time in the CCC, these men went on to serve on the home front, or they were deployed to combat theaters around the globe. Some did not live to see the end of the 1940s, did not survive to enjoy the recreational and aesthetic improvements on which they'd labored so hard as CCC enrollees. That fact alone makes a book like this all the more valuable to each and every one of us. These are our people, accomplishing great things in the places we know and love here in Arizona.

—Michael I. Smith
Past SW Regional Director, NACCCA/CCC Legacy
President NACCCA/CCC Legacy Chapter 44, 2003–2013
CCC Legacy Lifetime Member

Acknowledgements

This work owes much to the assistance and knowledge of many individuals.

First of all, we would like to acknowledge the CCC personnel and their families who through the years have told us of their experiences, shared their photographs, and allowed us to tell their stories. Their kindness, humor, and work ethic will forever stay with us. We would like to particularly thank enrollee and local experienced man Elson Alvarez and his children Martha, Al, and Sylvia; Ernest Bruss, son of camp commander Ernest H. Bruss; enrollee Eduardo "Buck" Quiroz Castillo and his son Daniel; Harold David Kennedy, nephew of enrollee Harold Patterson; enrollee Merle Timblin and his daughter Melissa; and enrollee Tomas H. Vega and his daughter Loretta Velasco.

The following individuals and institutions graciously provided images and information: the Baumgartner family; Andrea Bornemeir, Pipe Spring National Monument; Phil Brown, ranger, Saguaro National Park West; R. Sean Evans, Special Collections, Northern Arizona University Cline Library; Flagstaff City–Coconino County Public Library; William Gillespie, forest archaeologist, Coronado National Forest, US Forest Service; Gwenn Granados and Randy Thompson, National Archives and Records Administration–Pacific Region (Riverside); John M. Herron, BLM archaeologist, St. George, Utah; John Irish; Flagstaff author Jane Jackson, who graciously shared her interviews of CCC men; Daniel McGrew; Robert J. Moore; Eugene Morris, National Archives at College Park, College Park, Maryland; Mike Quinn, Grand Canyon National Park Museum Collection; Petrified Forest National Park; Matt Smith, Petrified Forest National Park Museum Collection; and Jim Steely.

Thanks from Sharon also go to editor Alyssa Jones of Arcadia Publishing, who provided timely and beneficial assistance.

The following abbreviations are used throughout for image courtesies: National Archives at College Park, College Park, MD (NARA MD); National Archives and Records Administration–Rocky Mountain Region [Denver] (NARA–RMR) / Pacific Region [Riverside] (NARA–PR); Harold David Kennedy (HDK); William Gillespie, US Forest Service (WG, USFS); US Forest Service, Southwestern Regional Office (USFS, SWR); Ernest Bruss (EB); Elson Alvarez (EA); Eduardo and Daniel Castillo (E&DC); Merle Timblin (MT); John Irish (JI); Petrified Forest National Park Museum Collection (PFNP); Robert J. Moore (RJM); Tonto National Forest (TNF); Grand Canyon National Park Museum Collection (GCNP); Kaibab National Forest (KNF); Flagstaff Monuments Museum Collection (FMM); Coconino National Forest (CNF); US BLM, Kingman Field Office (BLM); Pipe Spring National Monument Museum Collection (PSNM); Tomas H. Vega (THV); and author's collection (AC).

INTRODUCTION

Delay is fatal to a starving man.

—*Prescott Evening Courier*
April 4, 1933

America was at its most desperate during the time of the Great Depression. The stock market had collapsed, banks were failing, families were losing their farms, unemployment was at a staggeringly high level, and people were hungry.

Statistics from this era tell a grim story. The stock market had lost 80 percent of its value. Three states and over 1,300 cities, counties, and school districts were in bankruptcy. Thousands of banks had failed. Auto production was down 80 percent, while steel production and new housing starts were down 88 percent. Farm foreclosures exceeded 20,000 a month, and farm income had dropped 60 percent. One of the hardest-hit groups was single young men ages 15–24. Their unemployment rate was over 25 percent, with another 29 percent working only part time. Many of them had taken to "riding the rails" in search of employment.

The nation's natural resources were also declining. On the Great Plains, decades of indiscriminate plowing of the prairie followed by drought created the Dust Bowl. Tens of thousands abandoned their farms, resulting in one of the largest internal migrations in US history. Forested land had been reduced from 500 million to 100 million acres.

The federal government responded to these harsh realities by establishing the New Deal, a package of domestic economic programs enacted in the mid-1930s focused on the three Rs: relief, reform, and recovery. The relief programs included the Federal Emergency Relief Act (FERA), the Civil Works Administration (CWA), the Works Progress Administration (WPA), the Public Works Administration (PWA), and the Civilian Conservation Corps (CCC).

According to historian John Salmond, the CCC program was a catalyst bringing "together two wasted resources, the young men and the land, in an attempt to save both." Its origins were in the mind of Franklin Delano Roosevelt, a conservationist who as the New York governor sponsored Temporary Emergency Relief Administration legislation. Under this plan, by 1932, 10,000 men were employed planting trees, fighting forest fires, building roads and trails, and developing recreational facilities throughout the state. By the early 1930s, the idea of sending unemployed people to work in the forests had gained acceptance in at least a half-dozen European countries.

Roosevelt was sworn into office as president on March 4, 1933, and after meeting with his advisors March 9–14, he introduced draft legislation to Congress on March 21. Ten days later, after overwhelming congressional support, the president signed the legislation creating the CCC. Unemployed US citizens were to be given jobs "in the construction [and] maintenance . . . in connection with the forestation of [US] lands . . . which are suitable for timber production, the prevention of forest fires, floods and soil erosion, plant pest and disease control, the construction, maintenance or repair of paths, trails, and fire lanes in the national parks and national forests, and such other work . . . as the President may determine to be desirable." The authorizing legislation (PL 5-73) and implementing Executive Order 6101 (April 5, 1933) totaled just two printed pages. Labor leader Robert Fechner was appointed the director of the CCC on April 5.

As the March 1933 debate in Congress over Roosevelt's conservation measure progressed, a few Arizona newspapers weighed in with editorials. The Phoenix *Arizona Republic* opined that the measure was merely a stopgap and another dole: "It may be that there will never be an adequate return." A *Prescott Evening Courier* editorial took a more positive approach. The president was praised for his worthwhile efforts. The Prescott newspaper in a later editorial stated that enrollees will "feel a source of pride . . . that they are making a great contribution to the welfare of their country for years to come." The *Phoenix Gazette* was a bit more upbeat than its sister Phoenix paper, stating, "Action is the Roosevelt slogan."

As soon as the legislation authorizing the CCC was signed, the government moved into high gear, and Secretary of Agriculture Henry Wallace telegraphed state governors inviting them to send a representative to a conference in Washington, DC, on April 6. On April 5, the *Phoenix Gazette* noted that the first 25,000 CCC enrollees would be sent to conditioning camps with most coming from eastern US cities. The following day, the *Arizona Republic* announced that W.W. Lane, a former state highway engineer, would be at the Washington meeting as Arizona's representative. Apparently, the Washington, DC, conference supplied few details beyond the state quota of 1,000 enrollees. Although the state plan for the first year called for 1,000 junior enrollees, it also called for 825 locally experienced men, 100 veterans, and 5,484 American Indians.

Even though the April 6 meeting was said to be lacking in details, Arizona officials were quick to announce their plans. The following day in Flagstaff, county engineer J.B. Wright and Forest Service officials announced ambitious road-building plans. Wright stated that 3,000 men would be working in the Coconino National Forest when the program was in full swing. On the same day, the *Phoenix Gazette* announced plans for CCC work in the Coronado National Forest as well as in the Coconino and Tonto National Forests. In Holbrook on April 7, Sitgreaves National Forest Supervisor F.L. Kirby announced his list of CCC projects.

However, on April 8, controversy was aired when some Maricopa County State House representatives protested the transporting of out-of-state unemployed men into the state when Arizona already had 10,000 people out of work. Their views were shared in a telegram to Arizona senator Henry Ashurst. While Ashurst took the side of those protesting the out-of-state men, Gov. Benjamin Moeur vigorously defended the president. "There are no state lines regarding this work, as it is national in scope. I sincerely hope that every citizen in the state will co-operate with the President . . . We are sorely in need of every outside dollar we can obtain." He stated that $10 million would be coming to the state in federal programs and that much of that money would be used for the purchase of food and materials within the state. He concluded that Arizona would receive a generous share of federal monies and credited that to Lane's knowledge of forests and soil erosion and the influence of Senators Ashurst and Hayden. Moeur went on to vigorously support the CCC throughout his term as governor, 1933–1937.

The idea of rejecting outside labor was not held everywhere. A business group from Douglas in southern Arizona sent telegrams supporting "even outside labor" for the CCC program. In Flagstaff in northern Arizona, the chamber of commerce supported the CCC program, fearing that numerous protests would result in a net loss of jobs to the state. Ultimately, the controversy over outsiders was solved with the CCC agreeing to assign men first to their home state and to assign only men recruited in the Eighth Army Corps area to Arizona. Preference was to be given to locating CCC camps where local cooperation was evident.

Meanwhile, delays and confusion began to plague the new program. Fechner began a quick reorganization. Again, state officials were beckoned to Washington, DC, and Stuart Bailey of the State Board of Public Welfare and State Engineer T.S. O'Connell flew east. Bailey was designated the first Arizona CCC representative. Soon after, state enrollment agencies began to accept men. Florence Warner, executive secretary of the State Board of Public Welfare, was listed in the first

Washington reports. On April 21, Fechner announced Arizona would initially be given 28 camps, housing a total of 5,000 enrollees.

But the enrollment of Arizona boys was not going smoothly. The *Arizona Republic* reported on April 26 that the first recruits would leave the following day for conditioning at Fort Bliss, Texas. The next day, the newspaper reported that the men were delayed indefinitely as Fort Bliss was overcrowded. The Jerome newspaper, in a United Press story, faulted the lack of transportation. On May 4, Governor Moeur announced that Fort Sam Houston had advised him that Fort Huachuca in southern Arizona would take 250 enrollees. Moeur advised the military that Fort Tuthill near Flagstaff would be available for conditioning, but apparently he did not receive an answer regarding this suggestion. On May 5, Bailey told the *Arizona Republic* that nearly all the 1,000 young enrollees had been selected. As it turned out, Director Fechner, the Forest Service, and the War Department needed to streamline what was a slow and convoluted process.

On May 10, Fechner met with the CCC Advisory Council and requested that Col. Duncan Major, the War Department representative, determine how the CCC could speed up the process to meet the president's goal of 250,000 enrollees in camps by July. The military requested, and was granted, new powers to cut red tape and hold wide authority over the movement of new enrollees. "Where questions arise not covered by instructions or when necessary to change such instructions you are authorized to act" and report later, commanders were told. Quickly, the military enacted massive decentralization and set a goal of enrolling 8,540 men per day, a greater number than processed for World War I. On June 1, a peak daily enrollment of 13,843 men was reached.

Arizona began to enroll men a bit faster. On May 9, Bailey announced that 215 recruits were assembling in Tucson, Nogales, Bisbee, and Douglas for physical exams. Those accepted were to be moved by army trucks that afternoon to Fort Huachuca. Three days later, Governor Moeur requested that Arizona counties assist with enrollee transportation. On May 14, the *Arizona Republic* reported that he was promised the loan of vehicles by 10 of Arizona's 14 counties. Coconino County promised three dump trucks, three graders, and three tractors. Other counties and cities followed that example, even volunteering private vehicles. The new enrollees were soon to arrive.

Enrollees were organized into companies of 200 men. The CCC Eighth Corps area encompassed Arizona, Colorado, New Mexico, Oklahoma, Texas, and Wyoming (excluding Yellowstone National Park). Companies in this corps usually had an eight in their company number, such as Company 819, located at Grand Canyon, or Company 2855, located at Safford. Most CCC companies were composed of junior enrollees, ages 17 through 25. Companies composed of military veterans were designated with a V, for example, Company 1826V. Companies composed of only African American men were designated with a C, for colored, for example, Company 2871C. Arizona had only one African American company. This company, located at Fort Huachuca, was made up mostly of Texas enrollees and was listed on only one report. Their existence in Arizona was short-lived due to economic movement.

The designations of the camps were based on the technical agency overseeing the work. Camps at national parks were designated NP, for example, NP-1 at Grand Canyon. Forest Service camps were designated with F, for example, F-30 at Madera Canyon. For a complete list of these abbreviations, see appendix II.

The first companies to be established in Arizona were Company 805 at Safford (F-14, Crook National Forest) and Company 806 at Globe (F-16, Crook National Forest) on May 23, 1933. The following day, Company 807 arrived at Payson (F-23, Tonto National Forest). Many men arrived by a special train of 525 people originating in San Antonio, Texas. About three-quarters of the enrollees in these first three camps were Texans, with the rest being Arizonans. By August 31, 1933, the date of the first military report, a total of 23 companies were at work statewide. Additionally, over 30 Arizona CCC camps were planned for American Indian reservations.

The War Department was responsible for the administration, finance, transportation, and supervision of the camps. It oversaw the initial conditioning the enrollees underwent before being assigned to camps and transported enrollees to and from camps. The War Department also provided physical examinations, medical care, and hospitalization. Every camp had a physician who was almost always a commissioned military officer. A commanding officer and subaltern supervised and disciplined the enrollees while in camp. Although the enrollees' lives outside of work were controlled by the military, they were not governed by strict military discipline.

The Army pulled officers and noncommissioned officers from teaching and staff jobs in order to fill the frantic need for camp leaders. Equipment and clothing that had been in storage since the end of World War I were quickly distributed. Sometimes the clothing and equipment were so aged they had to be handled carefully.

Fred Lancaster, an enrollee in a Prescott National Forest camp in late 1933, described walking carefully in his boots lest the soles fall off. He wrote that "[you] soon became adept to sliding into your bunk from the head, lest putting all your weight on one spot would rip the rotten canvas out of your cot." At first, the meals were outdoors until the kitchen and mess hall were finished, so with a little wind everything was "well flavored with sand." Enrollees moved into their barracks even before they were finished. Candles supplied the light at night until a light plant arrived. At first, Lancaster reported all work was done by hand until the needed equipment arrived. They built 18 miles of road and 20 miles of fence with picks, shovels, and wheelbarrows.

A project superintendent and his staff from the governmental technical agencies involved in the CCC supervised the camp work projects. These agencies in Arizona included the Department of Grazing (now the Bureau of Reclamation), the Department of State Parks, the Federal Reclamation Project, the National Forest Service, the National Park Service, and the Soil Conservation Service. Local experienced men (LEMs) with specialized skills also assisted and supervised the enrollees' work projects.

To be eligible to enroll in the CCC, a young man had to be between the ages of 17 and 25, and priority was given to men from families on relief. Later in the program, the age limits would change slightly, and the relief requirement would be relaxed. The age requirements differed for people in three broad categories: veterans (Executive Order 6129, May 11, 1933); local experienced men (LEMs), who acted as role models and work project supervisors; and American Indians organized into separate Indian Division companies. The prospective young enrollee had to be a US citizen in good health. An enrollee could not be married, have children, or have a criminal record. They had to have dependents such as a mother, father, or siblings. The program provided his basic housing, food, and medical care. He was paid $30 per month for his work and was required to send home $25 of this to his family.

Service in the CCC was voluntary, and boys enrolled (they did not enlist) for six months. The CCC calendar was made up of six-month enrollment periods that generally began in April and October. Enrollees could serve longer than six months if their behavior was acceptable and the budget allowed it.

Enrollees could advance to the levels of assistant leader and leader and receive a higher rate of pay: $36 per month for assistant leaders and $45 per month for leaders. Enrollees who served honorably were given an honorable discharge certificate. Those completing a program of formal job training received a proficiency certificate. Upon the enrollee's discharge, these two documents were frequently helpful in obtaining civilian employment.

Over three million men served in the CCC, where they learned job skills, gained an education, and developed the ability to work as a member of a team. These men went on to serve their country honorably in World War II and rebuild the country after the war. Their substantial accomplishments in the CCC included planting three billion trees, spending 4.2 million man-days fighting forest fires, arresting soil erosion on more than 20 million acres of farmland, building 125,000 miles of road, and building or improving 800 national and state parks. Their work endures today in parks, forests, and farmland across the nation—a living legacy to their lives and work.

One

Southwestern and South-Central Arizona
Pima, Santa Cruz, and Yuma Counties

Southwestern and south-central Arizona are home to the Sonoran Desert, the Tucson metropolitan area, small communities, the Tohono O'odham Nation, cattle ranches, and sections of the Coronado National Forest. The work of the CCC in this part of Arizona focused largely on improving the forests, arresting soil erosion on grazing lands, and constructing recreational facilities. Tucson, the capital of Pima County, served as the headquarters for the Tucson District of the CCC, which stretched across Arizona from California to New Mexico and from the US–Mexico border to the Gila River south of Phoenix. District headquarters was responsible for staffing the camps and attending to the enrollees' transportation, housing, educational, medical, recreational, and food needs.

Pima County had forestry, grazing, soil conservation, and state park camps as well as a county park and a municipal area camp in Tucson. The CCC performed erosion-control work throughout the county. They developed many recreational areas, particularly in Tucson Mountain Park, the Coronado National Forest, Colossal Cave, and what is now Saguaro National Park. Residents and visitors to the area derive great pleasure from the CCC-constructed recreational facilities. The work the CCC accomplished helped lead to the Tucson area's phenomenal growth as a population center and as a tourist destination.

Santa Cruz County is the smallest Arizona county. Camps here included forestry and soil conservation camps. The CCC built recreational facilities, roads, water-control features, and fences in the Coronado National Forest and constructed water-control features in communities and ranches throughout this county.

Yuma County was split into two counties in 1983, with the northern part becoming La Paz County. Yuma County had two Bureau of Reclamation camps. These camps worked on the Yuma Project, a Colorado River irrigation project that included an extensive system of canals, laterals, and drains. They updated and improved many features of the system, constructing laterals, cleaning canals, lining canals and laterals with concrete, and leveling large piles of silt material removed from canals. They also eradicated weeds and gophers, did landscaping, strung telephone lines, improved roads along canals, and placed pipelines.

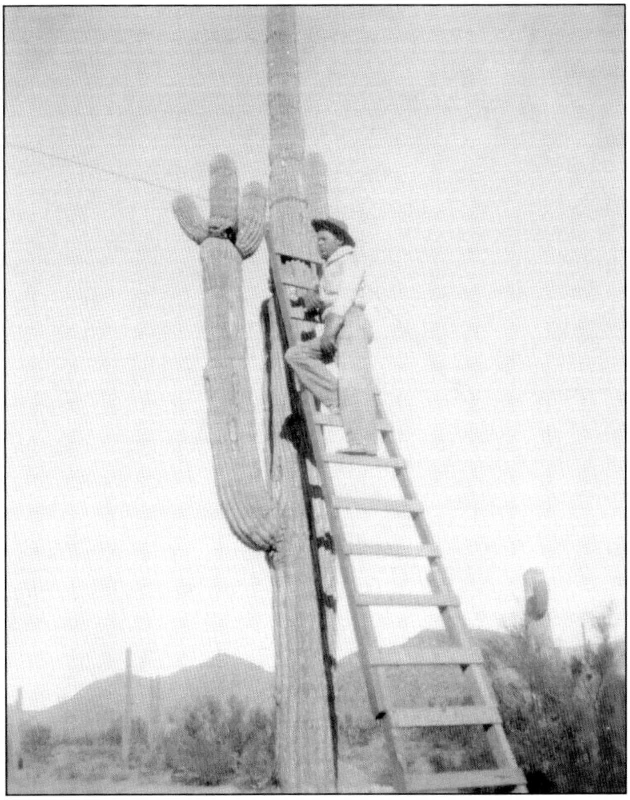

Tucson Mountain Park on the western edge of Tucson was established in 1929. When the CCC became available in 1933, two camps were requested for the park. Camp SP-7 lasted only one season, from October 1933 to May 1934, because the water supply was inadequate and unreliable. Here, a SP-7 enrollee is stringing a telephone line through the arms of a majestic saguaro, an iconic symbol of the Sonoran Desert, in March 1934. (NARA MD.)

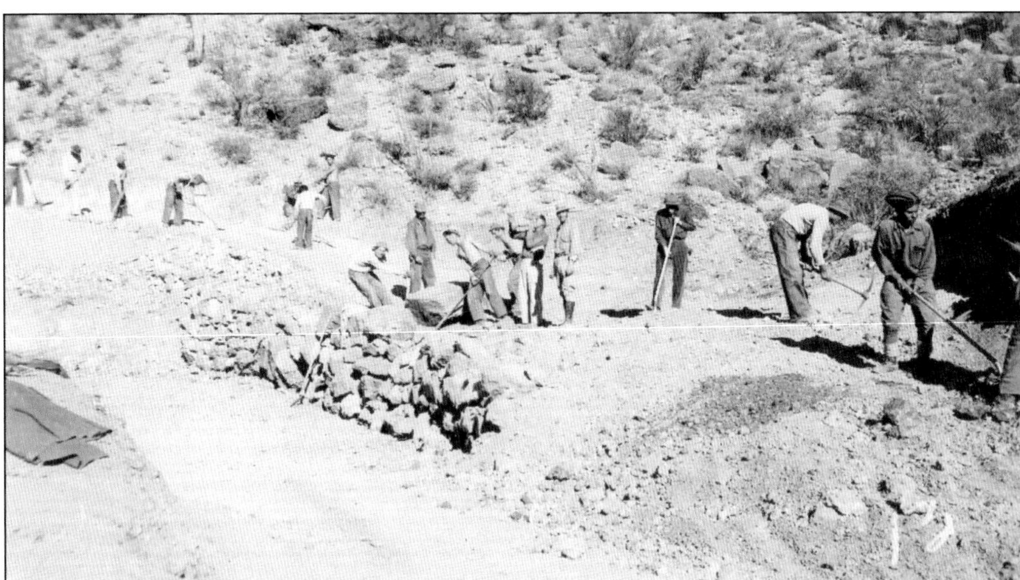

The men of Camp Pima are working on improving Gates Pass Road, a scenic route through the Tucson Mountains at the western fringe of Tucson. At the top of Gates Pass, the enrollees built a scenic overlook, parking area, restroom, and amphitheater. The amphitheater was composed of seating rocks lined up on one side of a canyon, with a speaker rock (a podium constructed of large stones and topped with a cement slab) perched on the opposite side. (NARA MD.)

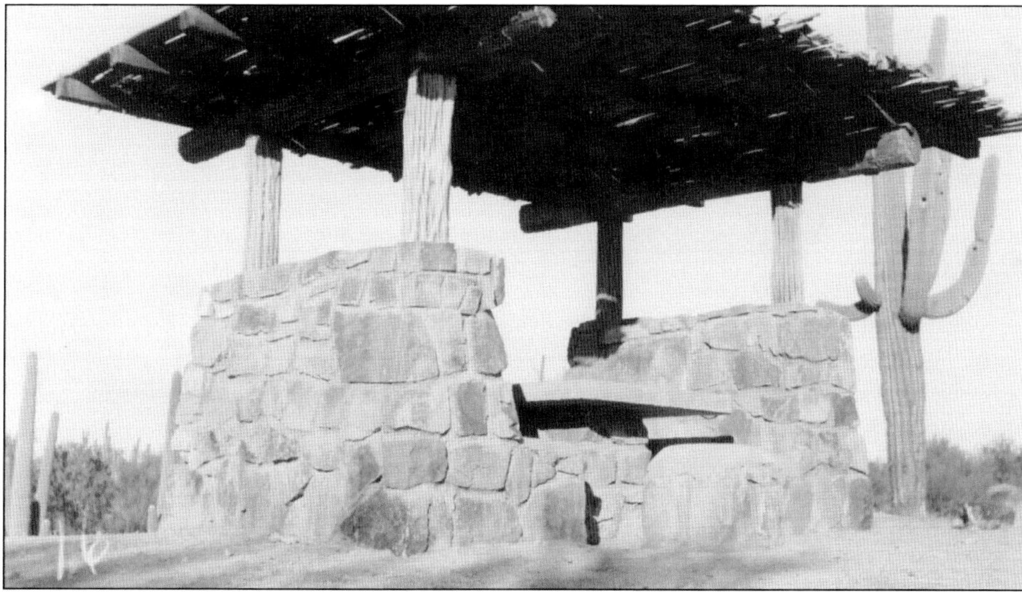

Throughout Tucson Mountain Park, the CCC built trails and recreational facilities, such as this ramada, picnic table, and bench built by Camp DSP-1 in 1934 at the Signal Hill picnic area. Saguaro ribs covered the roof and support posts, and local stone was used to construct the walls and the bottoms of the benches and table. The CCC also built structures such as ramadas, shelters, tables, fireplaces, restrooms, and benches in the Cam-Boh, Ez-Kim-In-Zin, Juan Santa Cruz, Mam-A-Gah, and Sus picnic areas. (NARA MD.)

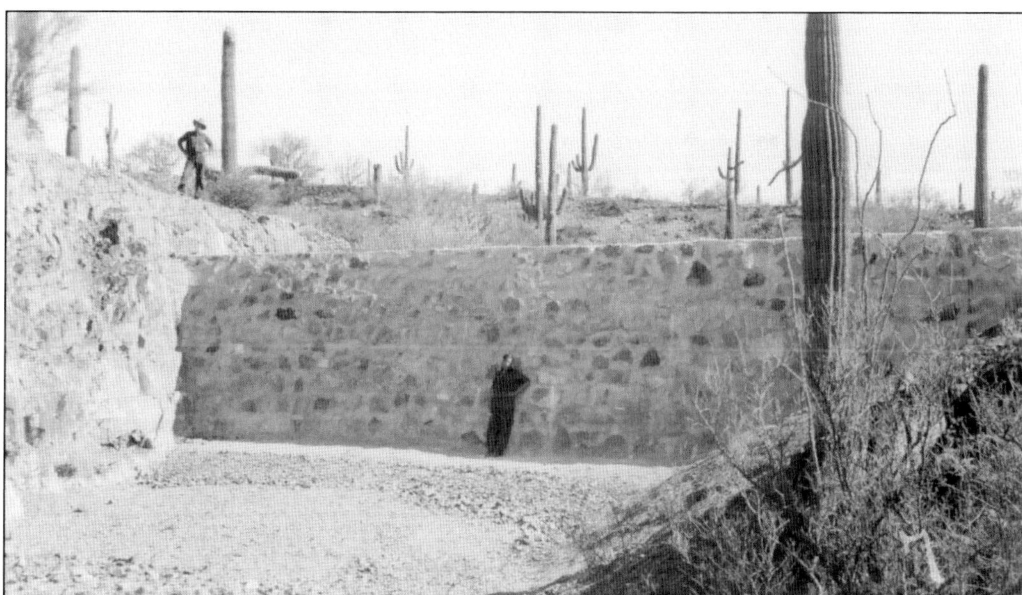

A Department of State Parks unit (DSP-1) occupied Camp Pima in Tucson Mountain Park in 1934. They worked on recreational-area and soil-erosion projects. In park canyons, they constructed check dams to control the water rushing through the canyons during flash floods, especially during the Sonoran Desert's torrential summer monsoons. This flood-control masonry dam at Red Canyon was built by the camp in 1934 and still exists, although it is badly damaged. (NARA MD.)

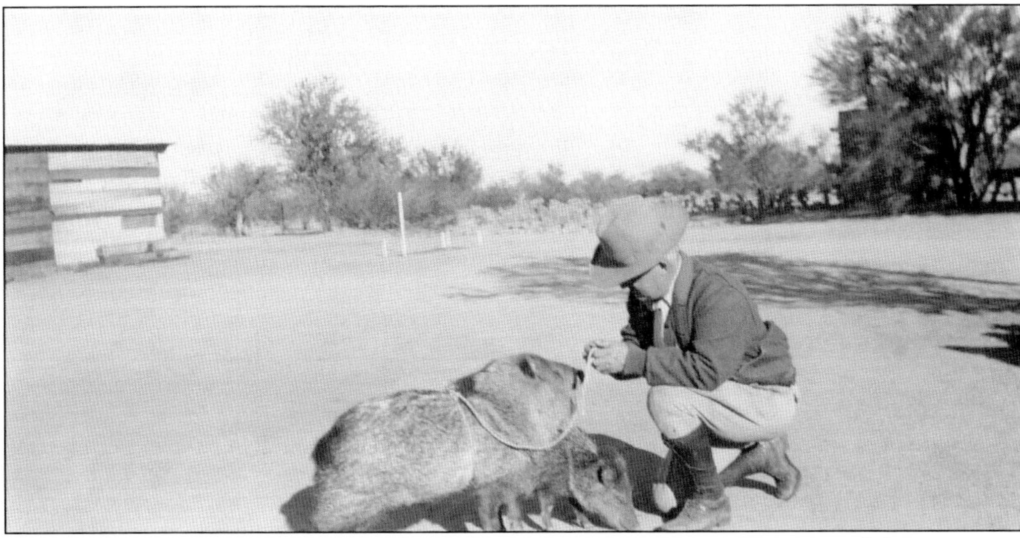

The javelinas, or collared peccaries, shown here are Sonoran Desert natives, and the companies who occupied Camp Pima in Tucson Mountain Park would tame the animals by feeding them table scraps. Camp members also would play a game of tag with the javelinas, using the barracks as a safe base. Many camps adopted animals as pets, particularly dogs, but also such desert creatures as Gila monsters, skunks, and even bears. (NARA MD.)

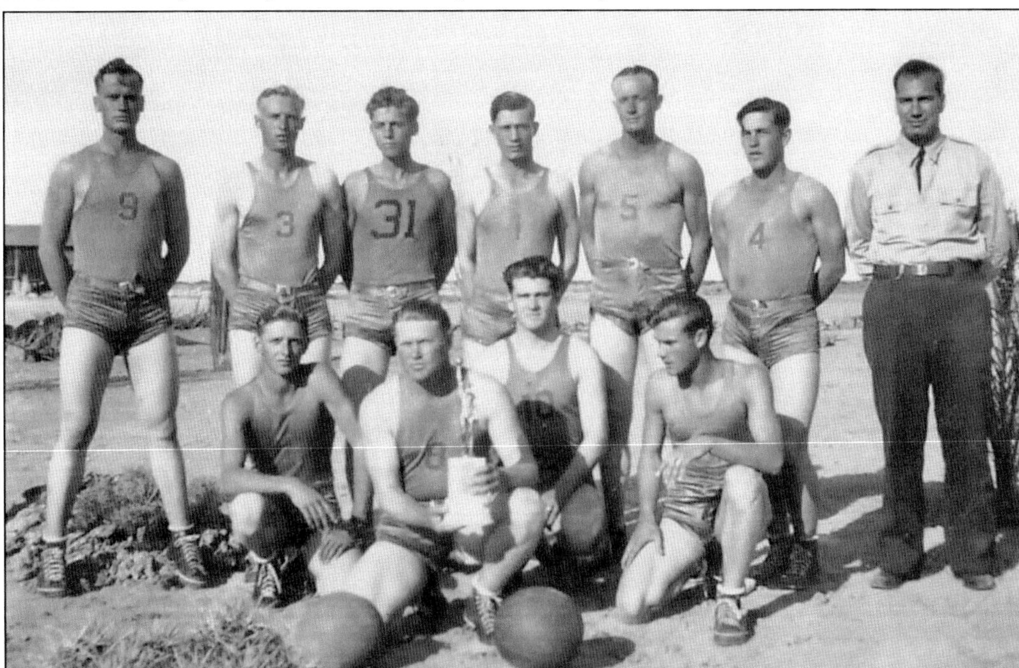

Sports were an important part of the CCC life. The enrollees played baseball, softball, basketball, volleyball, and football. Camp teams would play local teams as well as each other. This Company 2833 basketball team is from Camp SP-6, Tucson Mountain Park, where they served the winter of 1938–1939. Harold L. Patterson (far right in the front row) wrote home to his cousin who was considering joining the CCC, "You will learn things you never had dreamed about before and never will forget them." (HDK.)

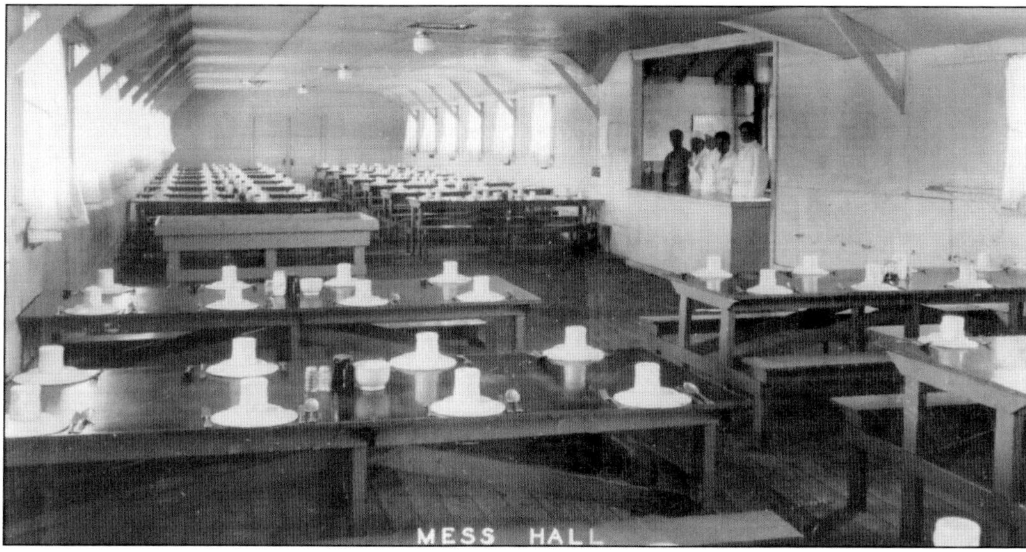

Breakfast and dinner were served in the camp mess hall, such as this one at Camp SP-6, Tucson Mountain Park, with lunch usually eaten at the worksite. The camp commander approved the daily menus. The CCC strove to provide plentiful and wholesome food to the hardworking men. Tucson-area camps' dinners typically included a beef entrée, boiled vegetables, bread and butter, and dessert. The cooks, shown at right, wore white. Enrollee Harold Patterson wrote home about all the "good eats," including ice cream on Sundays. (HDK.)

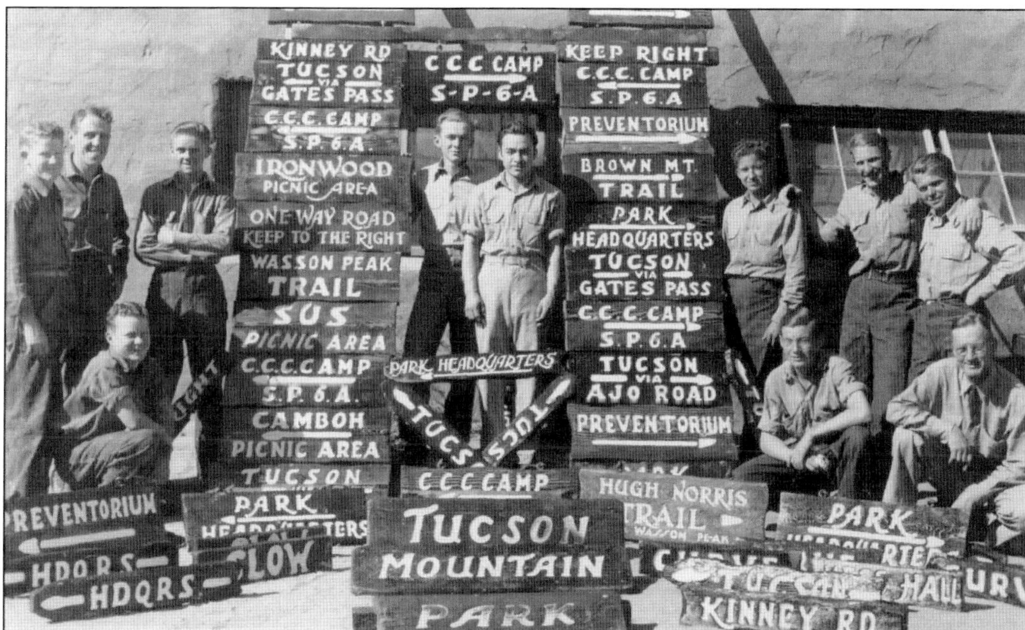

The men of Company 2833, Camp SP-6, Tucson Mountain Park, pose in spring 1939 in front of an adobe building at their campsite with the signs they eventually erected on park roads to direct visitors to trails and picnic areas. These recreational facilities are still in heavy use today. The campsite is also still there, although only some cement slabs, crumbling adobe walls, and posts remain. (HDK.)

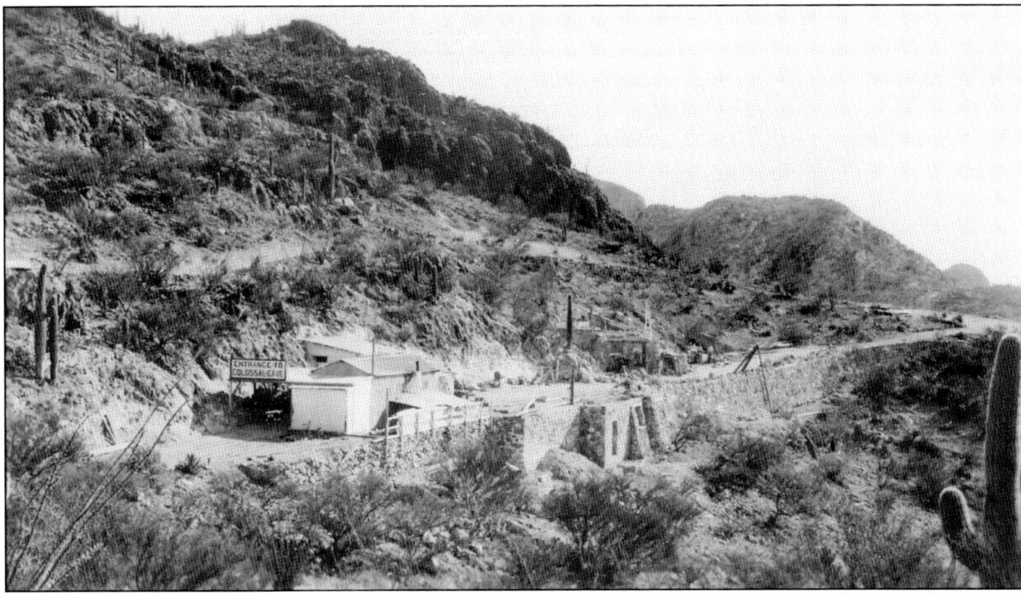

The men of Camp SP-10 constructed the hewn-limestone administration buildings at the mouth of Colossal Cave in Vail. Shown here in March 1935 are the temporary ticket booth (left), garages building (back), and the 20-foot-high retaining wall (right). A cave custodian's residence was later built at the site of the ticket booth. The limestone was quarried nearby and selected so that the buildings would blend in with the landscape. The administration buildings are still in use today. (NARA MD.)

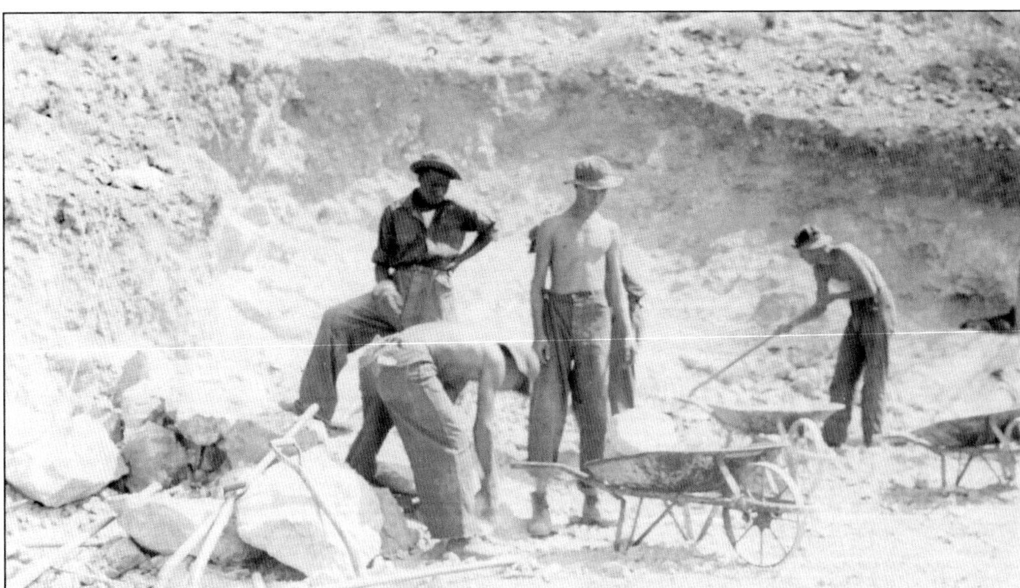

The men of Camp SP-10 are excavating land for a garages building at Colossal Cave in Vail in 1934. Much of the work they did was backbreaking, using wheelbarrows, picks, shovels, and muscle to move rock and soil. Many of the enrollees were underweight when they entered the CCC, but due to the regular, filling food and hard labor, enrollees gained an average of 12 pounds in their first three months. (NARA MD.)

Before the CCC, access to and through Colossal Cave was limited. Here, the men of Camp SP-10 are installing a water pipeline into the cave from the pump house they had constructed about a half-mile away. They also enlarged the entrance; widened passageways; and installed handrails, rock walkways, and lighting. Their work resulted in greater accessibility of the cave and expanded its value as a tourist attraction. Some of the enrollees worked as tour guides in the cave. (NARA MD.)

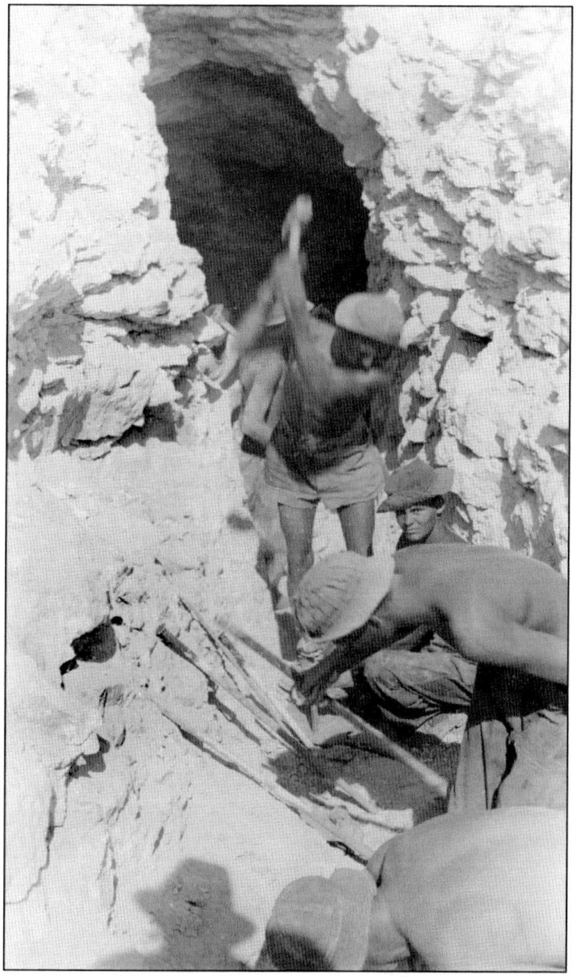

The men of Camp SP-10, Colossal Cave, are shown here building a road in 1936. In the area surrounding Colossal Cave, they did landscaping, built a parking lot and roads, and constructed restrooms, a ramada, and a drinking fountain in two picnic areas. The man to the right is a member of the Technical Services, an employee of the State Park Service who oversaw the work projects and supervised the enrollees. (NARA MD.)

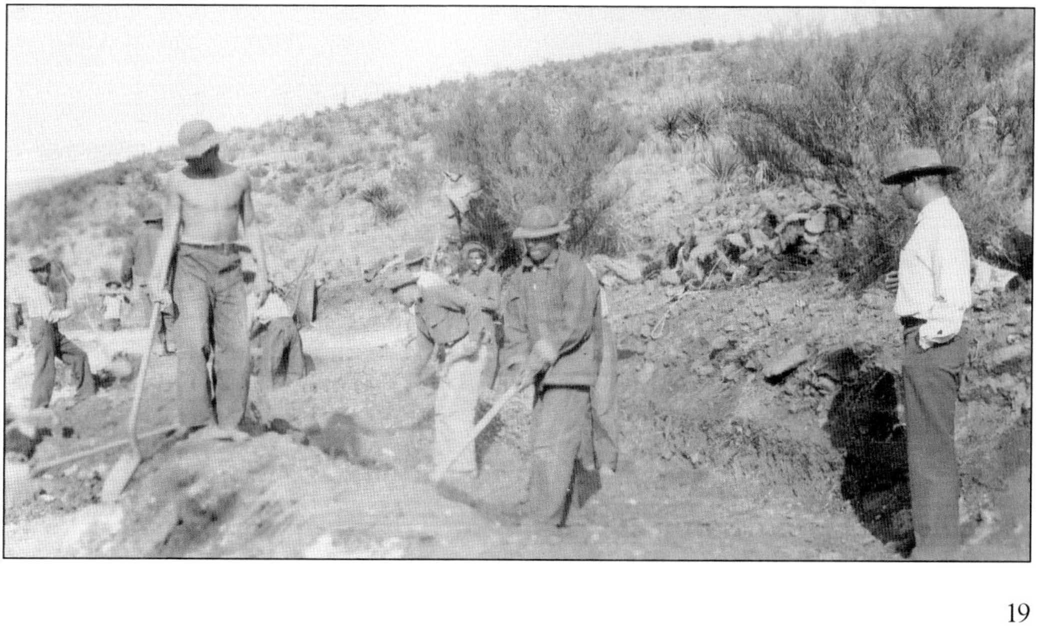

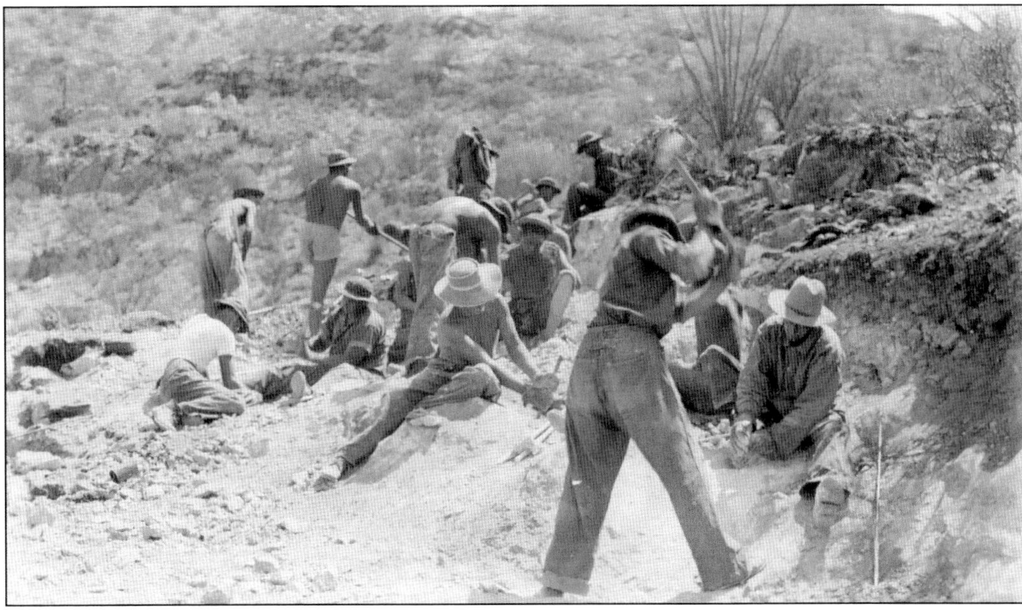

The limestone used in the construction of the administration buildings at the mouth of Colossal Cave and of the ramada, bathrooms, and drinking fountain in the picnic areas came from a nearby quarry. Here, the Camp SP-10 enrollees are constructing the road to the quarry. The men in this camp hailed from Arizona, Oklahoma, or Texas, and organized themselves into separate barracks by state. They engaged in friendly inter-barrack sports rivalries. (NARA MD.)

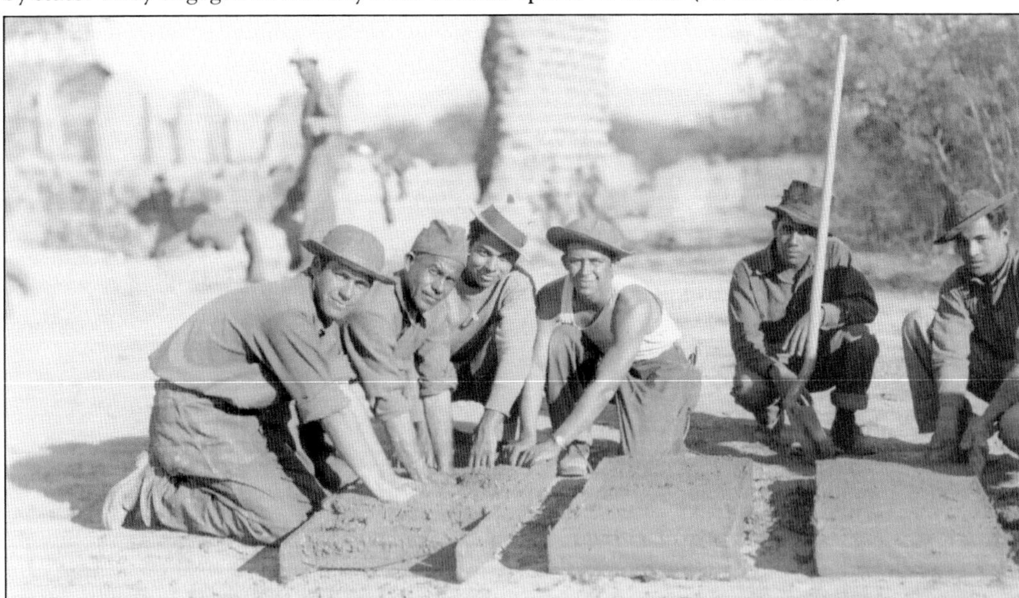

Camp SP-11, Tanque Verde, enrollees are making adobe bricks. This camp worked at Saguaro Forest State Park (now Saguaro National Park East), fencing in grazing land; constructing the skyline loop road; building dams; and removing old roads, trails, and buildings. They built an adobe administration building, which became the custodian's residence and visitor contact station. This camp's William V. Cudd, at 330 pounds, was perhaps the heaviest enrollee ever enlisted. (NARA MD.)

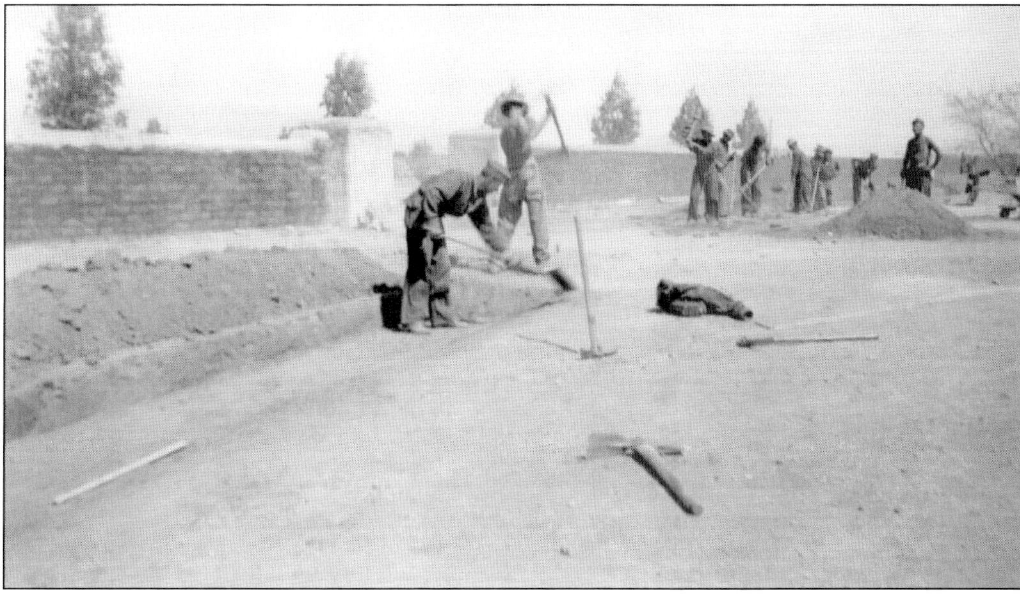

Camp SP-1 was located at Randolph Park in central Tucson. Here, the camp is excavating a drainage ditch in March 1934. This campsite was a winter camp for several companies transferring from colder states during the winters. Enrollee Lyon Strong from the Randolph Park camp made this statement about his CCC service: "I'll tell you, it saved my life. I would have been on a street corner, with no money in my pocket." (NARA MD.)

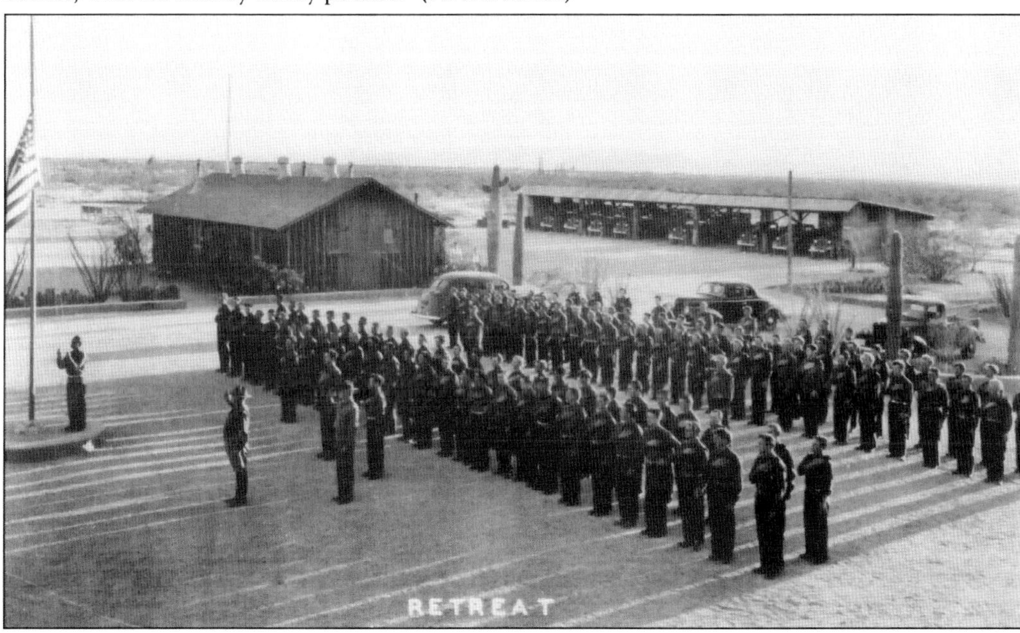

Camp MA-1 was a municipal area camp located at Randolph Park in central Tucson that worked on irrigation and recreational projects. Retreat was held at 5:00 p.m. followed by dinner at 5:30 p.m. The enrollees then engaged in sports, recreation, and educational activities until lights out at 10:00 p.m. The US Army personnel who ran the camps instilled military discipline into the enrollees, which helped ensure the smooth operation of the CCC and was invaluable training for the boys who subsequently went on to serve in World War II. (WG, USFS.)

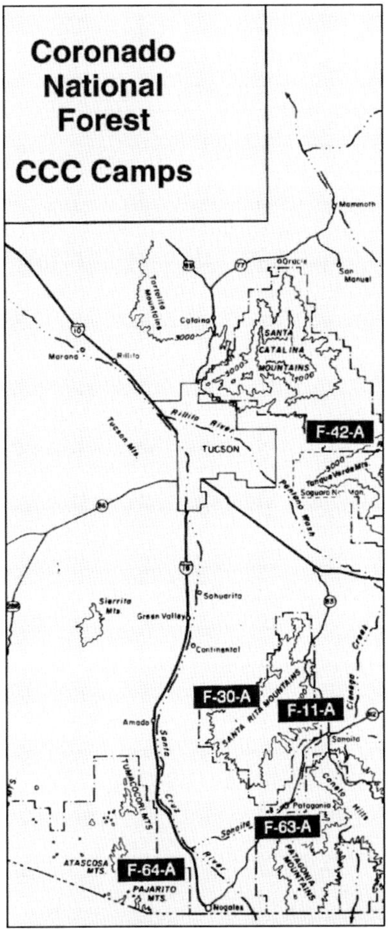

Pima and Santa Cruz Counties contain noncontiguous sections of the Coronado National Forest. The CCC performed a great deal of work here, building recreational facilities and ranger stations, fighting forest fires, battling erosion, and improving the health of the woods. Camp F-42, Tanque Verde, was located between the Rincon and Santa Catalina Mountains; F-11, Box Canyon, and F-30, Madera Canyon, in the Santa Rita Mountains; F-63, Flux Canyon, in the Patagonia Mountains; and F-64, Peña Blanca, in the Pajarito Mountains. (US Forest Service, *The Civilian Conservation Corps: Coronado National Forest, 1933–1942*.)

The men of Camp F-42, Tanque Verde, built roads in the Santa Catalina and Rincon Mountains area of the Coronado National Forest in the second enrollment period, October 1933 through March 1934. Camp SP-11 took over the F-42 campsite in July 1935 and continued its roadwork. These camps built the Redington Pass Road, shown here, between the Santa Catalina and Rincon Mountains northeast of Tucson. (USFS, SWR.)

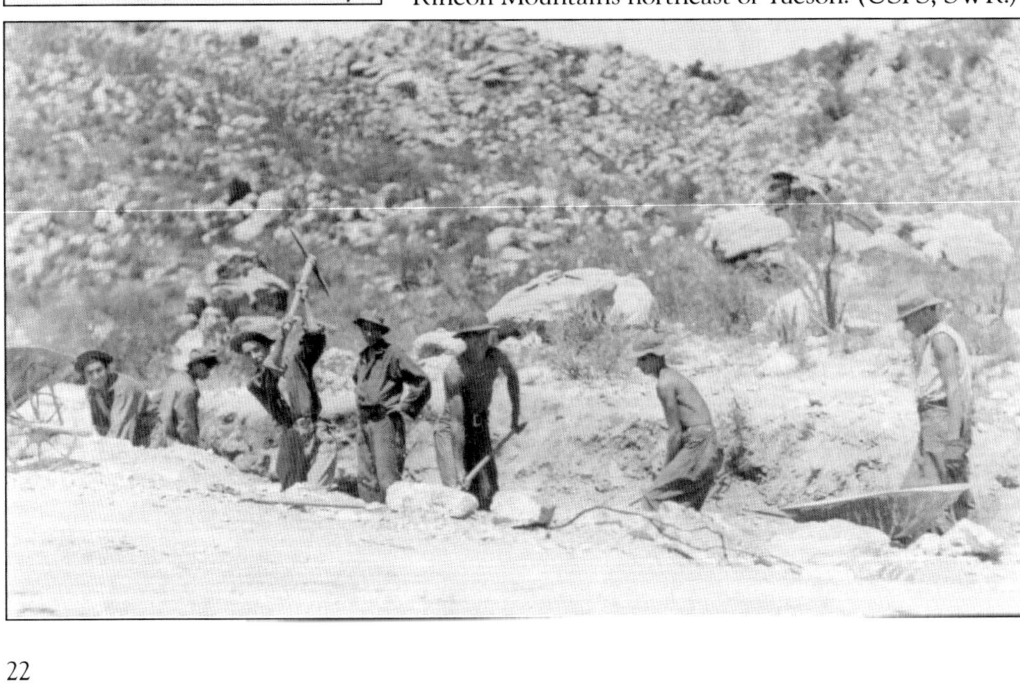

Local experienced men (LEMs) were workers with specialized skills hired from the nearby area by the Technical Services, the government agencies overseeing the work of the CCC. They helped supervise and train the enrollees on work projects. This LEM powder man from Camp DF-42, Tanque Verde, is inserting electrical wire in sticks of dynamite to blast rock for a road construction project in 1934. (Photograph by F.L. Kirby; WG, USFS.)

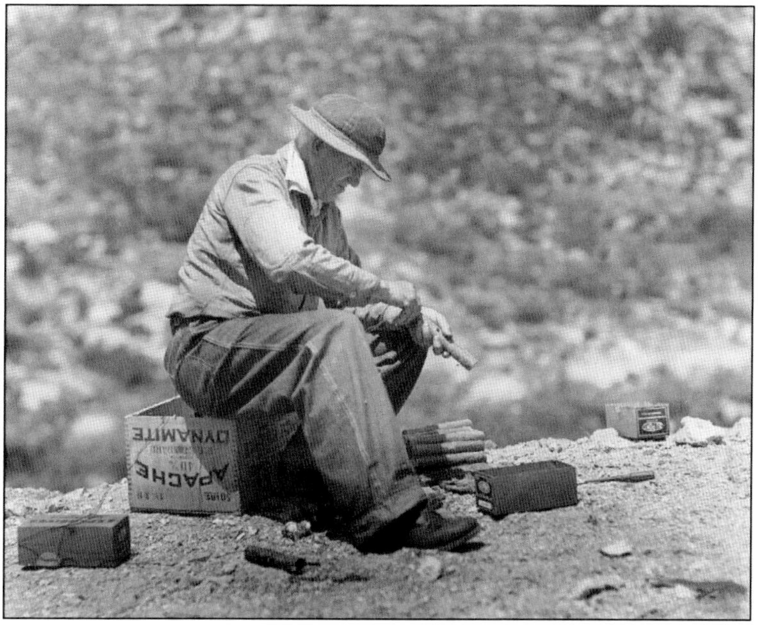

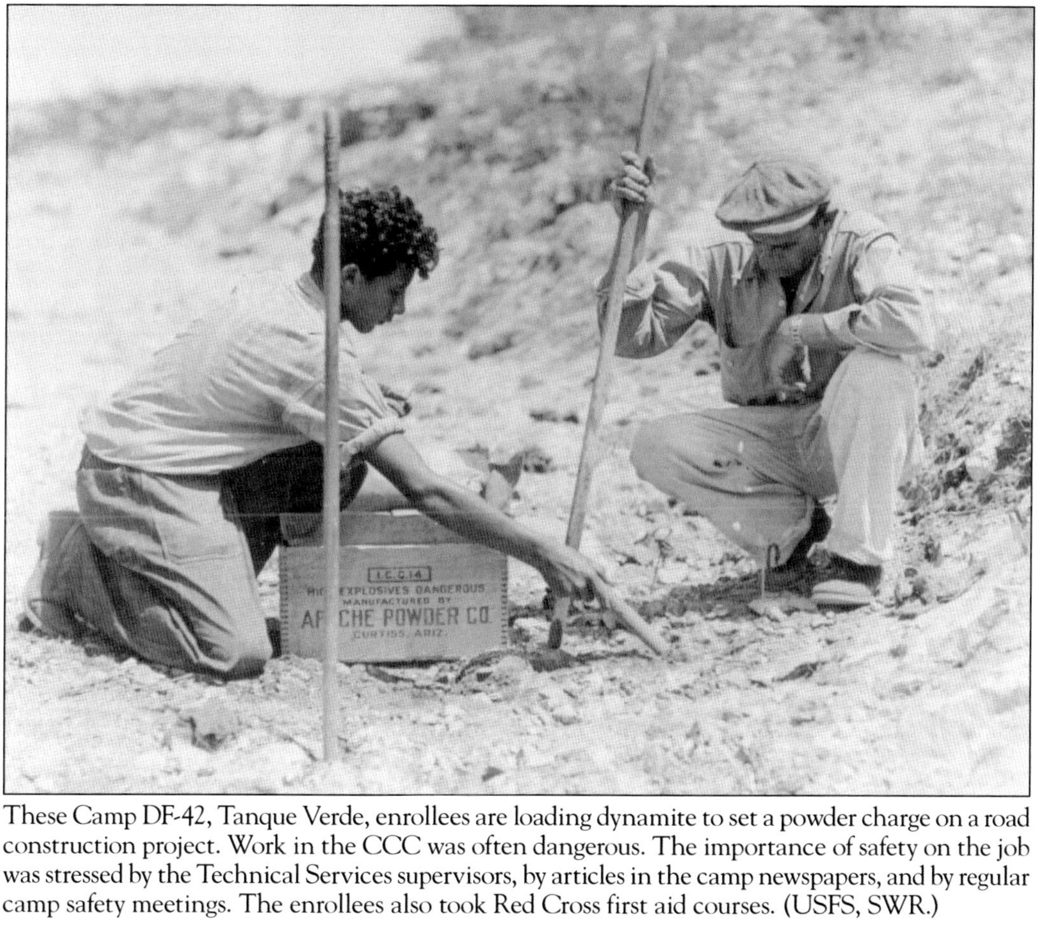

These Camp DF-42, Tanque Verde, enrollees are loading dynamite to set a powder charge on a road construction project. Work in the CCC was often dangerous. The importance of safety on the job was stressed by the Technical Services supervisors, by articles in the camp newspapers, and by regular camp safety meetings. The enrollees also took Red Cross first aid courses. (USFS, SWR.)

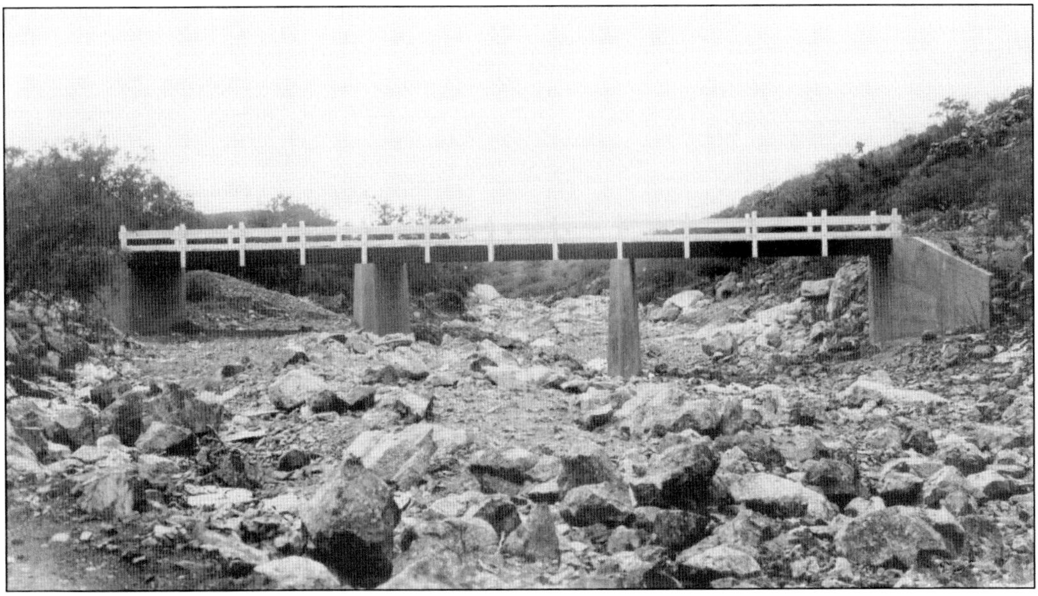

Box Canyon is located in the Santa Rita Mountains of the Coronado National Forest. In 1933 and 1934, Camp F-11 worked for five months on construction of the Box Canyon Road, and the World War I veterans of Camp F-30, Madera Canyon, then completed the work. Box Canyon Road officially opened on May 6, 1934, with a ceremony and official motorcade. In September 1935, a violent storm caused major damage to the road, but it was rebuilt eventually and is still in use today. (NARA MD.)

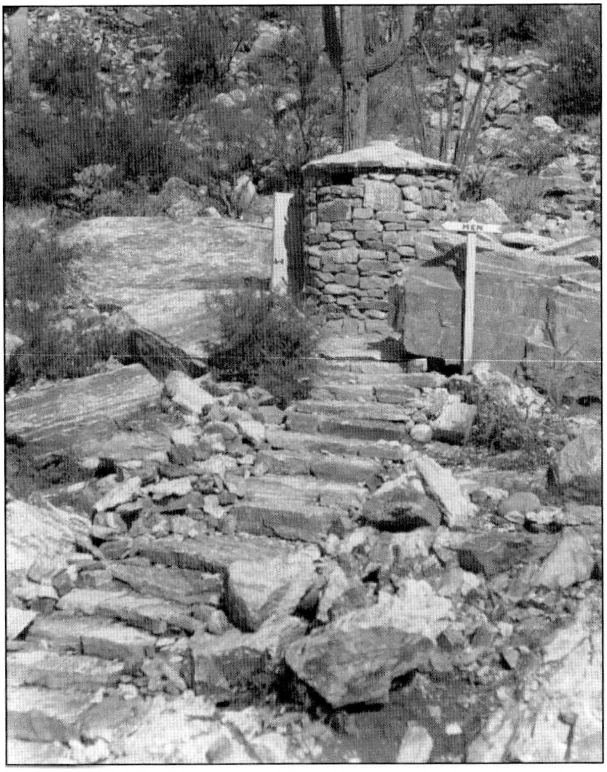

At times, personnel from various New Deal programs would work at the same site, such as at the Sabino Canyon Recreation Area in northeastern Tucson. Here, men from the WPA, FERA, and CCC labored on recreational facilities, roads, and trails. This men's toilet at Sabino Canyon was built by Camp SP-11 of stone from the area and was meant to blend in with the landscape. (Photograph by F.L. Kirby; WG, USFS.)

The men of Camp SP-11, Tanque Verde, built this caretaker/custodian's residence at the Sabino Canyon Recreation Area in northeastern Tucson using rocks from the area. They also constructed picnic tables, toilets, retaining walls, Sabino Dam, the Lowell Ranger Station, and low-water crossings. Unfortunately, this building is no longer standing. (Photograph by F.L. Kirby; WG, USFS.)

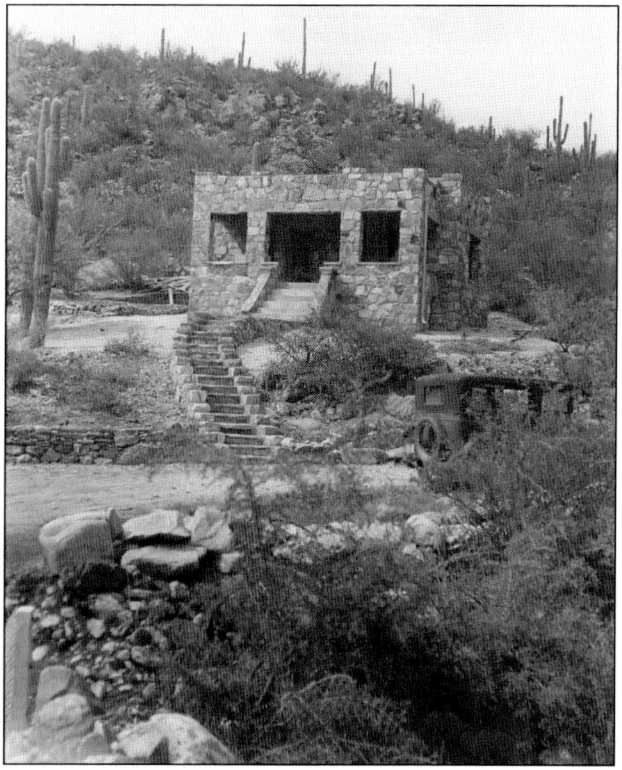

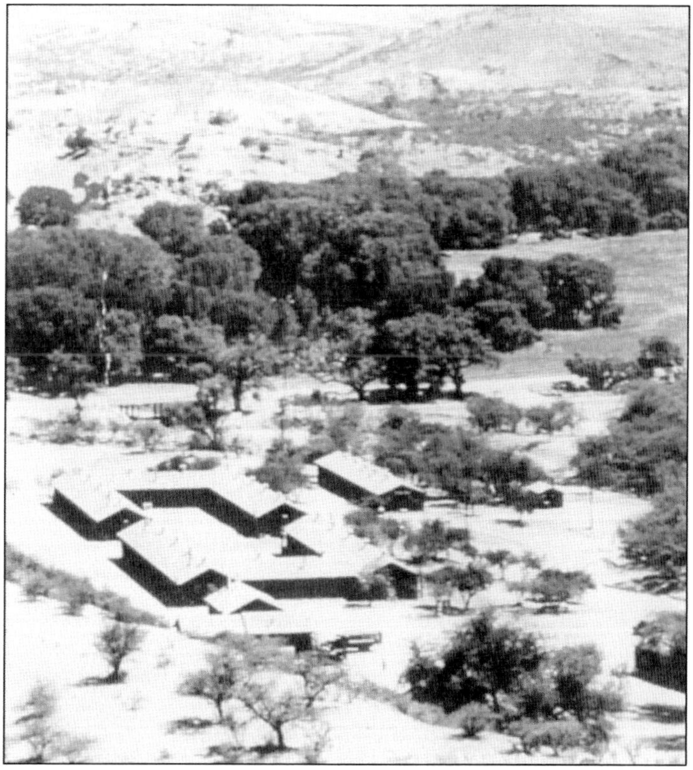

Camp SCS-26, Patagonia, built dams and other water-control features in the Patagonia Mountains and helped arrest soil erosion on nearby cattle ranches. Camp commander Ernest Bruss would climb the hill overlooking the camp so he could watch the supply building with binoculars to catch whomever was stealing food. Bruss would also tell moonshiners to move along. At nearby Gardner Canyon, he had an encounter with a moonshiner whom he later found out was gangster Pretty Boy Floyd, whose son was at the Gardner Canyon camp. (EB.)

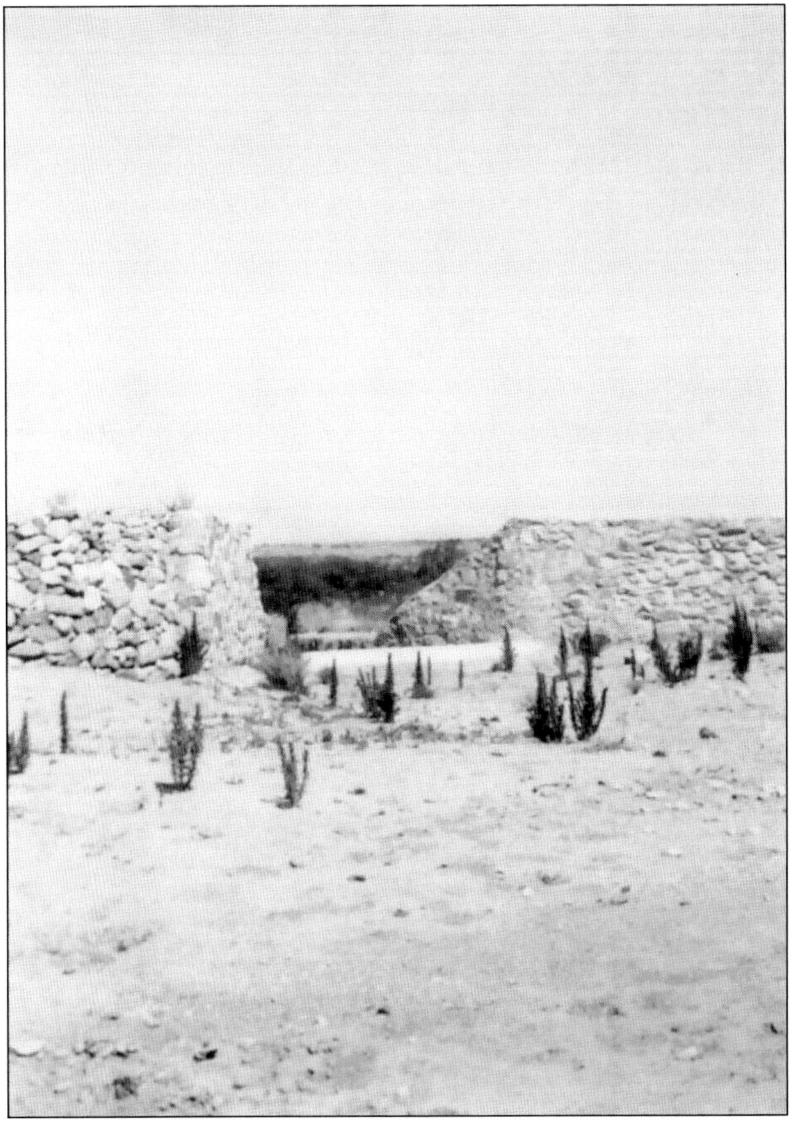

This stone dam in Flux Canyon in the Patagonia Mountains is one of many constructed by the men of Camp SCS-26, Patagonia. The summer monsoons in the Sonoran Desert bring torrential rains, with the water runoff causing soil erosion and other damage. The men of this Soil Conservation Service camp built stone dams, dikes, rock spreaders, and other features to control the water rushing through the canyons of these mountains and prevent erosion. (EA.)

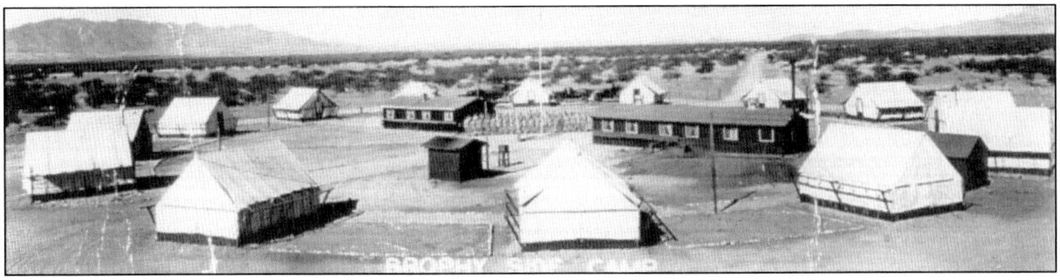

The fly, or side, camps were small, temporary camps for work projects at locations remote from the main camp. The Brophy Side Camp enrollees from Camp SCS-26, Patagonia, lived in surplus World War I tents while they worked on the Babacomari Ranch near Whetstone and the Louis Sands Ranch near Fairbank. Their work on these cattle ranches included constructing stock tanks, dams, and dikes to control water runoff and slow down soil erosion. (EB.)

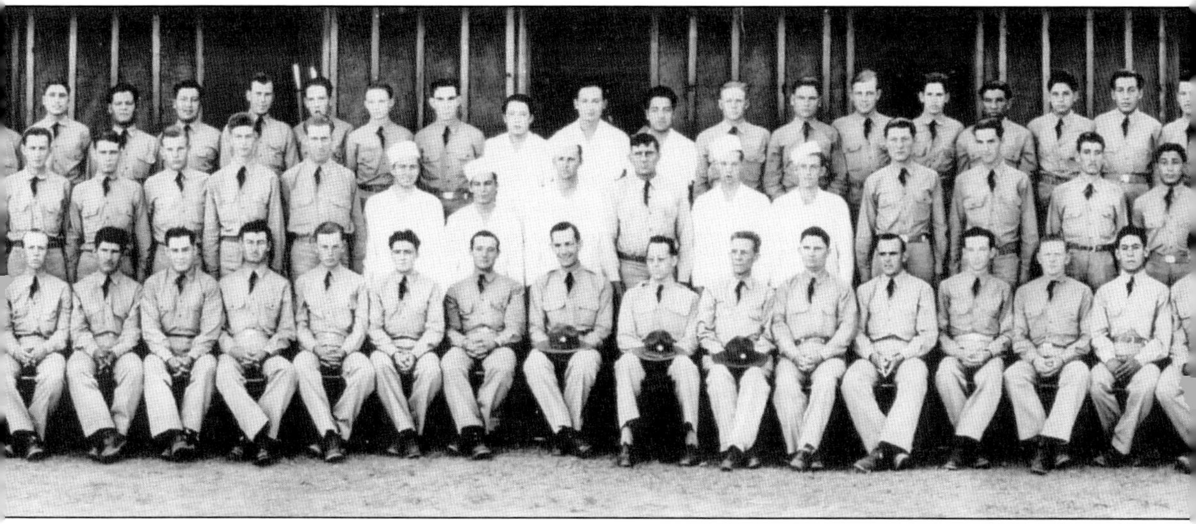

Company 3840, Camp SCS-26, Patagonia, is dressed up for this 1940 official group photograph. Technical Services and US Army staff are in the bottom row, and the cooks are in white. Camp commander Ernest H. Bruss, ninth from the left in bottom row, joined the CCC as a US Army Reserve officer in 1933 and was camp commander at the following southern Arizona camps: Ash Canyon, Black Rock, Box Canyon, Duncan, Patagonia, Rucker Canyon, St. David, and Sunnyside. The enrollees held him in high esteem, as this *The Gila Whisperings* camp newspaper poem shows: "A friend who taught us loyalty / and always to do right; / One who stood by royally / When we were in a tight." A notable enrollee from this camp was L.C. Wade, ace fighter pilot for the Royal Air Force in World War II. (EB.)

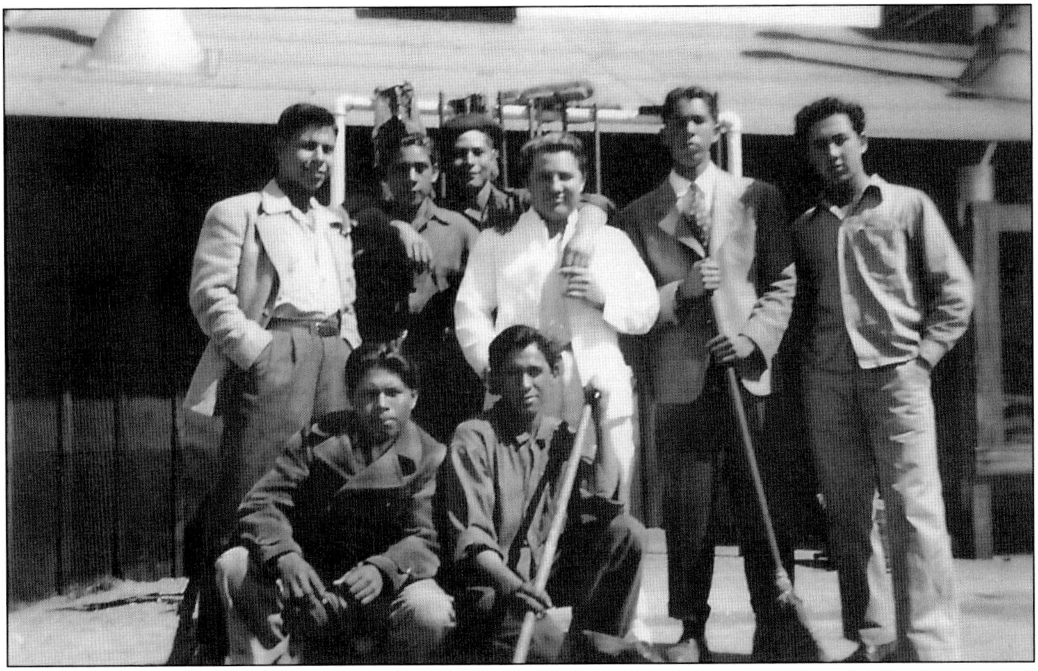

This group of buddies from Camp SCS-26, Patagonia, includes Eduardo "Buck" Castillo (back row, third from left), an ace pitcher from Nogales who was recruited into the CCC by the camp commander to play baseball. The enrollee at the left in the back row is no doubt dressed up for a night on the town. The camp cook in the middle is dressed in his "whites." The short pants on the enrollee holding the broom were probably due to his inability to tailor his clothes or to a teenage growth spurt. (E&DC.)

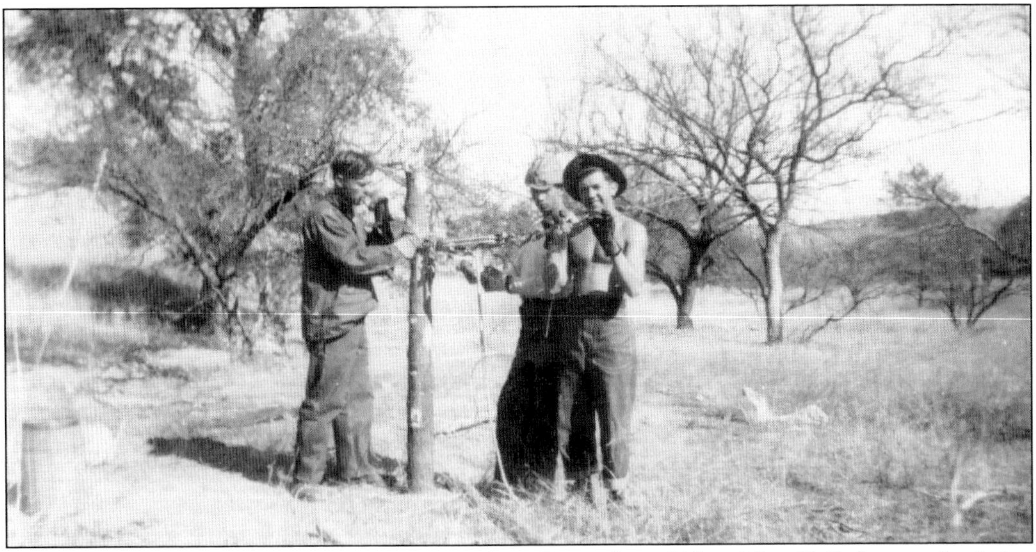

Camp F-64, Peña Blanca, was a winter camp from December 1935 to May 1940. Its men built fire trails, built and maintained the Ruby-Calabasas Road, strung telephone lines, constructed recreational facilities at the Peña Blanca Recreation Area, and performed erosion- and fire-control work. They also maintained a side camp at Madera Canyon. During the winters of 1938–1940, Company 3348 erected many fences, including 16 miles of fence line from the US–Mexico border in Nogales to Ruby Road and the Coronado Forest Valley. The fence corners were triple posted. (MT.)

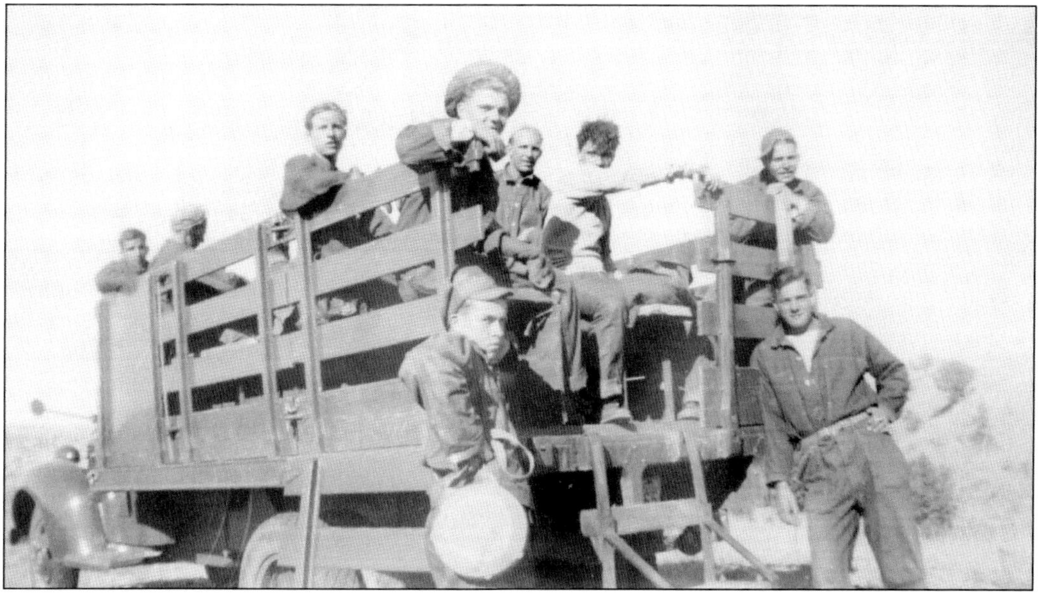

Truck driver Merle Timblin (standing, left), Camp F-64, Peña Blanca, drove the fence crew and their equipment in his 1939 Dodge truck close to the worksites, where the barbed wire and tools were loaded onto mules and the crew set off on foot. His frown was meant to discourage horseplay on his truck. Merle would make coffee at the worksite and—typical for an enrollee—help the crew line up fence posts even though it was not part of his job to do so. (MT.)

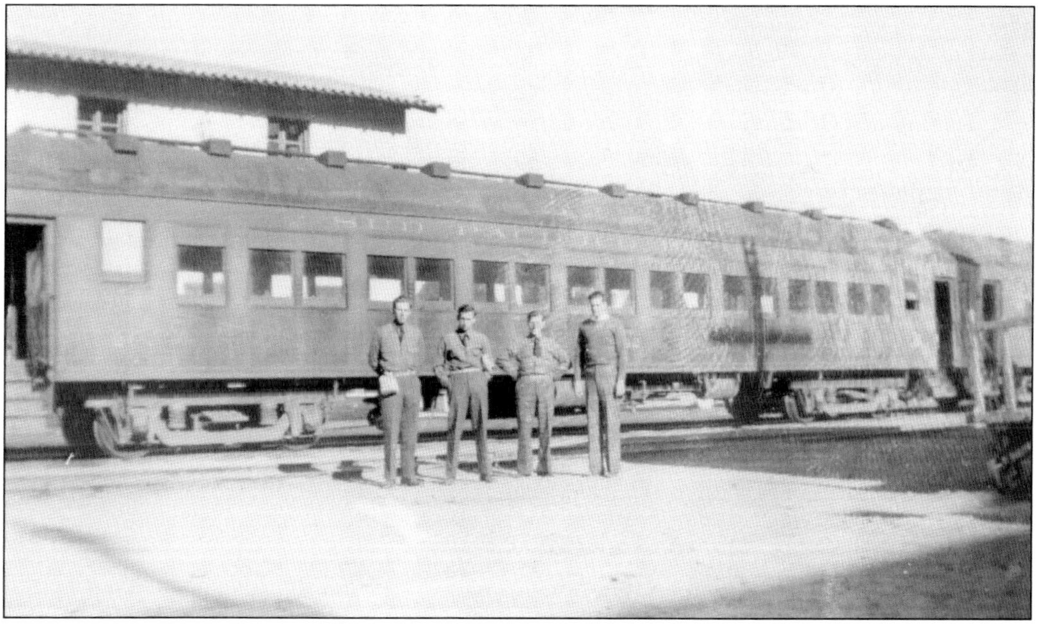

Company 3348, Camp F-28, Williams, moved to southern Arizona during the winters of 1938–1940. Here, enrollees pose before boarding the train for their trip to Camp F-64, Peña Blanca. Several companies from northern Arizona and other western states came to sunny southern Arizona during the cold winters at their home camps, and companies would move from southern Arizona to cooler climates during the hot southern Arizona summers. The US Army handled transportation, and personnel were moved from site to site by train and then by truck. (MT.)

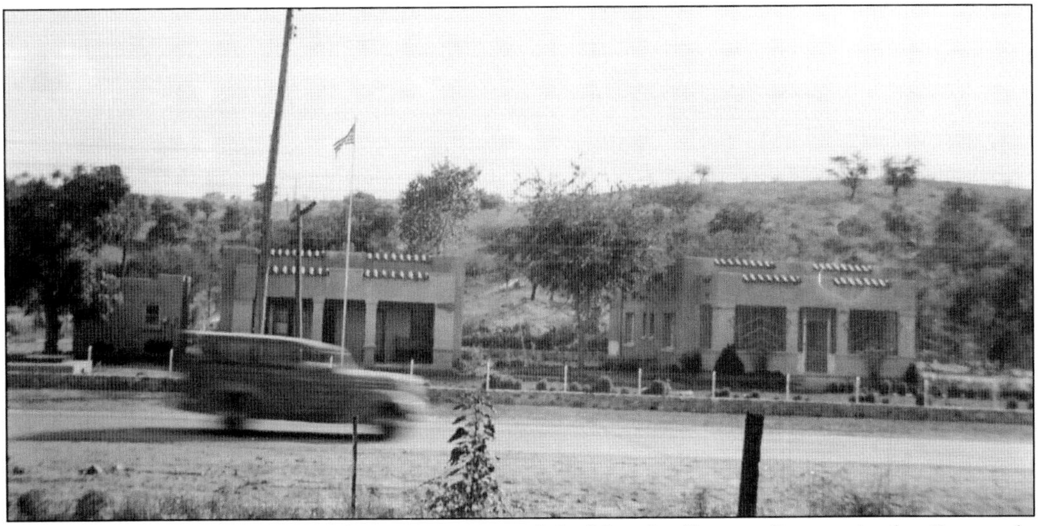

The men of Camp F-64, Peña Blanca, constructed the Nogales Ranger Station in the Coronado National Forest, shown here in 1941. They also constructed a storage house at the Patagonia Ranger Station and improved the Washington Camp road. Because of the lack of Army leadership, this camp suffered from tense race relations between whites and Hispanics. Tragically, in May 1941, a boxing match at this camp turned into a riot. An enrollee was killed in the melee, five were dishonorably discharged, and eight were transferred to other camps. (WG, USFS.)

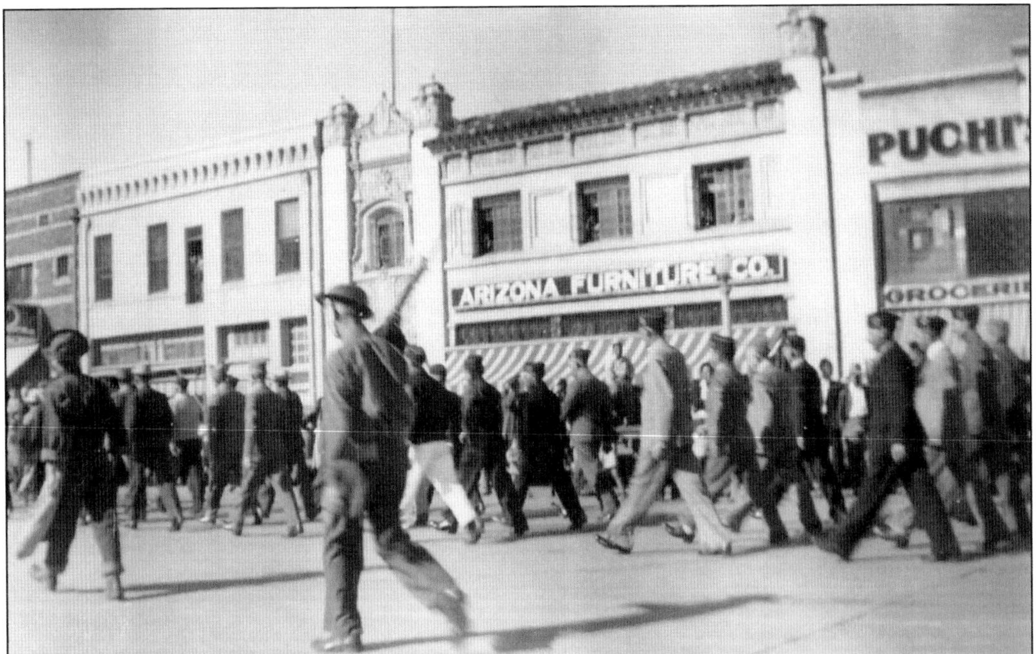

A color guard from Camp F-64, Peña Blanca, marched in the Thanksgiving Day parade in the nearby town of Nogales in 1939. The CCC worked to maintain good relationships with neighboring towns. Residents were invited to visit camps and attend dances, plays, and special events. After this parade, the mayor and other dignitaries went to the campsite for a special feast. Unfortunately, a cook had allowed the ice cream to melt and then refroze it. The local dignitaries and enrollees were very sick with food poisoning for the next few days. (MT.)

Two

Southeastern Arizona

Cochise, Graham, and Greenlee Counties

Southeastern Arizona is sparsely populated, with small communities, large cattle ranches, and sections of the Apache-Sitgreaves and Coronado National Forests. The CCC work in Cochise, Graham, and Greenlee Counties focused on improving the rangeland and the forests.

Due to drought and overgrazing, the land was in dire need of assistance when the CCC was established. Soil conservation, grazing, and forestry camps in these counties built dams and other structures to control water runoff and soil erosion. They built stock tanks for cattle and educated cattle ranchers on range management principles.

The Douglas, Sierra Vista, and Safford Ranger Districts of the 1.78-million-acre Coronado National Forest are located in the southeastern Arizona counties. The work of the camps here included building and maintaining roads, constructing cattle guards and water-control features, erecting fences, building bridges, stringing telephone lines, and developing campgrounds, picnic areas, and trails.

In Cochise County, the CCC had forestry, national park/national monument, and soil conservation camps. A segregated company of African American enrollees was at the Fort Huachuca Army reservation in 1935, the only such company in Arizona. The fort also functioned as an orientation and conditioning camp for the Arizona CCC. In the Coronado National Forest, the camps worked extensively in the Huachuca and Chiricahua Mountains and at Chiricahua National Monument, known as the "Wonderland of Rocks."

In Graham County, the CCC had forestry, grazing, and soil conservation camps. These camps battled erosion, built roads, and made improvements to the Coronado National Forest.

In Greenlee County, the CCC had forestry, grazing, and soil conservation camps. Many of these camps were very isolated, and the men struggled with getting supplies and entertaining themselves. There were a large number of desertions and turnovers. The forestry camps worked in Apache National Forest (now the Apache-Sitgreaves National Forests) and the Crook National Forest (now incorporated into other forests), building and maintaining roads, stringing telephone lines, constructing bridges, fighting forest fires, developing springs, and building campgrounds. They helped local ranchers and residents by building stock tanks, erecting fencing, and building water-control features.

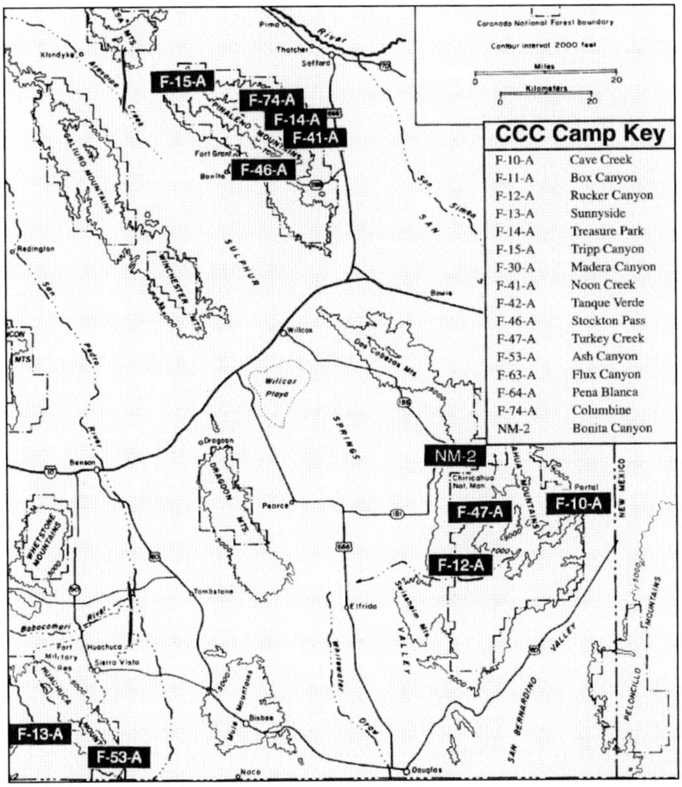

Sections of the Coronado National Forest are located in Cochise and Graham Counties. The CCC work in this forest involved improving the health of the timber stand and building recreational facilities. Camps F-13, Sunnyside, and F-53, Ash Canyon, were in the Huachuca Mountains. Camps F-10, Cave Creek; F-12, Rucker Canyon; F-47, Turkey Creek; and NM-2, Bonita Canyon, were in the Chiricahua Mountains. Camps F-14, Treasure Park; F-15, Tripp Canyon; F-41, Noon Creek; F-46, Stockton Pass; and F-74, Columbine, were in the Pinaleño Mountains. (US Forest Service, *The Civilian Conservation Corps: Coronado National Forest, 1933–1942.*)

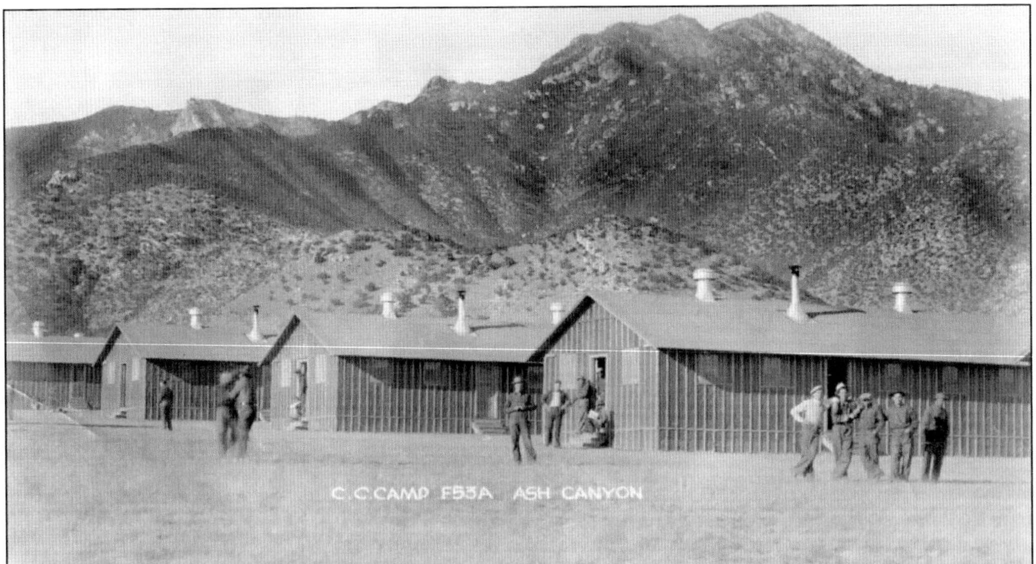

A company from Colorado occupied Camp F-53, Ash Canyon, in the Huachuca Mountains of the Coronado National Forest in the winter of 1933–1934. The camp buildings had wood frames with tar-paper covering and asphalt roofing. As were many forestry camps, this camp was isolated, reachable only by a dirt road that wound through the mountains. The camp personnel worked on a road through Montezuma Canyon; maintained several other roads; and built cattle guards, a bridge, a powder magazine, two stone fences, and two telephone lines. (EB.)

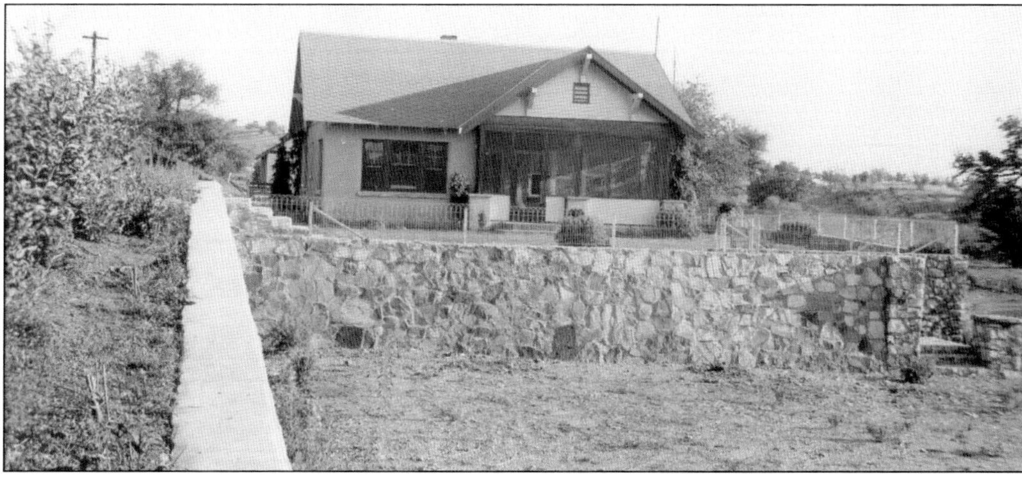

Camp F-13, Sunnyside, was located in Parker Canyon of the Huachuca Mountains of the Coronado National Forest and occupied for five six-month enrollment periods from June 1933 to October 1935. Major work projects were the construction and maintenance of roads and the building of fences and cattle guards to divide the range. The camp also worked on the Canelo Ranger Station, including the stone retaining walls and paths shown here. (USFS, SWR.)

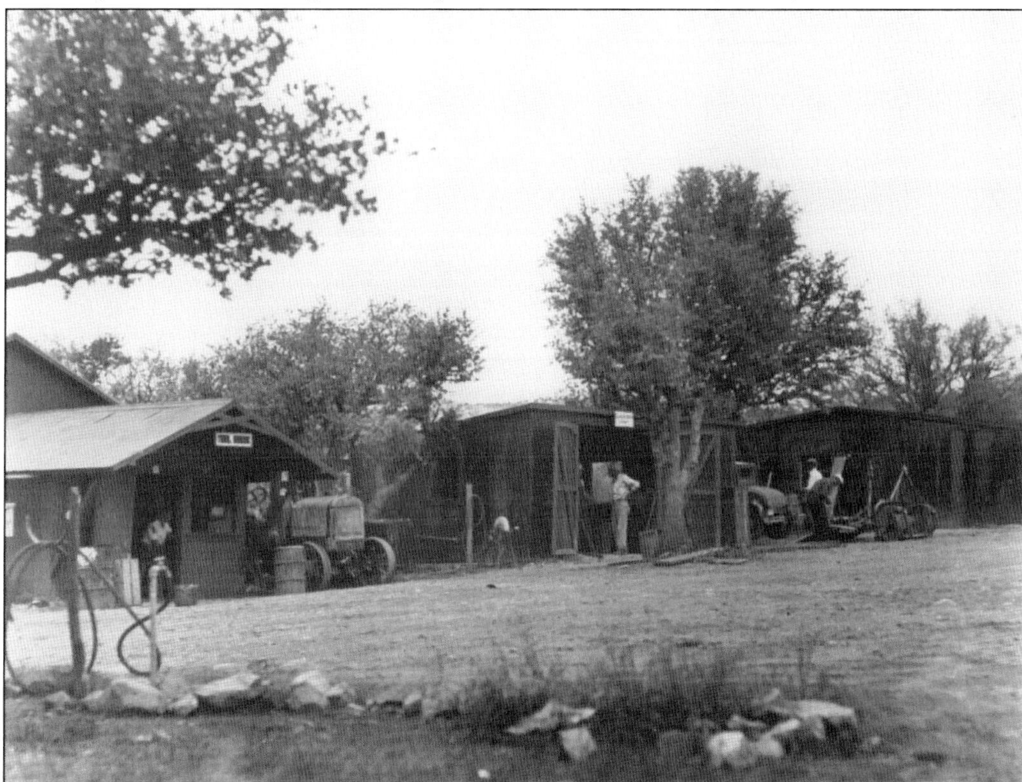

Shown here is the Camp F-13, Sunnyside, gas pump (front left), garage (back left), and tool shed (back right). The men of this Coronado National Forest camp worked on building check dams, improving the rangeland, and improving roads, including building the Lyle-Parker Road. A hole dug between two trees and covered with canvas served as the camp's icehouse. (WG, USFS.)

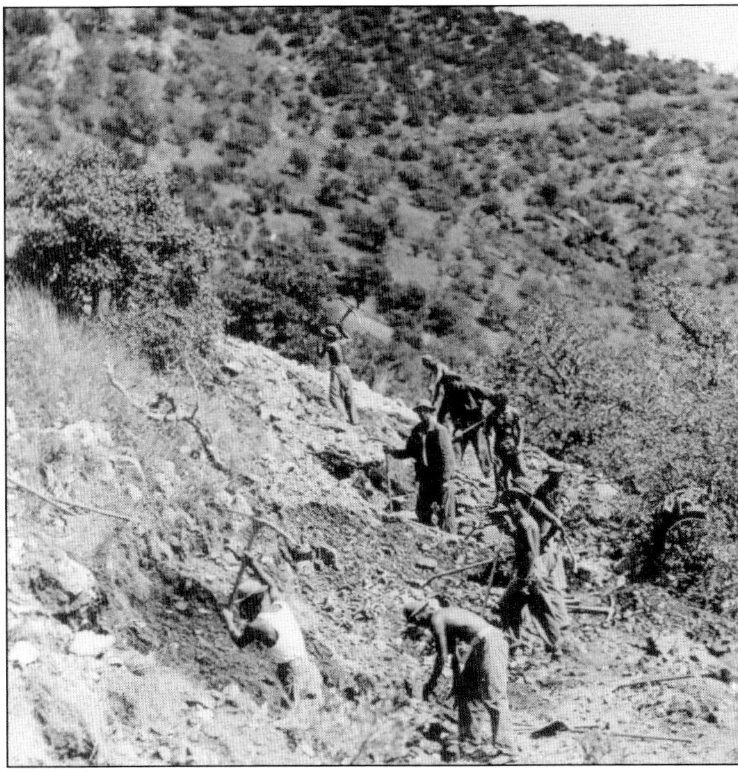

Enrollees from Camp F-13, Sunnyside, are working on a trail in Montezuma Pass, now part of Coronado National Memorial, in September 1934. In addition to building trails, this camp developed springs, constructed check dams to control erosion, erected fences, and built and improved roads. The camp received an Outstanding Camp in the Area award in February and again in April 1934. (USFS, SWR.)

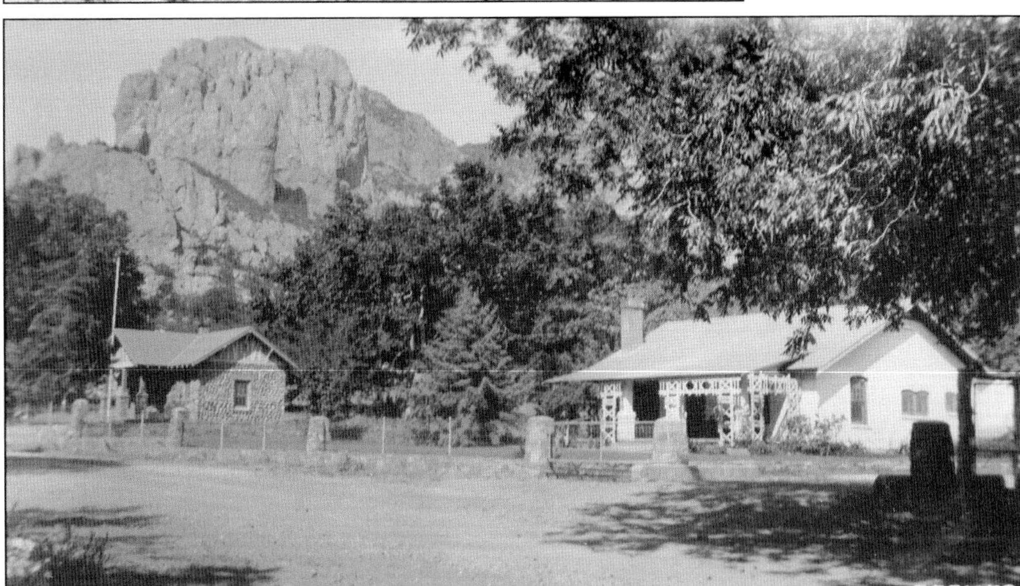

Camp F-10, Cave Creek, was located on the east side of the Chiricahua Mountains near the town of Portal. The camp was occupied almost continuously from 1933 to 1942 and constructed the Portal Ranger Station office shown on the left. The camp was renamed Camp Harold C. Riley in honor of this enrollee, who was killed on July 18, 1933, when an unexploded dynamite charge went off unexpectedly at a work site. In 1940, enrollees Arnold Garrett, Nalty Lee, and Ralph Case were killed in a culvert cave-in. (USFS, SWR.)

The work of Camp F-10, Cave Creek, in the Chiricahua Mountains of the Coronado National Forest included boxing springs and installing waterlines. Here, enrollees are stocking trout. The camp constructed the Rustler Park Fire Guard Station and completed South Fork Campground. Special Investigator A.W. Stockman in his March 1939 camp inspection report lauded them for their "valuable and splendid work." (USFS, SWR.)

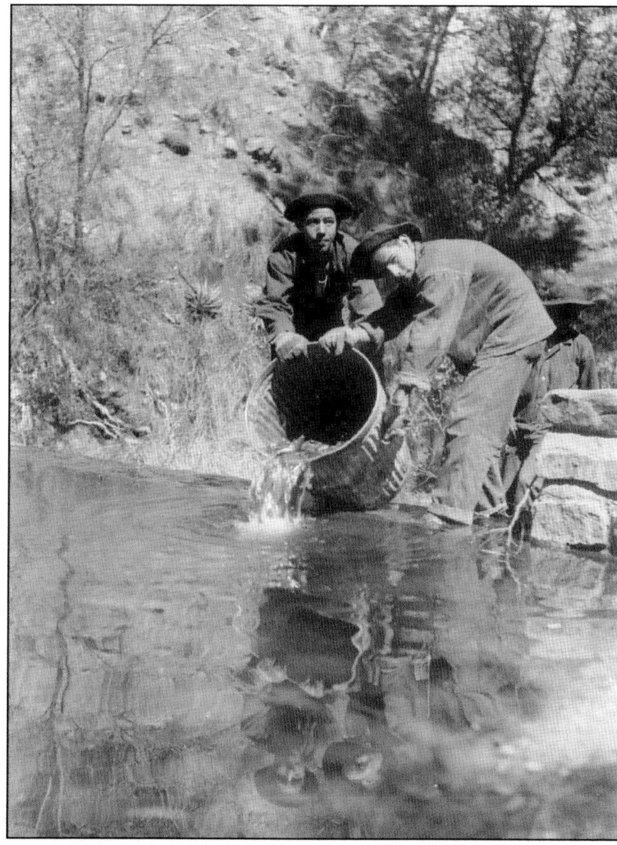

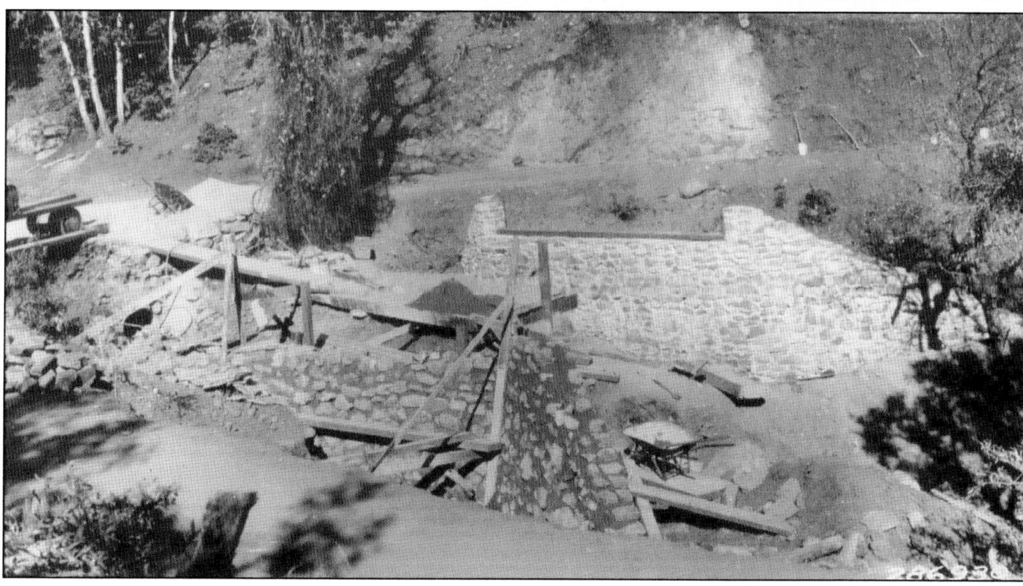

Camp F-10, Cave Creek, built and maintained many miles of mountain roads, which required a considerable amount of blasting and jackhammer work. Pictured here is a bridge built by the camp, which also fenced rangeland, built trails, developed campgrounds, and strung telephone lines. (USFS, SWR.)

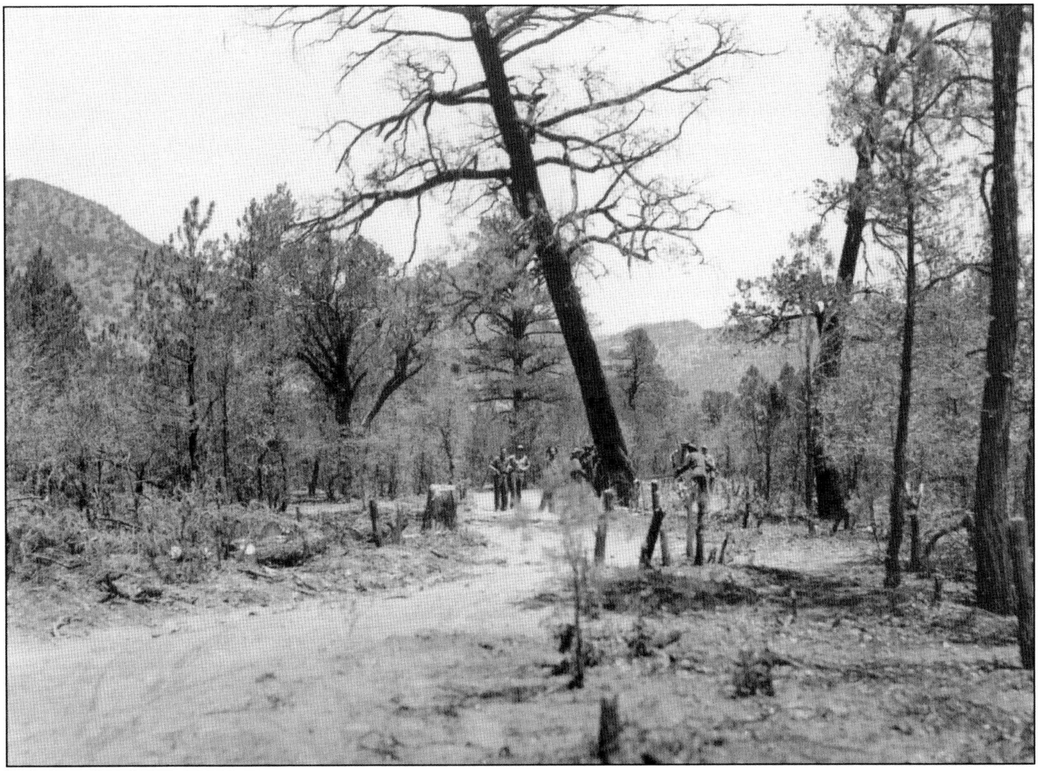

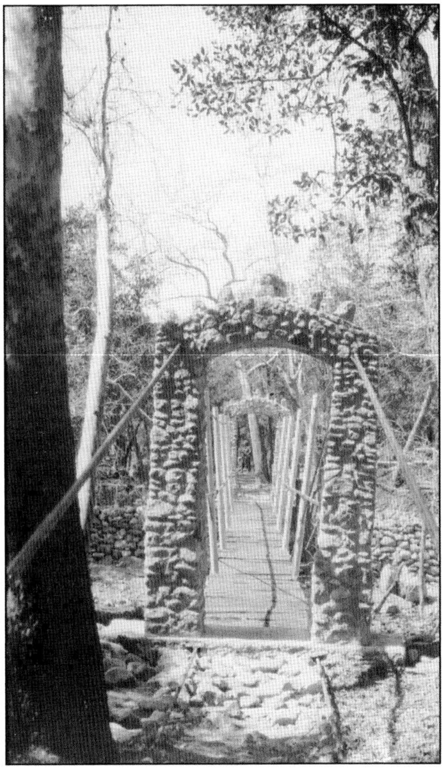

Camp F-12, Rucker Canyon, was on a hillside on the west side of the Chiricahua Mountains and occupied sporadically from summer 1933 until fall 1938. The buildings were widely separated and connected by walkways. The men constructed roads and bridges, strung telephone lines, fought forest fires, developed campgrounds, and improved the timber stand. Range improvement activities included developing springs, performing revegetation, building dams and cattle guards, and erecting fences and stock tanks. The camp constructed Rucker Canyon Road to allow recreational access and to aid in fire protection. (USFS, SWR.)

The men of Camp F-12, Rucker Canyon, in the Chiricahua Mountains constructed recreational facilities at Rustler Park, Rucker Park, Cypress Park, Bathtub Park, and Hermitage Park. This suspension bridge was built in the Hermitage Campground. The camp was located 40 miles northeast of the town of Douglas, and it struggled with a venereal disease outbreak. The Douglas chief of police cooperated with the camp commander and ordered women from bawdy houses out of town. The CCC maintained a prophylaxis station at the Douglas City Hall on weekends. (USFS, SWR.)

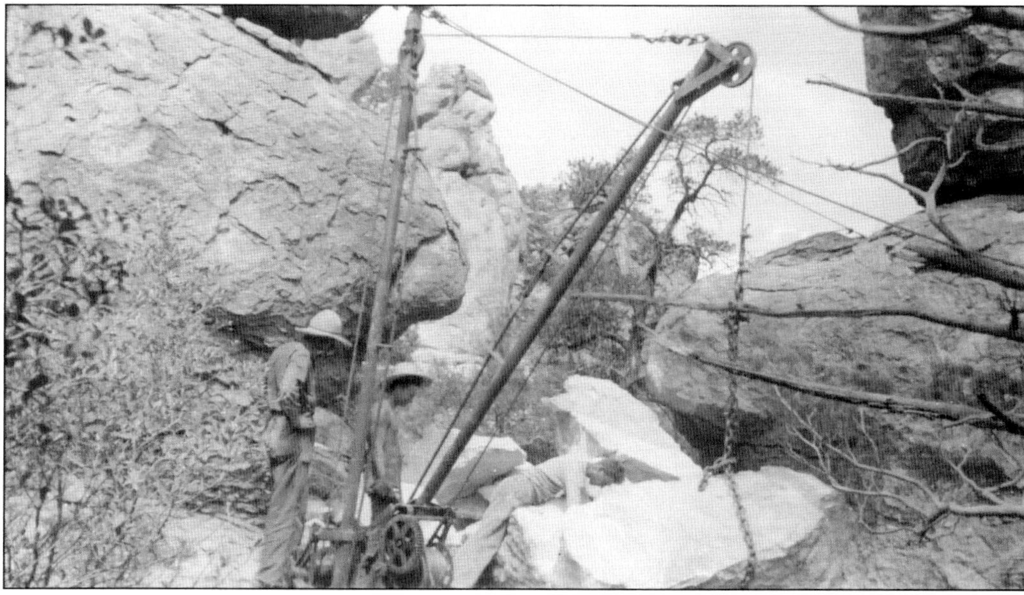

Camp NM-2, Bonita Canyon, labored in the Chiricahua National Monument to construct trails, roads, and recreational facilities to highlight and increase access to the wonders of this area, dubbed the "Wonderland of Rocks" because of its fascinating rock formations. Here, the enrollees are constructing a rock wall in Echo Canyon in 1935. This work would have been formidable, requiring much labor to carve out paths through this wilderness. (NARA MD.)

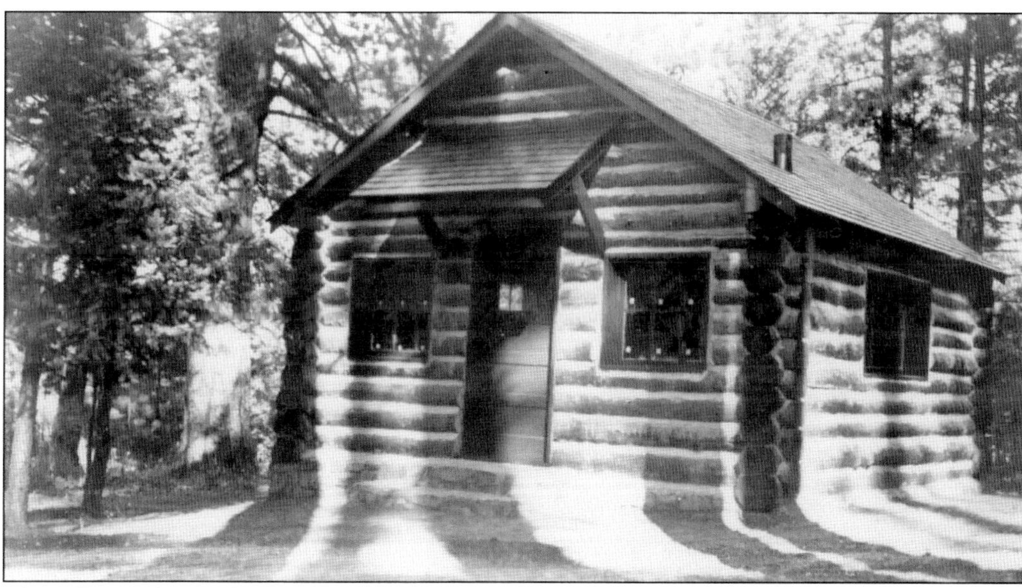

This cabin in the Rustler Park Campground of the Chiricahua National Monument was constructed by Camp NM-2, Bonita Canyon. From June 1934 to June 1940, this camp built campgrounds, fire lookouts, fireplaces, sewer systems, restrooms, bathhouses, a public contact station, houses for National Park Service staff, and a maintenance facility. Many of these structures are still in use today. (NARA MD.)

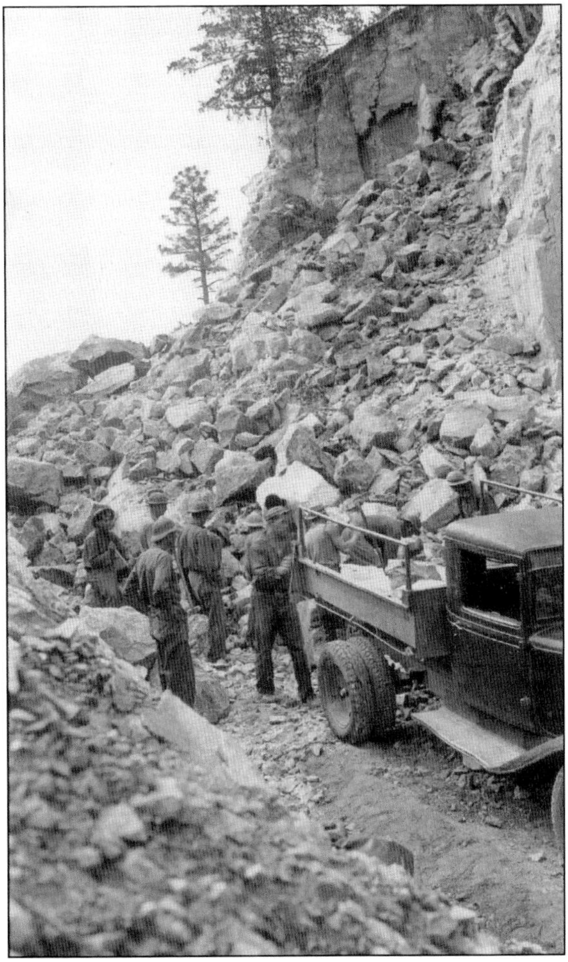

Camp NM-2, Bonita Canyon, constructed roads in the rocky Chiricahua National Monument. The camp was located in Silver Spur Meadow and administered by the National Park Service, but the enrollees worked extensively on US Forest Service projects. This photograph shows a rockslide at the Massai Point Road. Massai Point, named for a Chiricahua Apache, is 6,870 feet above sea level. (NARA MD.)

Throughout the Chiricahua National Monument, Camp NM-2, Bonita Canyon, built trails, including the Heart of Rocks, Rhyolite Canyon, and Echo Canyon Trails. This is an example of a typical finished trail section built by the camp. The trails, campgrounds, picnic areas, and other recreational facilities the CCC developed in the monument have allowed generations of visitors to enjoy the wonders of this area. (NARA MD.)

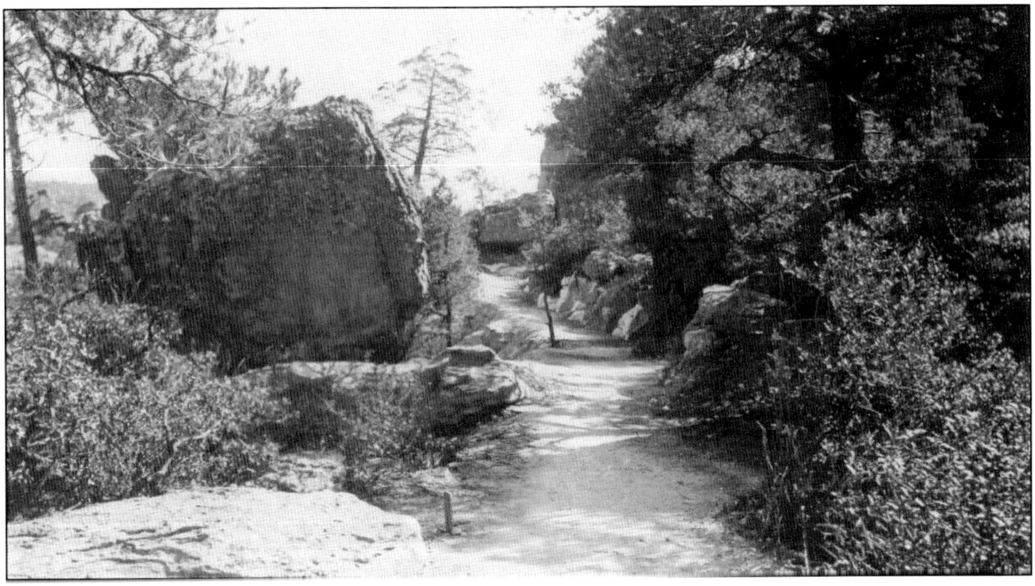

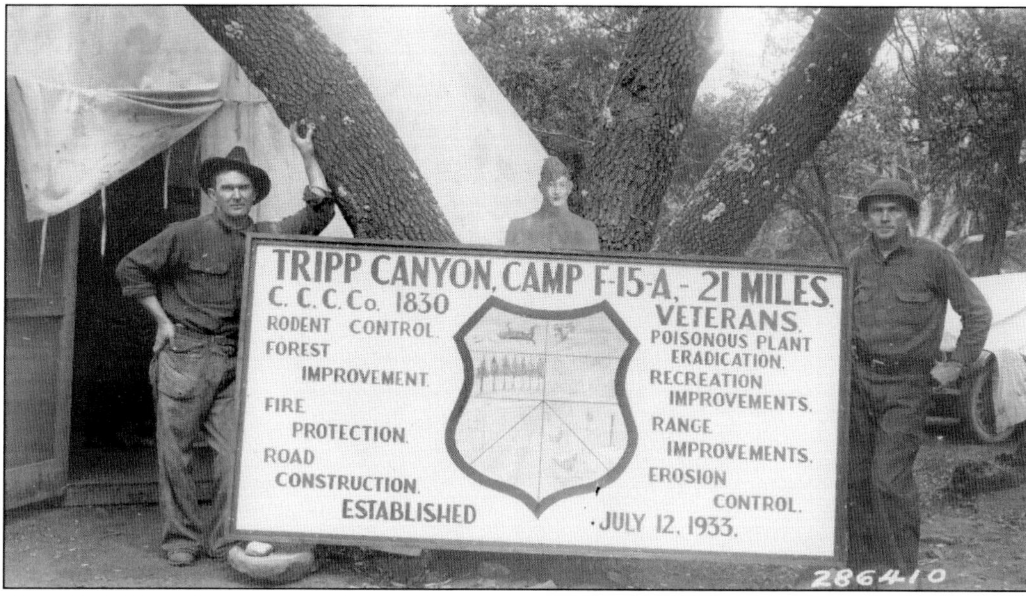

Camp F-15, Tripp Canyon, near the small town of Pima at the north end of the Pinaleño Mountains, was occupied in 1933–1934 by Company 1830V, a World War I veterans' company. Veterans could enroll in the CCC if approved by the Veterans Administration. They lived in separate camps, had no age restrictions, and could be married. The camp worked on building roads, controlling rodents, eradicating poisonous plants, controlling erosion, stringing telephone lines, fighting fires, and improving the forests. After they left, the camp was used as a side camp by other CCC camps. (USFS, SWR.)

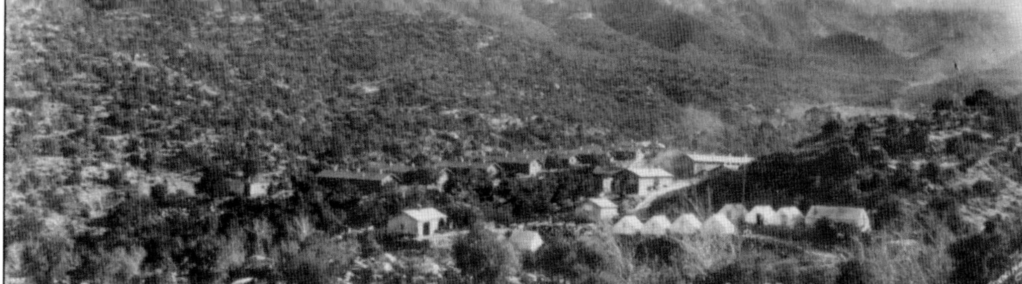

Camp F-41, Noon Creek, is shown in this 1935 photograph. The camp was located at the eastern base of Mount Graham in the Pinaleño Mountains and was occupied during the winter months beginning in 1933. The barracks were located on the opposite side of a small wash from the other camp buildings and had to be reached via a footbridge. (WG, USFS.)

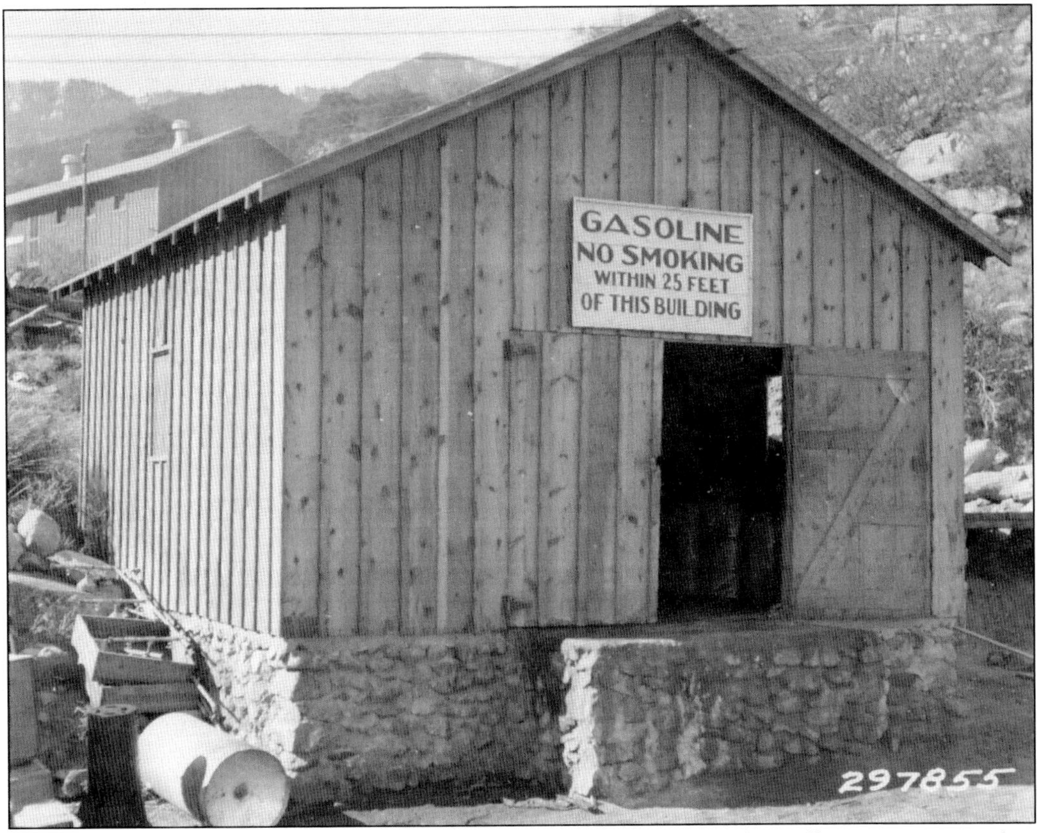

The sign on the F-41, Noon Creek, gas and oil storage house cautioned enrollees to practice safety and refrain from smoking in the building's vicinity. This camp did considerable work building and maintaining roads and stringing telephone lines in what was then the Crook National Forest. It also built fences, developed springs, fought forest fires, built check dams to arrest soil erosion, collected seeds, and built campgrounds. (USFS, SWR.)

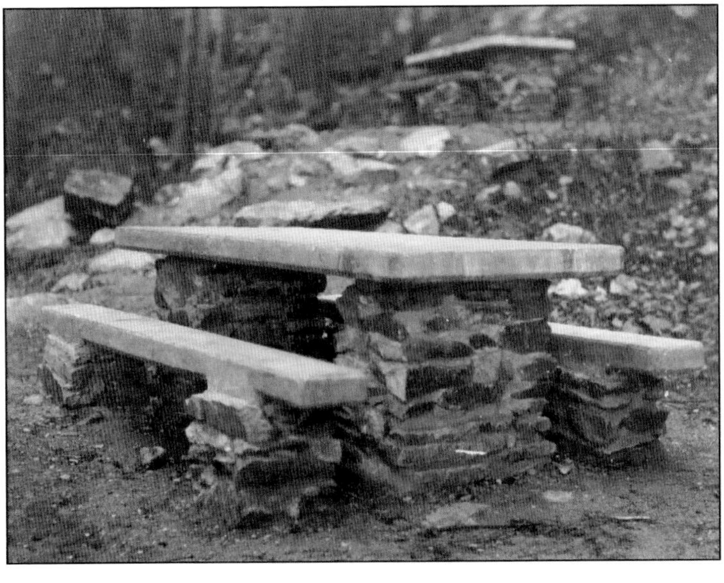

Camp F-41, Noon Creek, constructed recreational facilities in the Pinaleño Mountains of Graham County in what was then the Crook National Forest. This picnic table is typical of many the CCC built in picnic areas throughout the state. The tables and benches were made of uncoursed local stone with concrete tops. (USFS, SWR.)

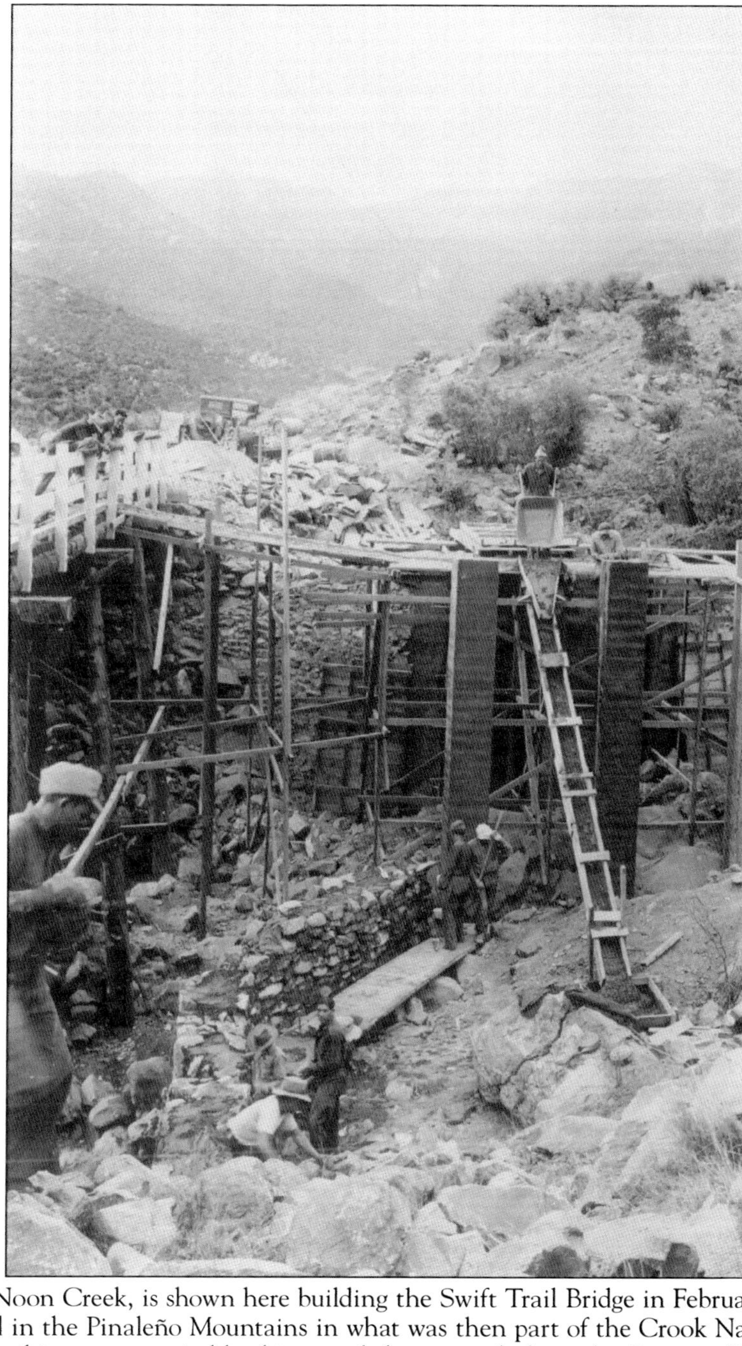

Camp F-41, Noon Creek, is shown here building the Swift Trail Bridge in February 1934. This camp worked in the Pinaleño Mountains in what was then part of the Crook National Forest. The Swift Trail is a steep, switchbacking road that ascends from the Sonoran Desert cacti of the Gila Valley at 2,900 feet above sea level to alpine forests and meadows on the ridges of the Pinaleño Mountains at 9,000 feet. Camp F-74, Columbine, also worked on this road. In 1939, the technical agency supervisor for this camp had the reputation of being overzealous in completing work projects (to the detriment of enrollee welfare) and of trying to terminate enrollees without the proper hearings. The Arizona district commander had to confer with him on many occasions about the situation. (JI.)

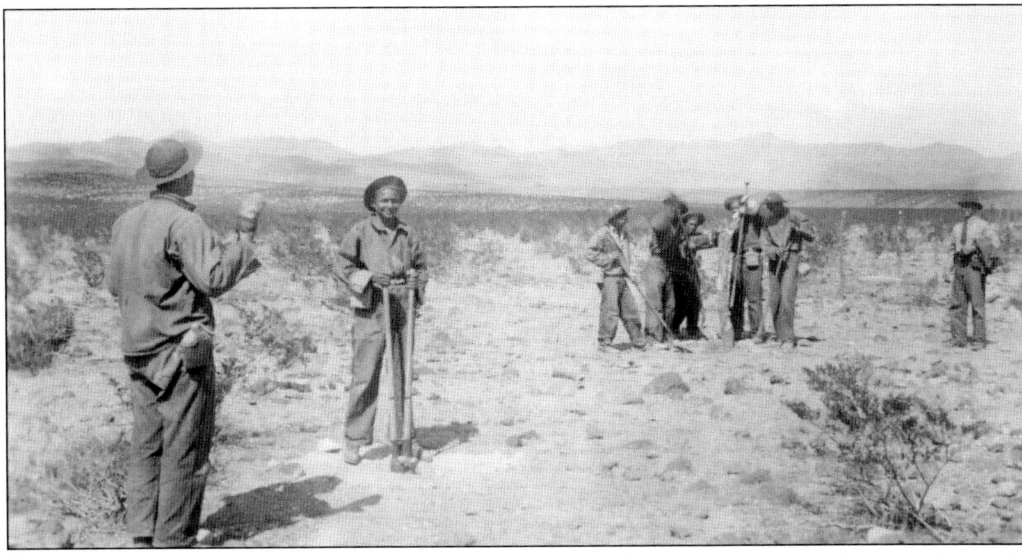

Camp DG-61, Teague Springs, was located across the Gila River from Fort Thomas, five miles south of the Gila Mountains. This camp worked on range management projects to combat soil erosion and lack of vegetation caused by overgrazing. Here, enrollees are setting posts for the Bryce-McEuen Fence to separate two grazing allotments in 1937. Fencing involved not only digging holes and stretching wire but also constructing miles of roads and cutting thousands of posts and stays. (NARA-RMR.)

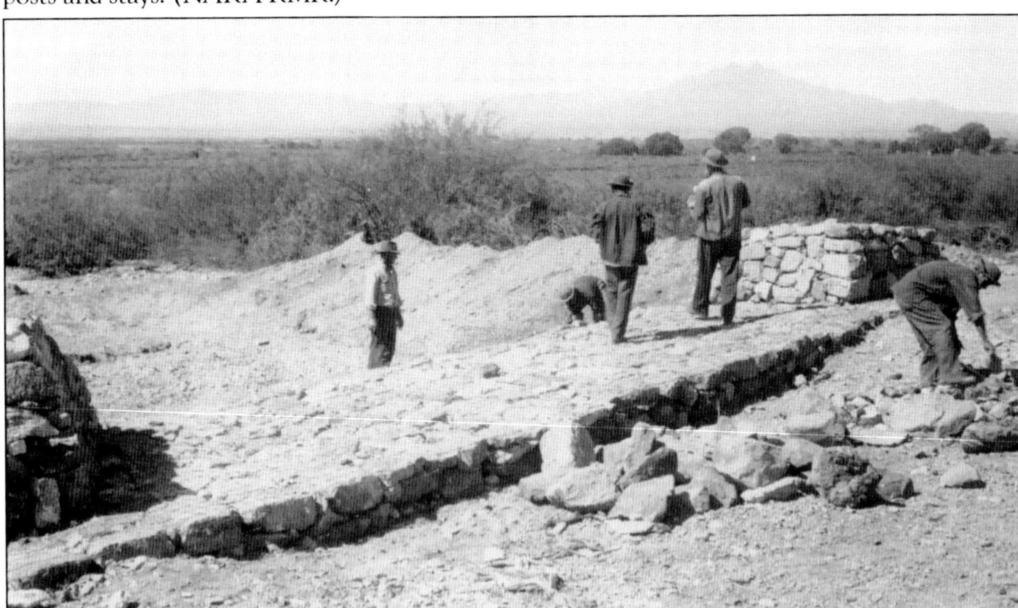

Camp DG-61, Teague Springs, is shown here constructing dip (slanted) walls for the Sunny Side Truck Trail in 1937. This road was constructed in accordance with CCC policy to aid nearby communities and to provide transportation for future work. The community of Sunny Side was cut off when the Gila River flooded, but this road enabled them to reach the bridge at Pima. The camp had two side camps, one at Thatcher and one near Pima, that worked on controlling rodents, eradicating poisonous plants, and erecting fences. (NARA-RMR.)

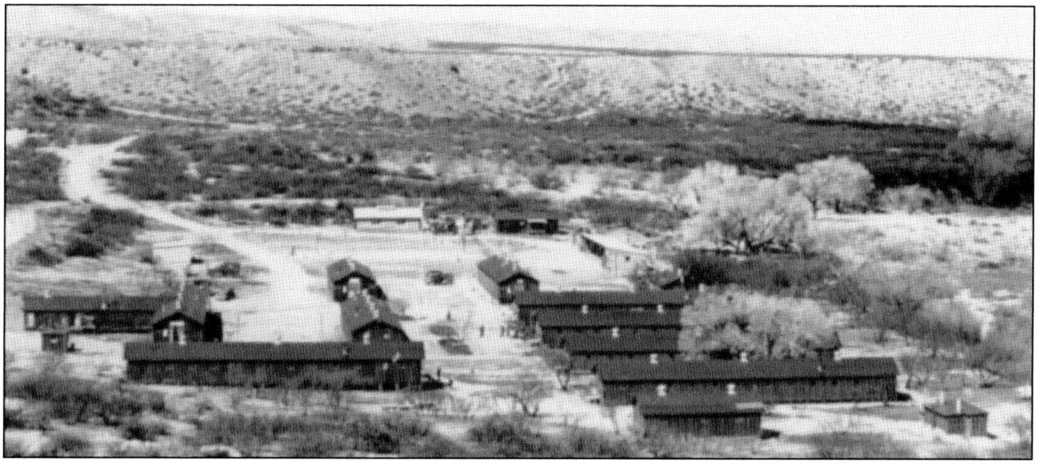

Camp SCS-19-N, Duncan, Arizona/Virden, New Mexico, worked on projects to arrest soil erosion on nearby cattle ranches, such as building dams, erecting stock tanks, developing springs, and erecting fences. It was known as Camp Mesquitita. This isolated camp suffered from the lack of entertainment for the enrollees and time delays in getting supplies. The enrollees often had to wait to have their shoes repaired and replaced. Most camp buildings in Arizona are gone, often taken down at the end of the CCC era for materials to support the war effort. (EB.)

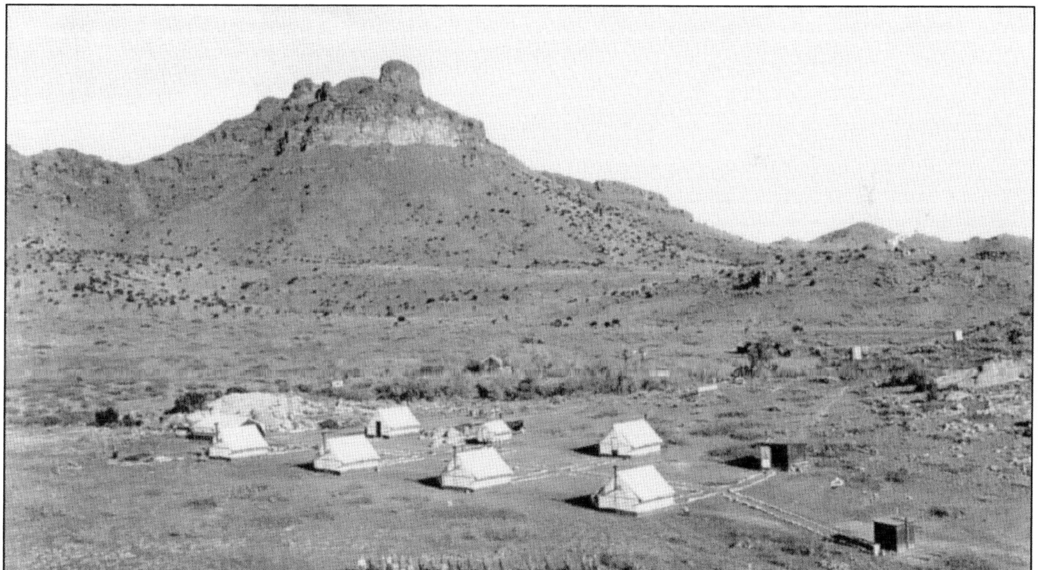

The Lazy B Ranch near the Arizona-New Mexico border was owned by Harry Alan Day, father of US Supreme Court Justice Sandra Day O'Connor, in the 1930s. Day was a "cooperator" with the CCC, which meant that in exchange for materials and equipment he got CCC labor to work on his ranch. The work projects were not "ordinary" ranch duties, but approved projects such as building roads. The Gruwell Side Camp from SCS-19-N, Duncan, Arizona/Virden, New Mexico, worked on the ranch in 1938. (EB.)

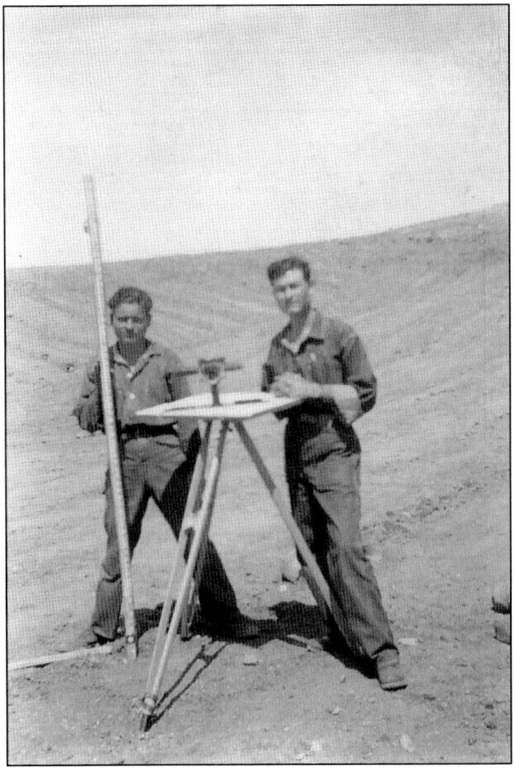

Enrollees Jack Hale (left) and Elson Alvarez from Camp SCS-19, St. David, are surveying on a Cochise County cattle ranch. This camp worked extensively on area ranches, building water-control structures such as dikes, dams, and rock spreaders, many of which are still in use. Elson is using the level on the plane table to determine elevation in conjunction with the level rod Jack is holding. The soil erosion in this area at this time is evident in the background. (EA.)

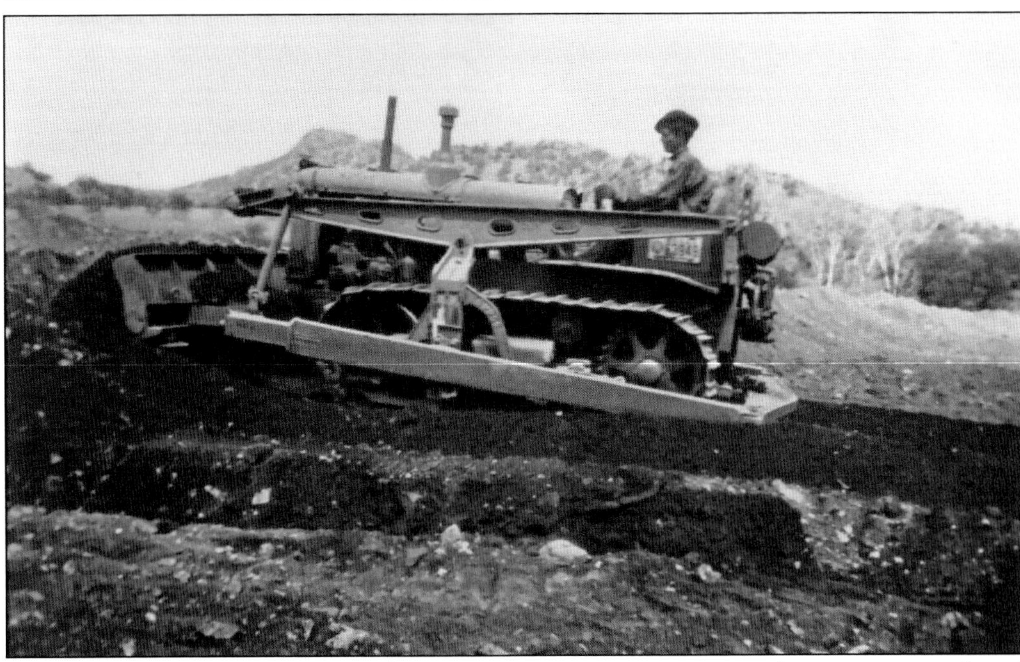

This Camp SCS-19, St. David, enrollee is using a tractor in preparation for erecting a stock tank on a Cochise County cattle ranch. The many stock tanks this camp erected ensured that the cattle did not have to walk far to reach water, a process that leads to soil erosion. Many of the men who worked as tractor operators in the CCC went on to become tank drivers in World War II. (EA.)

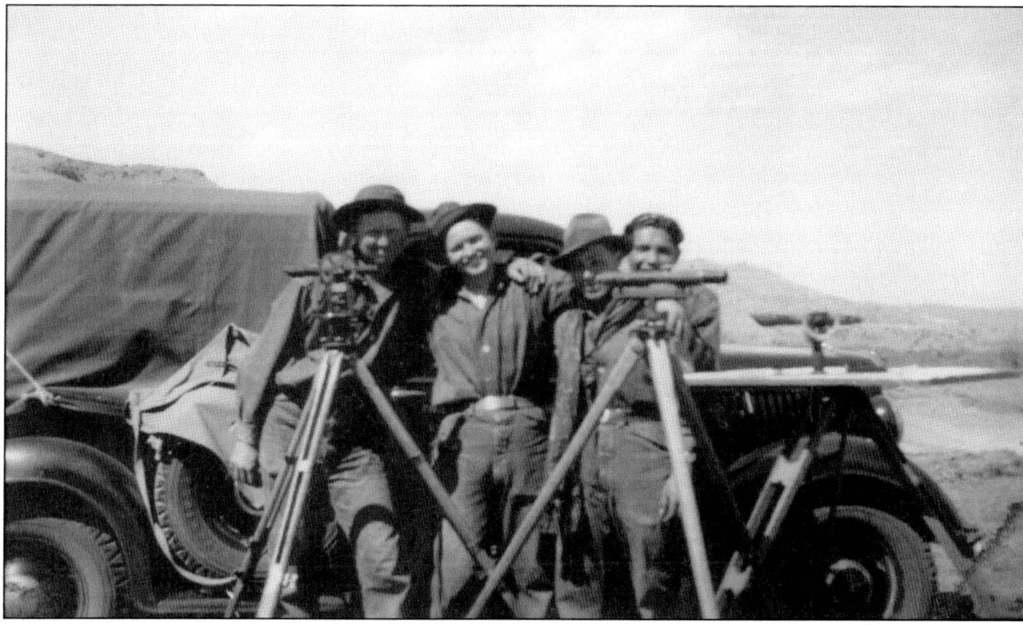

This survey crew is from Camp SCS-19, St. David. One of the benefits of the CCC was that the enrollees learned to work together as a team and get along with people from different places and backgrounds. Many formed lifelong friendships from their CCC days. The older man second from the right is a member of the Technical Services staff, who supervised the work projects. These staff members were generally held in high esteem by the enrollees. (EA.)

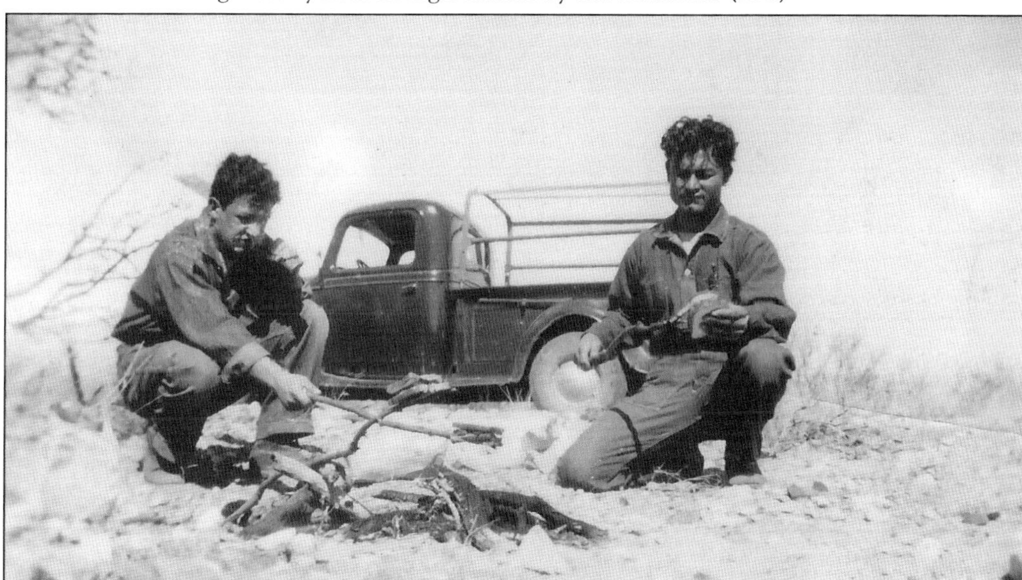

Camp SCS-19, St. David, enrollees Robert Garcia (left) and Elson Alvarez are grilling bologna and jam sandwiches over a fire while on their lunch break. The February 1939 camp inspection report noted that there "was almost united complaint against cold field lunches" by the enrollees. Tucson District headquarters instructed the camp commander to vary the content of lunches and to add dessert. Still, Elson says, they "just wanted a hot meal" while working, and the camp commander told them to build a fire. (EA.)

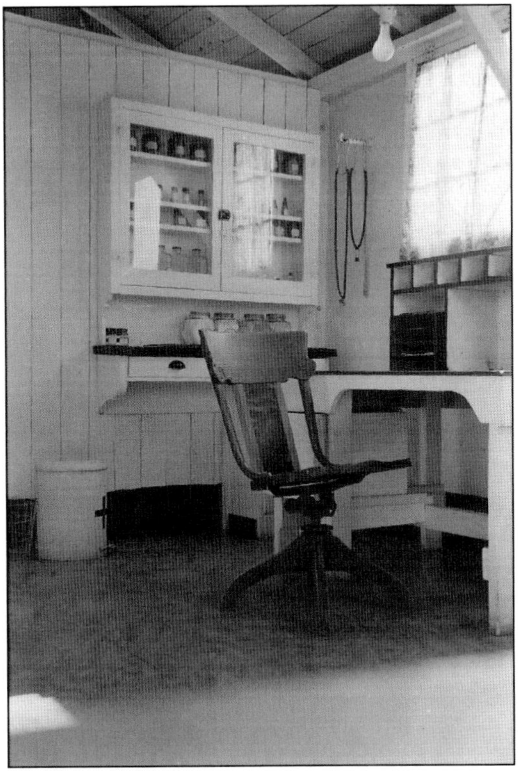

The US Army was responsible for providing medical care to the enrollees. Each camp had an infirmary, like this one at SCS-19, St. David. A camp physician gave vaccinations, provided health and hygiene tips in the camp newspaper, attended to minor ailments, and taught a Red Cross first aid course. Special investigators from the CCC regularly visited camps to check on safety issues, and the camps held regular safety meetings. (EA.)

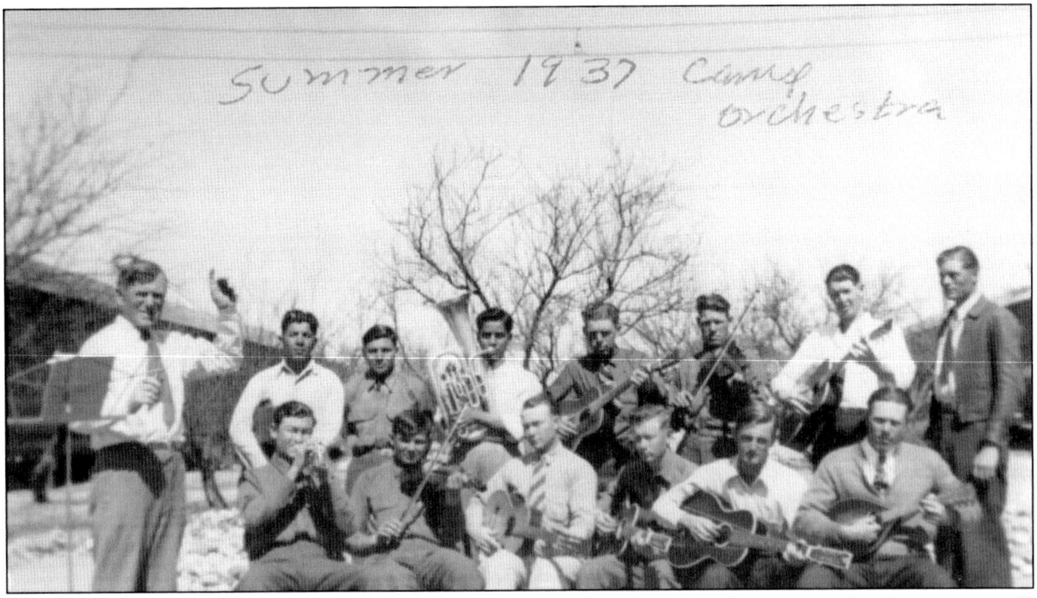

The camp educational program offered instruction in academic and vocational subjects, as well as opportunities to participate in the arts. Camps had drama, music, and choir classes, and they presented plays and provided musical entertainment to camp visitors. This camp orchestra from Camp SCS-19, St. David, was given many of its musical instruments by the surrounding community, although some of the enrollees came to camp with their own guitars. Enrollee Elson Alvarez (far left, bottom row) learned to play the trumpet while in the CCC. (EA.)

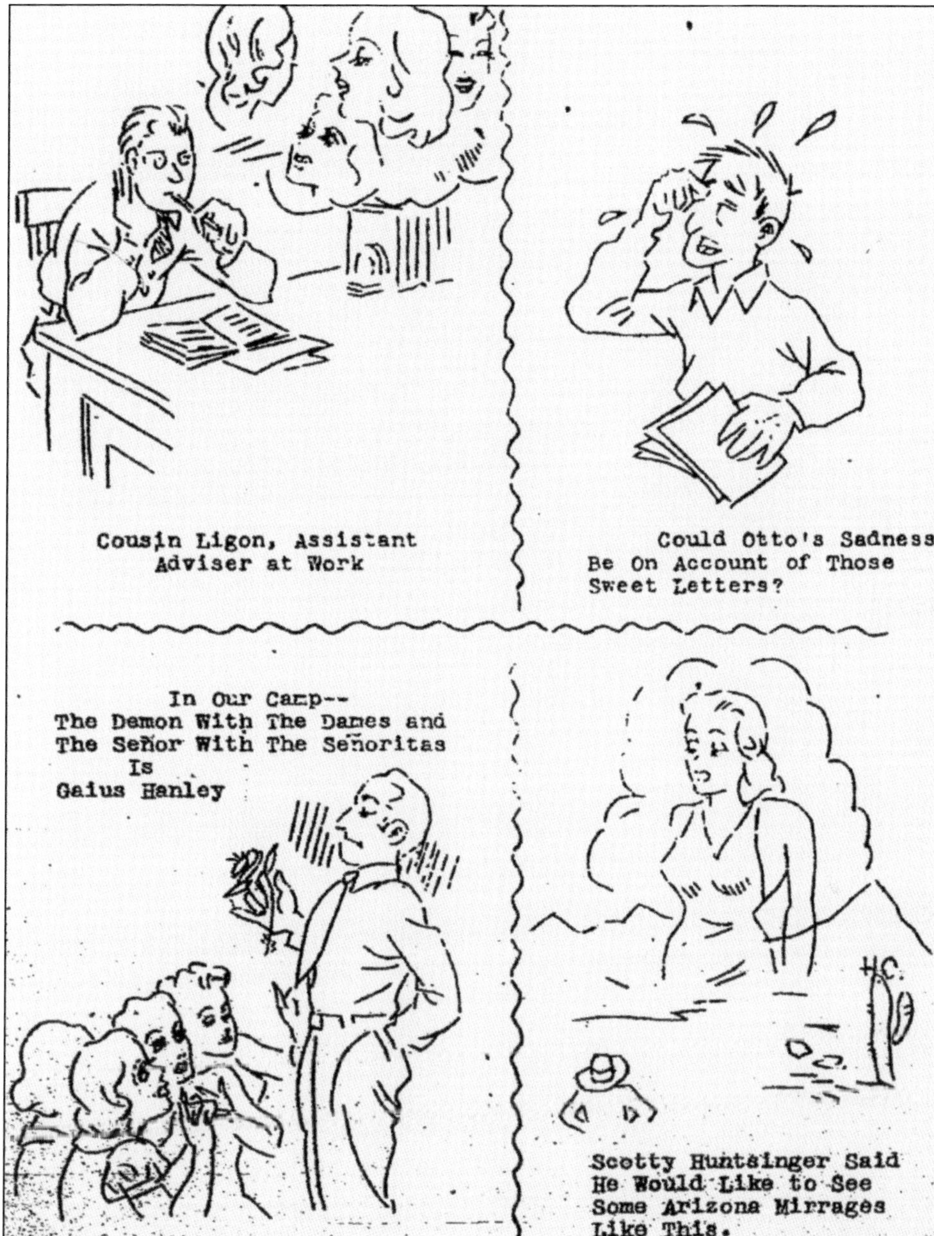

The camp newspapers helped combat illiteracy, bolster camp morale, and build team spirit. They were forums for opinions, complaints, and advice. The enrollees in the camp's educational program produced the newspaper under the guidance of the camp educational advisor. Names ranged from descriptive to amusing (*The Eight-Holer*, Flagstaff, and *Cactus Bites*, Safford). The quality of these newspapers varied widely, with some having excellent writing and artwork. A typical camp newspaper issue would contain jokes, amusing illustrations, health and safety articles, words of wisdom on appropriate behavior, poems, and updates on the camp's sports, work, educational, and recreational programs. The pages had plenty of jokes, gossip, stories, and illustrations about the enrollees' real or imagined love lives. Not surprisingly, the local boys were not usually very fond of the CCC boys. (AC.)

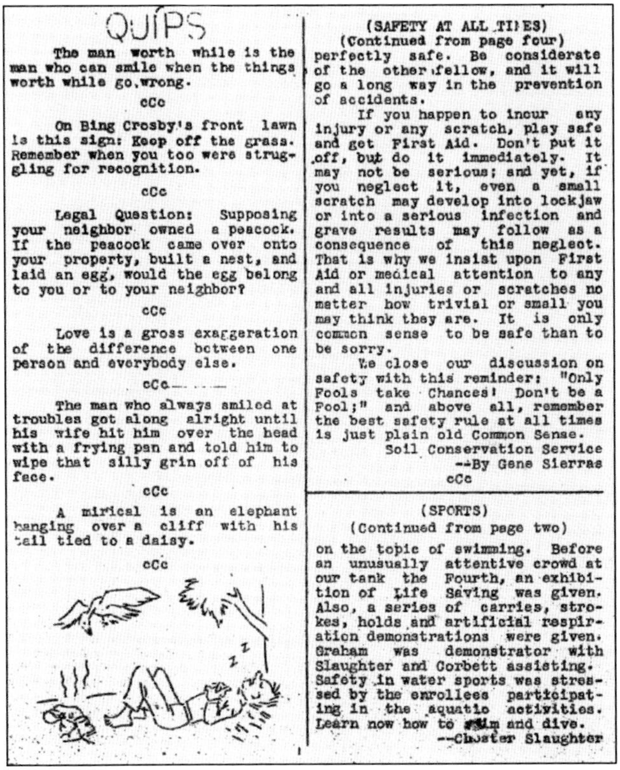

QUIPS

The man worth while is the man who can smile when the things worth while go wrong.

cCc

On Bing Crosby's front lawn is this sign: Keep off the grass. Remember when you too were struggling for recognition.

cCc

Legal Question: Supposing your neighbor owned a peacock. If the peacock came over onto your property, built a nest, and laid an egg, would the egg belong to you or to your neighbor?

cCc

Love is a gross exaggeration of the difference between one person and everybody else.

cCc

The man who always smiled at troubles got along alright until his wife hit him over the head with a frying pan and told him to wipe that silly grin off of his face.

cCc

A mirical is an elephant hanging over a cliff with his tail tied to a daisy.

cCc

(SAFETY AT ALL TIMES)
(Continued from page four)
perfectly safe. Be considerate of the other fellow, and it will go a long way in the prevention of accidents.

If you happen to incur any injury or any scratch, play safe and get First Aid. Don't put it off, but do it immediately. It may not be serious; and yet, if you neglect it, even a small scratch may develop into lockjaw or into a serious infection and grave results may follow as a consequence of this neglect. That is why we insist upon First Aid or medical attention to any and all injuries or scratches no matter how trivial or small you may think they are. It is only common sense to be safe than to be sorry.

We close our discussion on safety with this reminder: "Only Fools take Chances! Don't be a Fool;" and above all, remember the best safety rule at all times is just plain old Common Sense.

Soil Conservation Service
--By Gene Sierras

cCc

(SPORTS)
(Continued from page two)
on the topic of swimming. Before an unusually attentive crowd at our tank the Fourth, an exhibition of Life Saving was given. Also, a series of carries, strokes, holds and artificial respiration demonstrations were given. Graham was demonstrator with Slaughter and Corbett assisting. Safety in water sports was stressed by the enrollees participating in the aquatic activities. Learn now how to swim and dive.
--Chester Slaughter

Illiteracy among enrollees was a major concern of the CCC administration, and the camp newspaper published by the enrollees in each camp helped them develop reading and writing skills. The newspapers were usually produced on mimeograph machines, and their frequency varied from weekly to monthly to occasionally. Enrollees were encouraged to send copies home to their families. The newspapers are a rich source of information on camp activities and on what the CCC experience was like for the enrollees. (AC.)

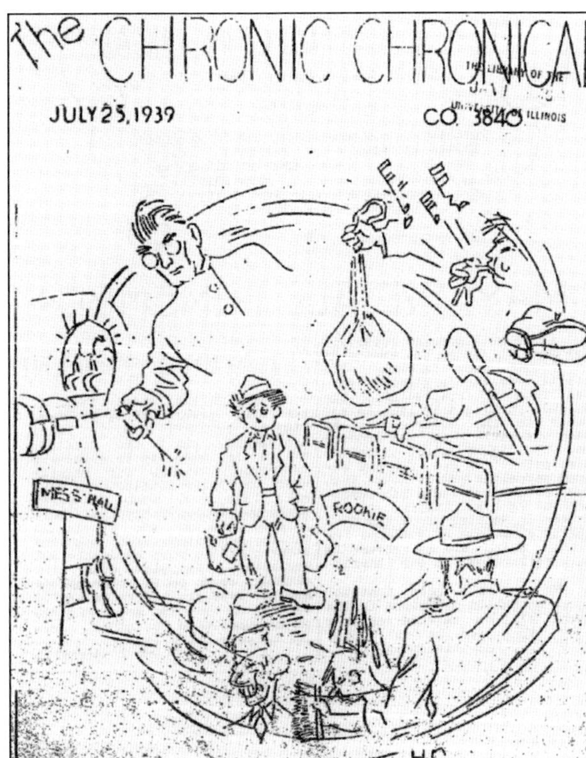

This Camp SCS-19, St. David, newspaper cover shows how a rookie enrollee would have experienced his first days in the CCC. He had to learn when meals were served, how to follow orders from the Army officers, what the camp work projects were like, how to keep his living space clean and neat, and how to get along with other enrollees. The newspapers helped in this orientation process by welcoming new enrollees to camp and helping them figure out how to fit in. (AC.)

Three

Central Arizona
Maricopa and Pinal Counties

By 1930, Maricopa County was the most populous county in the state, tallying 150,970 people of the state's total 435,573. It had nine CCC camps, three of these at South Mountain Park. Other camps included F-34 at Ashdale and Cave Creek, Bureau of Reclamation camps at Tempe and Papago Park, SP-5 at Papago Park, and two Department of Grazing camps at Arlington (DG-109 and G-109).

The Arlington camps did typical grazing projects such as fences, stock reservoirs, and spring development. They had side camps at Vekol Valley near Mobile as well as at Kofa Mountain near Vicksburg in present-day La Paz County. This side camp was unusual in that some of the time the enrollees were from the CCC Indian Division, yet the Bureau of Indian Affairs supervised them rather than the Army and the Division of Grazing. At the Kofa and Cabeza Prieta Game Preserves, they assisted the Fish and Wildlife Service with bighorn sheep habitat. Some of their completed projects include Owl Head Tank, Cholla Tank, New Well–Squaw Peak Truck Trail, Four Peaks Silt Trap, Four Peaks Tank, Kofa Side Camp, Bighorn Sheep Tanks, and the Kofa Patrol Station.

Pinal County had only three camps; all occupied less than two years. Much like the Arlington camps, no photographs were located. Camp SCS-20 near Apache Junction constructed small check dams, flood-control dams, water-spreading dikes, and contour ditches as well as revegetating land. Camp DG-48 at Winkelman had side camps at Eloy and Dripping Springs. Its most notable work was the near completion of the Aravaipa Truck Trail. In addition, it completed the Barkerville and Dripping Springs Truck Trails. It also strung telephone lines, did erosion and flood control, developed springs, dug wells, and erected stock tanks. The work of DG-49 at Eloy included constructing dams, drilling wells, and constructing the Eloy-Silver Bell and the Red Rock Silver Bell Roads.

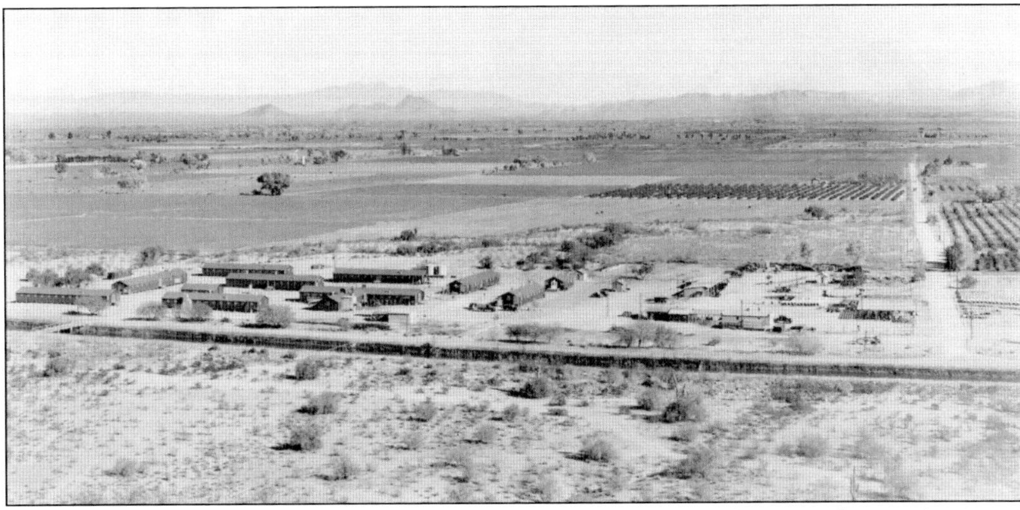

Camp BR-19 was located in Tempe near Papago Park and occupied from October 1935 to March 1938. Many of its first inhabitants were West Virginia boys who were welcomed by state and local dignitaries, including Phoenix mayor Joseph S. Jenckes and the Phoenix Chamber of Commerce. Gov. Benjamin Moeur noted that the camp's work was "recognized as one of the outstanding activities of the past two years and we in Arizona are very appreciative of the splendid work that has been done." (NARA MD.)

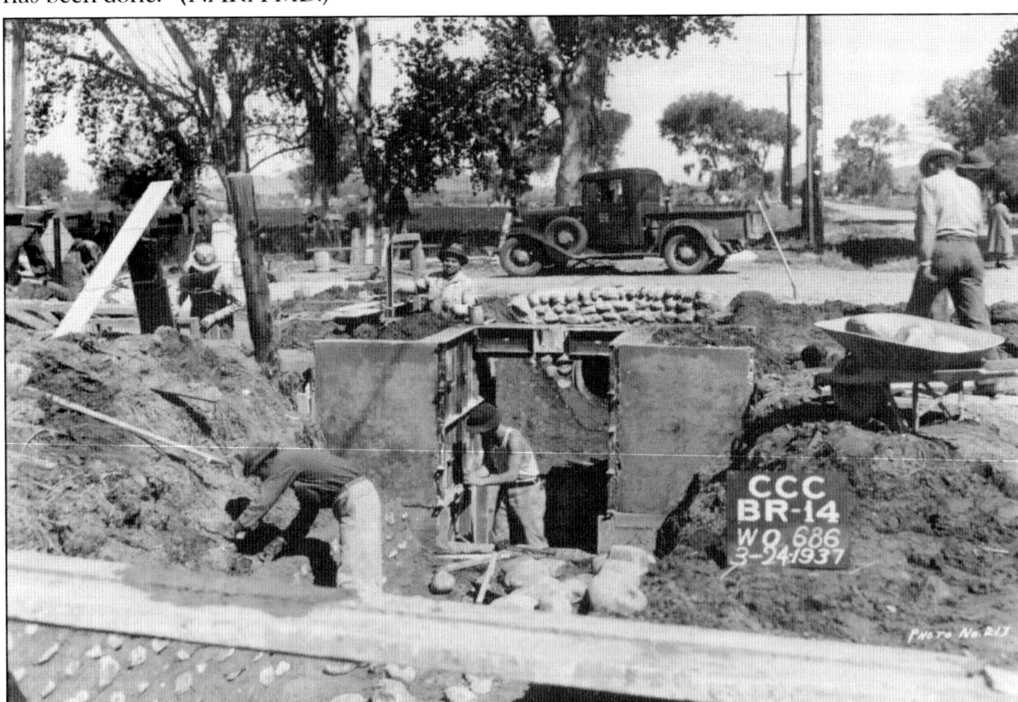

Camp BR-14, like BR-19, did considerable work for the Salt River Irrigation Project. Located at Papago Park, it built roads and riprap along canal banks and installed precast concrete irrigation pipes. Much of its work involved replacing old wooden irrigation structures with modern ones made of steel and concrete. The two camps had installed over 35,000 feet of concrete irrigation pipe by the time both closed in 1938. (NARA-RMR.)

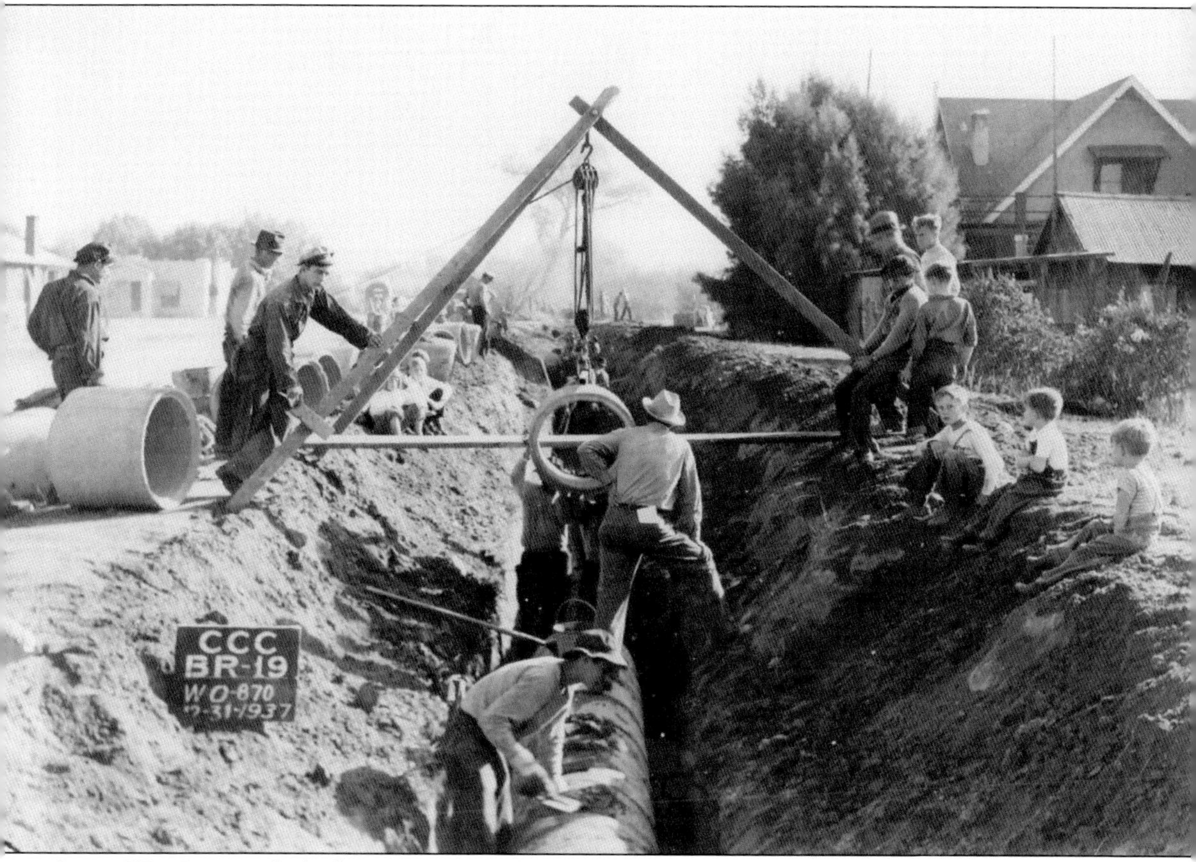

Camp BR-19 not only laid irrigation pipe but also staffed a plant that manufactured concrete pipe for BR-19 and BR-14 and a sand and gravel processing plant. They constructed buildings, including a four-room structure for ditch riders, and they made the adobe bricks for the walls. Other work included controlling rodents, razing undesirable structures, and constructing dams. BR-19 was first staffed by Company 2544, which was mostly West Virginia boys, and then by Company 2849, which was mostly Arizona, Texas, and Oklahoma boys. In this photograph, enrollees install irrigation pipe. Note the children on the right near the excavation—something that would be forbidden today. (NARA MD.)

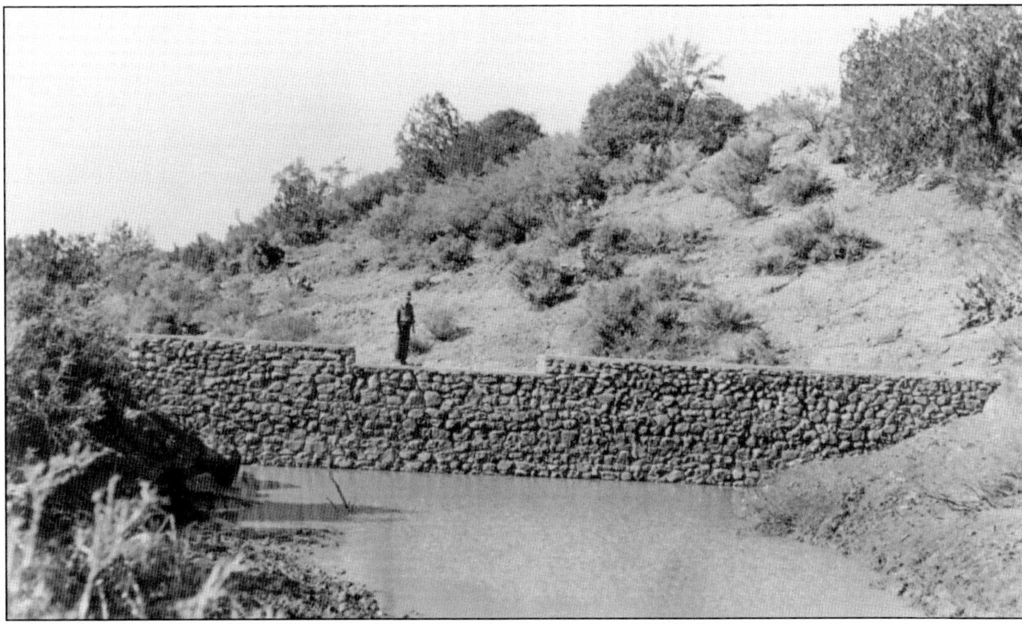

Camp F-34, located at Ashdale and Cave Creek, was occupied almost continuously from 1933 to 1941. Its work included erosion control, firefighting, search and rescue, fence construction, and the Mount Ord fire lookout tower. Considerable effort was put into road construction, including building the Camp Creek Road and widening the Bloody Basin to Ashdale Road. The Cartwright Dam, pictured here, was completed in December 1933. (JI.)

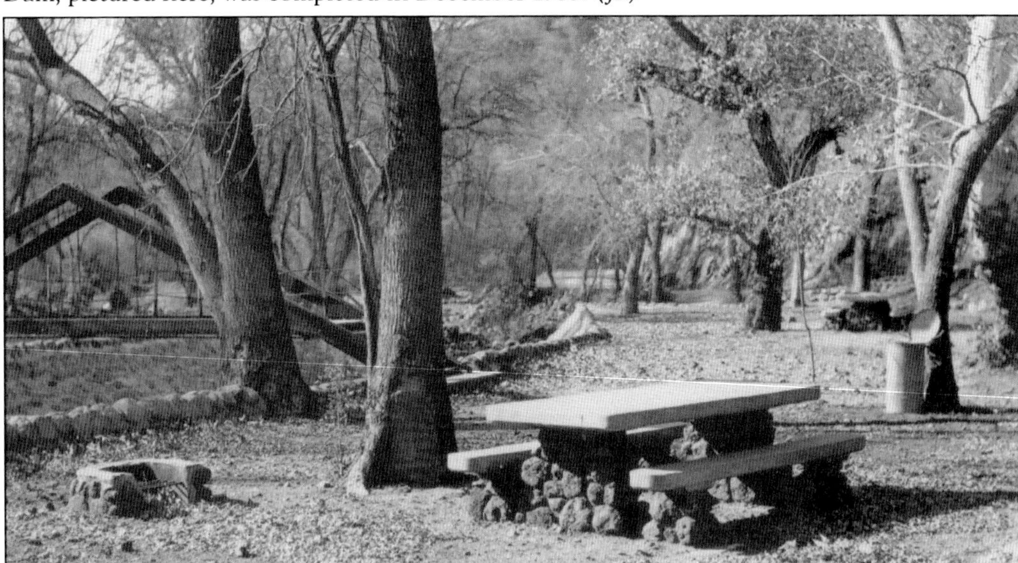

Camp F-34 completed recreation developments at Ashdale (seen here in 1934), Seven Springs, and Camp Creek. The enrollees not only built picnic tables but also constructed water and sewage systems and did the landscaping at the recreation areas. Work in the Tonto National Forest was initially oriented to resource protection such as constructing roads, stringing telephone lines, and erecting fences but over time expanded to include recreational-facilities development. (Photograph by F.L. Kirby; USFS, SWR.)

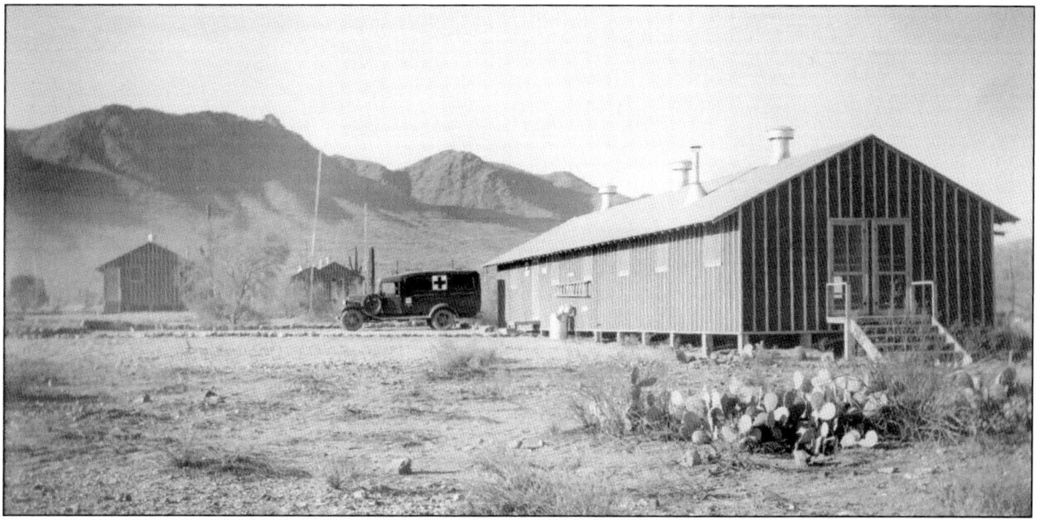

South Mountain Park (SP-3, SP-4, and MA-2) was occupied by junior CCC companies seasonally during the winters of 1933–1937, with Company 1826V occupying it in June 1938–1941. The latter accomplished a great deal, but Special Investigator A.W. Stockman reported, "This company has always been difficult to handle. There are from 20 to 39 heavy and constant drinkers among the veterans. The proximity of a beer and wine dispensary (one-half mile from camp) has been the cause of a disturbing influence on the camp." Here is the SP-3 camp infirmary in 1934. (NARA MD.)

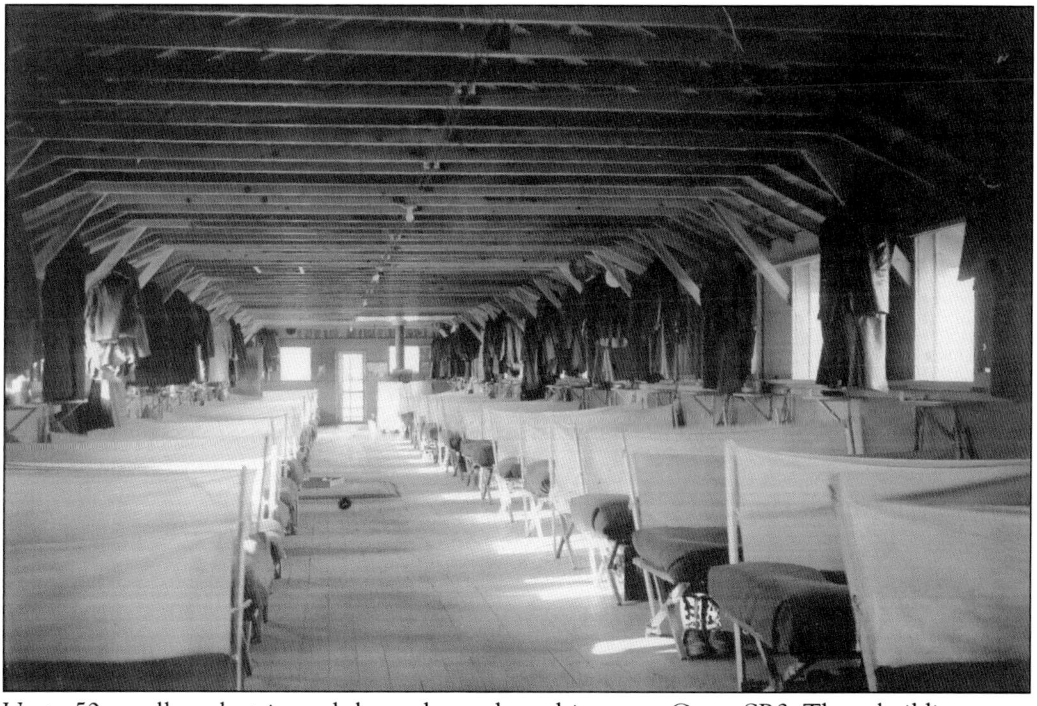

Up to 50 enrollees slept in each barracks, such as this one at Camp SP-3. These buildings were built in matching sections, easily assembled and disassembled and transported by truck or train. As they were made almost wholly of wood, they were very susceptible to fire. Typically, an enrollee fire "watchman" patrolled the barracks during the night in order to alert enrollees of an incident. (NARA MD.)

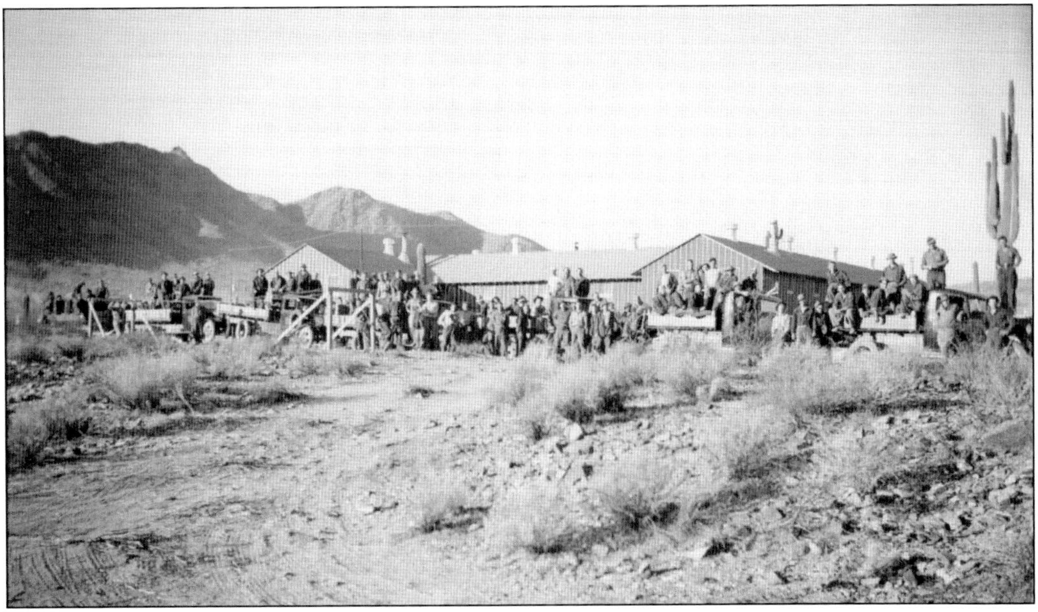

Camp SP-3 enrollees of Company 831 pose in March 1934, ready to drive to their work assignments. Reveille was sounded at 6:00 a.m., enrollees then shaved and showered, and breakfast was served at 7:00 a.m. After breakfast, enrollees cleaned up the area and reported for work at 8:00 a.m. Lunch lasted for one hour, with the work day ending at 4:00 p.m. Retreat was at 5:00 p.m. and dinner at 5:30 p.m., with lights out at 10:00 p.m. (NARA MD.)

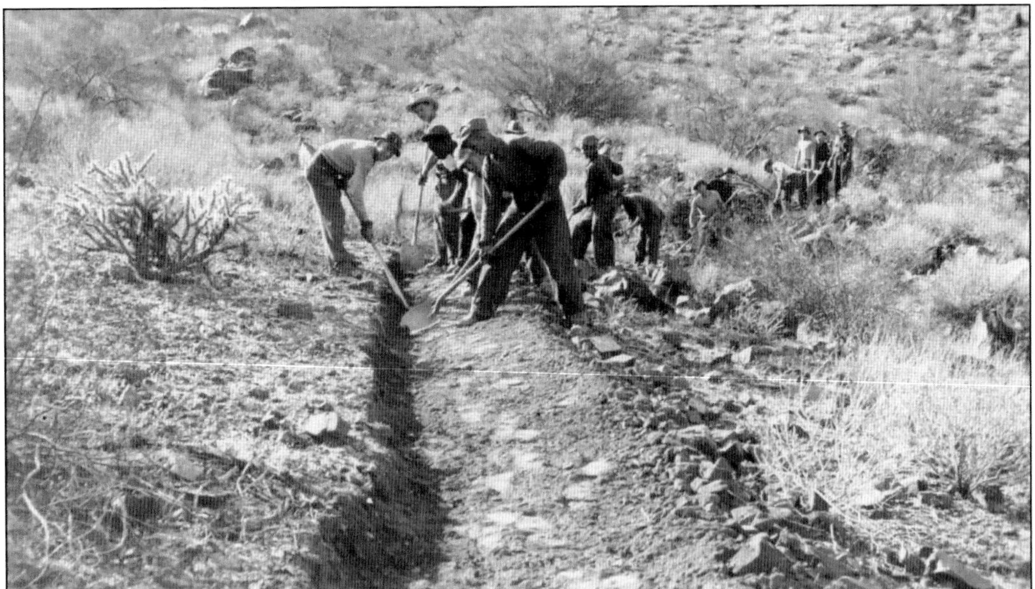

Enrollees of Company 831 constructed the Estrella Trail in 1934. Here, African American enrollees are working with white enrollees, an uncommon practice. The 1930s was a time of segregation across the United States, and African American enrollees were frequently given jobs that others did not want, such as cooking and cleaning. This company had three to seven black enrollees out of the 200 in the company. After 1936, Washington, DC, ordered strict segregation and black Arizona enrollees were shipped out of state to work in segregated companies. (NARA MD.)

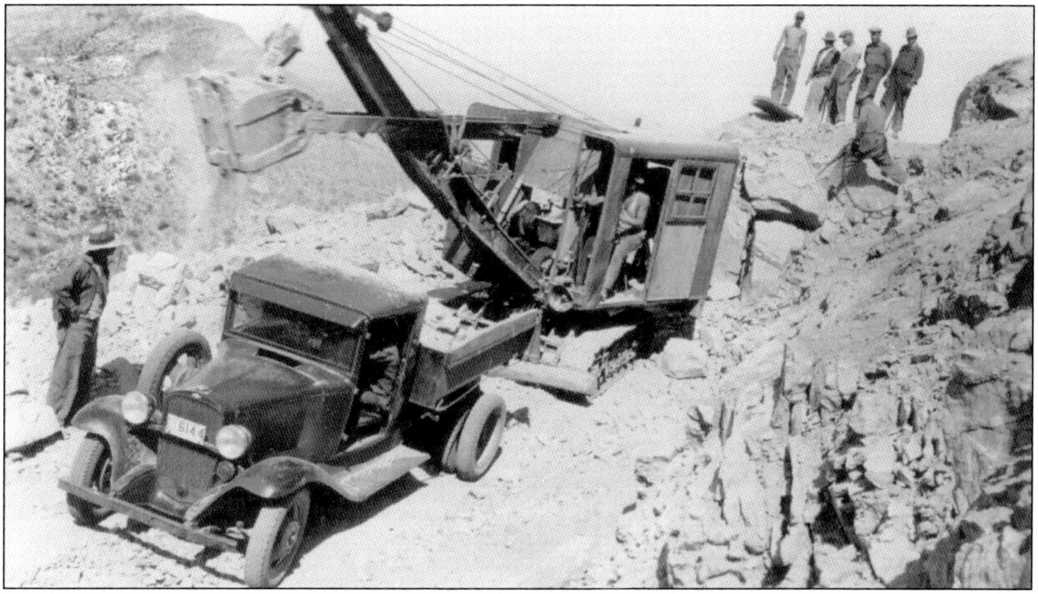

A gasoline-powered shovel is used on a road rock cut in March 1934, with the enrollee crew at the rear with the jackhammer. Enrollee Louis Purvis, a member of Company 818 while at Grand Canyon's bottom and at South Mountain Park, noted the work in both locations was almost identical. He stated that 818 had experienced jackhammer and powder men, surveyors, compressor operators, rock masons, concrete workers, and truck drivers—with all of them "experienced with shovel and wheelbarrow." (NARA MD.)

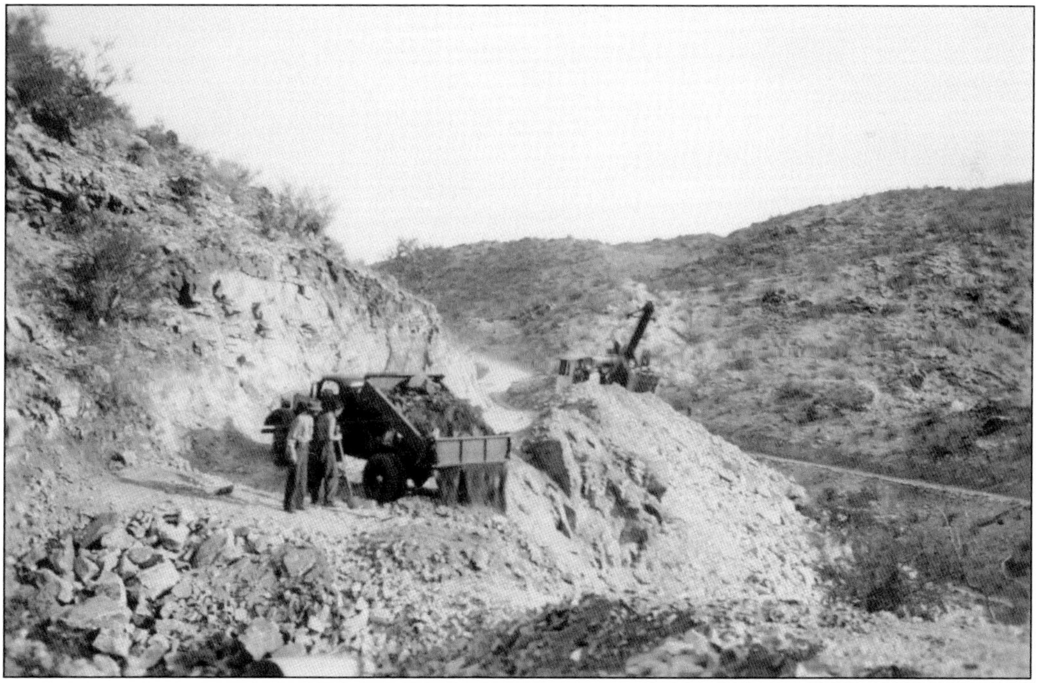

The work of enrollees of Company 2545 at Camp SP-3 in April 1936 included substantial work on South Mountain Park's roads. By May 1941, the CCC had completed 24 miles of roads, parking facilities for 1,500 automobiles, 11,000 feet of pipelines, and 10,000 feet of power lines. (NARA MD.)

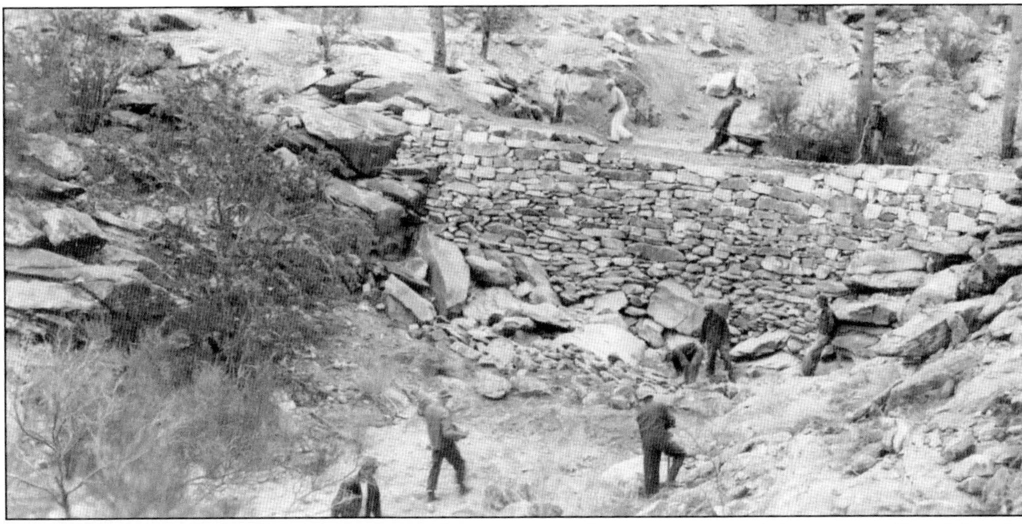

Camp SP-4 enrollees (shown here in 1935) constructed erosion-control dams as well as 26 miles of trails by 1941. Other CCC work at South Mountain Park included stringing telephone lines, installing guardrails along roads, landscaping, collecting and planting seeds, obliterating old roads, surveying, and making park signs. (NARA MD.)

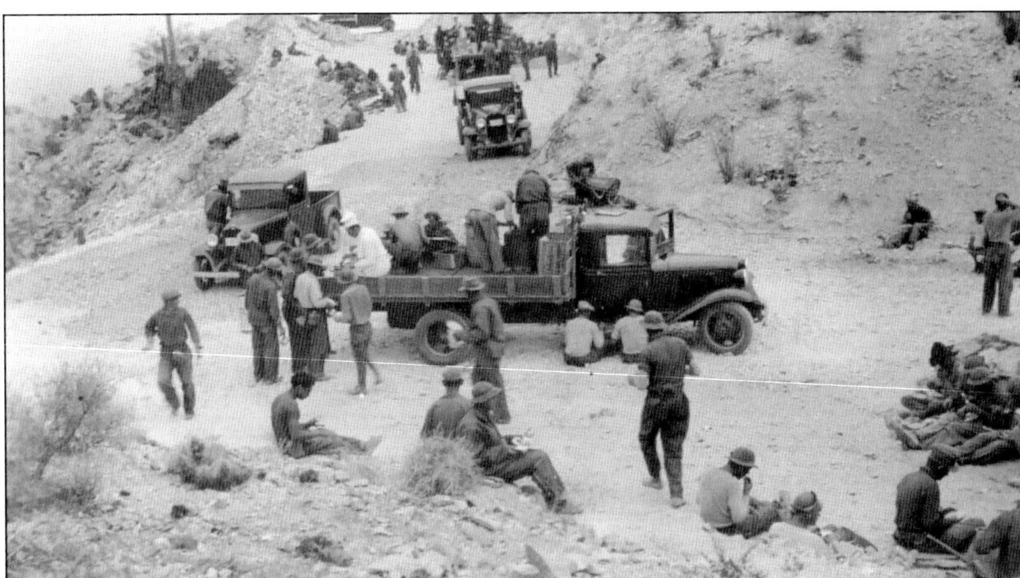

With the mess hall not far away, Camp SP-4, South Mountain Park, enrollees received a hot noon meal each work day, as shown here in February 1934. Many enrollees were from very poor families, so they looked forward to the regular food they did not get at home. Nationwide, the average enrollee gained 8–14 pounds during his first six months of enrollment. CCC meals were almost always from Army menus. As their work was mostly hard physical labor, they were served 5,000 calories a day. (NARA MD.)

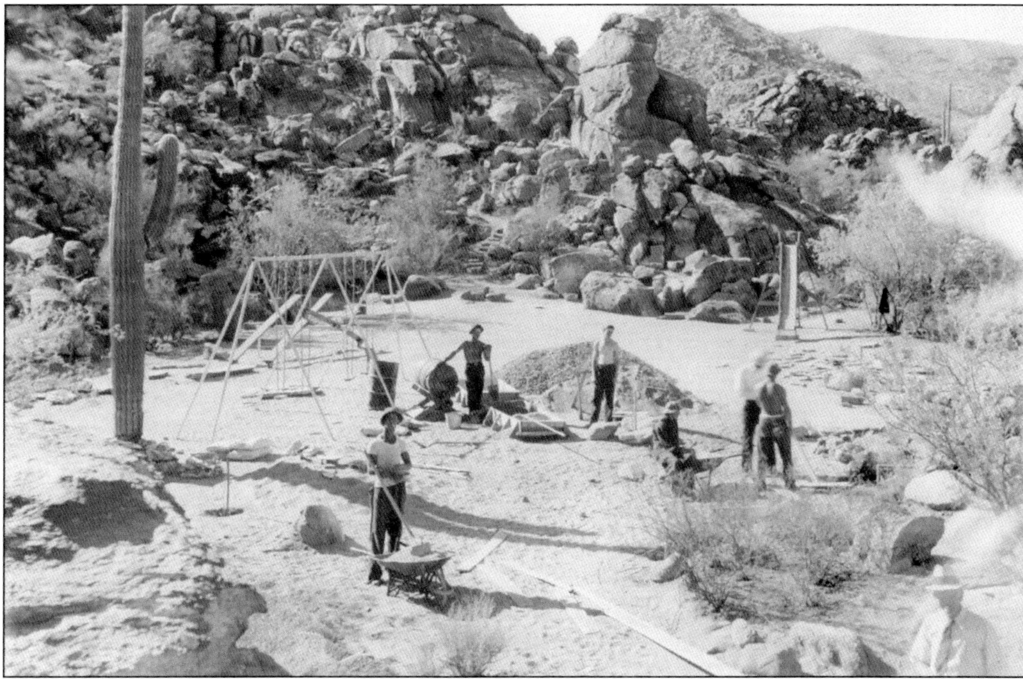

Camp SP-3, South Mountain Park, enrollees constructed picnic areas as shown here in March 1934. Other work included building a dance platform, ramadas, lookout houses, an administration building, a utility building, a blacksmith shop, and a caretaker's house. Picnic areas often included fireplaces, pipelines for water and sewer, and drinking fountains. Present-day South Mountain Park would not exist without the substantial planning of the National Park Service, the resources of the city of Phoenix, and the considerable labor of the CCC. (NARA MD.)

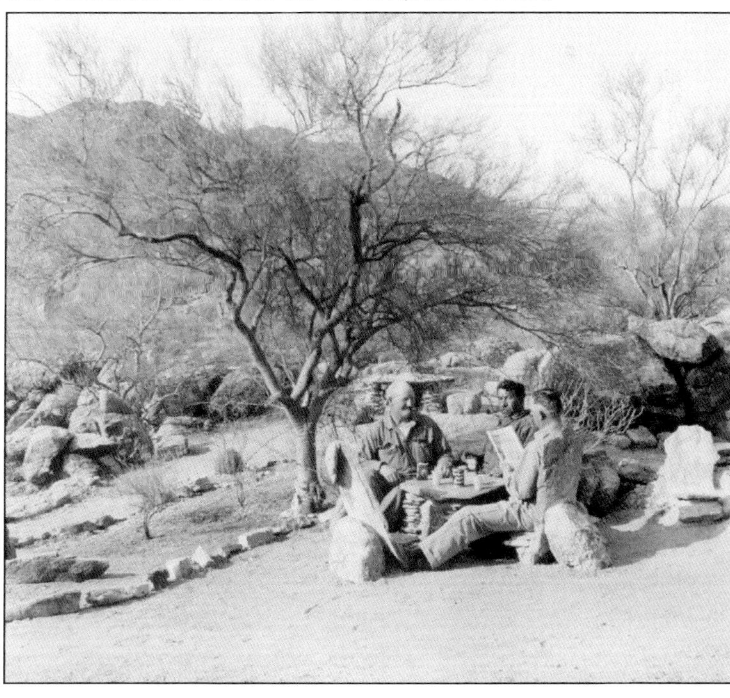

Visitors enjoy a CCC-constructed picnic area at South Mountain Park in 1934. Enrollees of Camps SP-3, SP-4, and MA-2 did substantial work at Pueblo Grande. Crews of 8 and sometimes 24 worked on the archeological dig there. They manufactured over 80,000 adobe bricks to restore the ruins. They also installed a water system consisting of drinking fountains and a 29,000-foot-long pipeline. (NARA MD.)

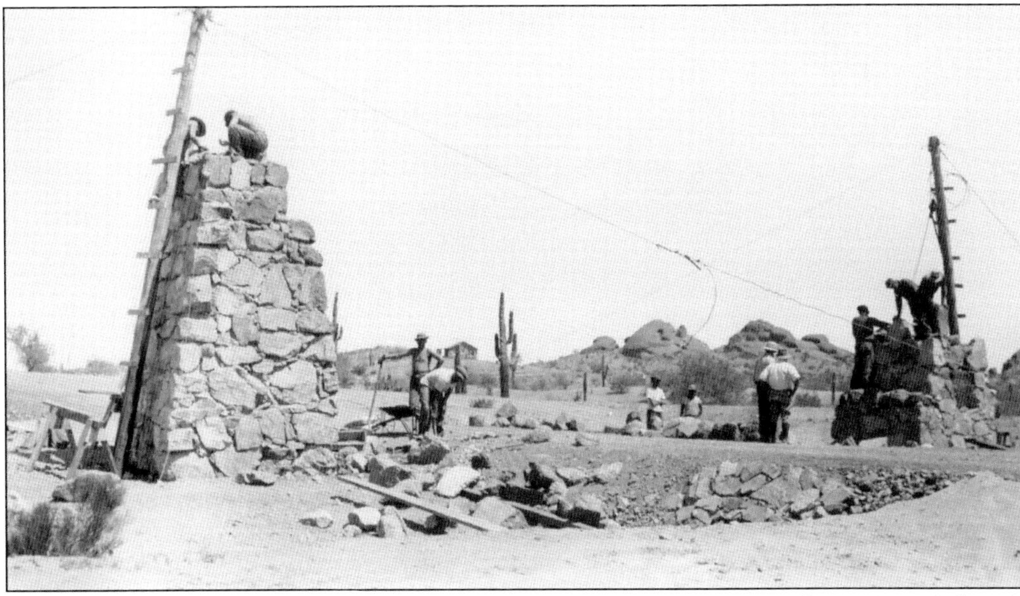

Companies 874 and 1826V occupied Camp SP-5, Papago Park, from October 1933 to July 1934 and from October 1934 to May 1935. Gov. Benjamin Moeur spoke at the camp's dedication in December 1933 and was quoted in the *Phoenix Gazette*: "There is more good done through the CCC camps than in any other organization of mankind in many years." In this April 1934 photograph, enrollees construct the park's entrance monuments. (NARA MD.)

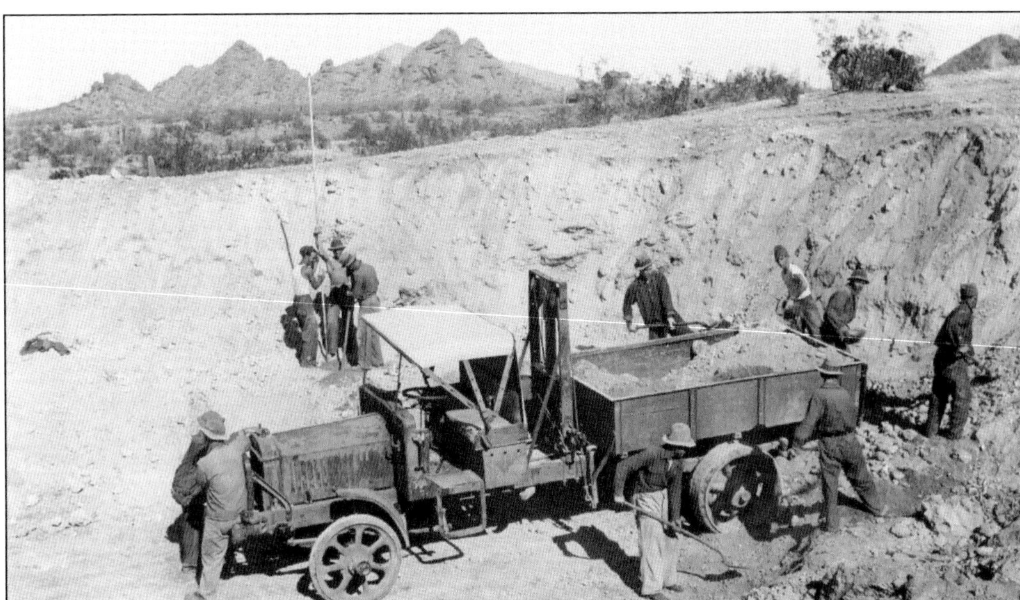

Camp SP-5 work at Papago Park included the construction of a fish hatchery, dams, canals, bridges, and six lakes. Company 874 had an active social life with frequent dances at the camp. In this January 1934 photograph, enrollees load materials for Dam No. 7. (NARA MD.)

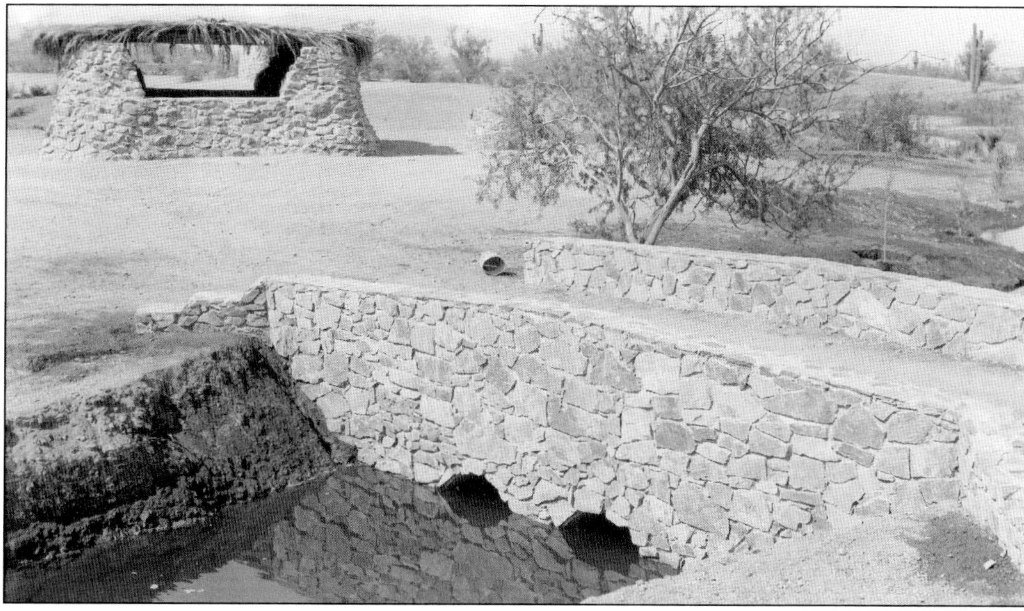

Work done by Camp SP-5, Papago Park, included building picnic shelters, a storage house, and a garage; constructing the Hole in the Rock Trail; and participating in the archeological dig at Pueblo Grande. This April 1934 photograph shows their fine masonry work. (NARA MD.)

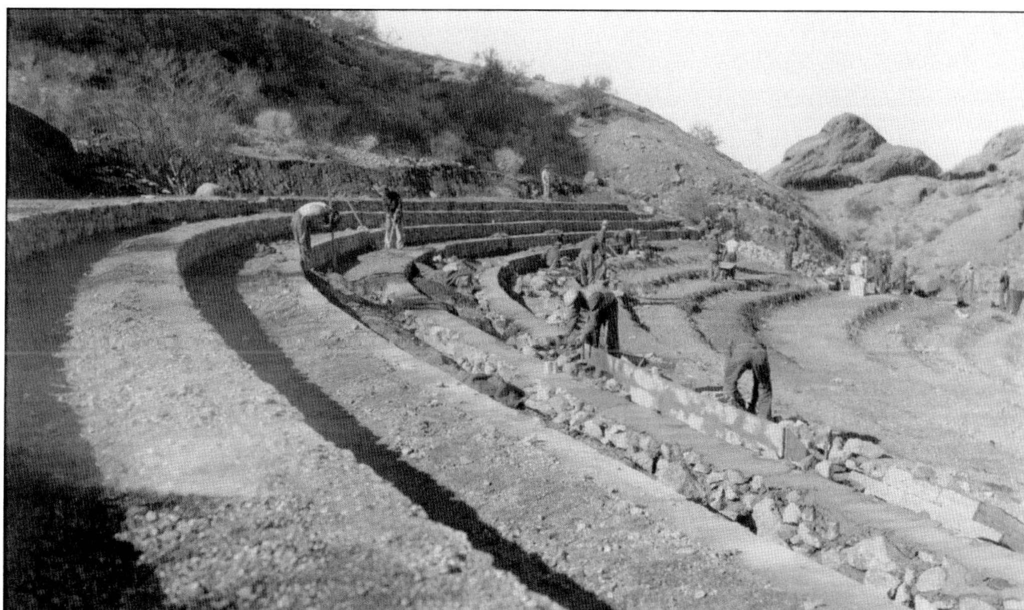

Company 874 at Papago Park spent over 7,000 man-days constructing an outdoor amphitheater said to seat 3,500, which is seen here in January 1934. According to the March 30, 1934, *Arizona Republic*, it was ready for dedication. The article went on to say that Company 874 had only one desertion since they arrived in October—an envious record. Company 874 was composed of boys from Texas, Arizona, or Wyoming. (NARA MD.)

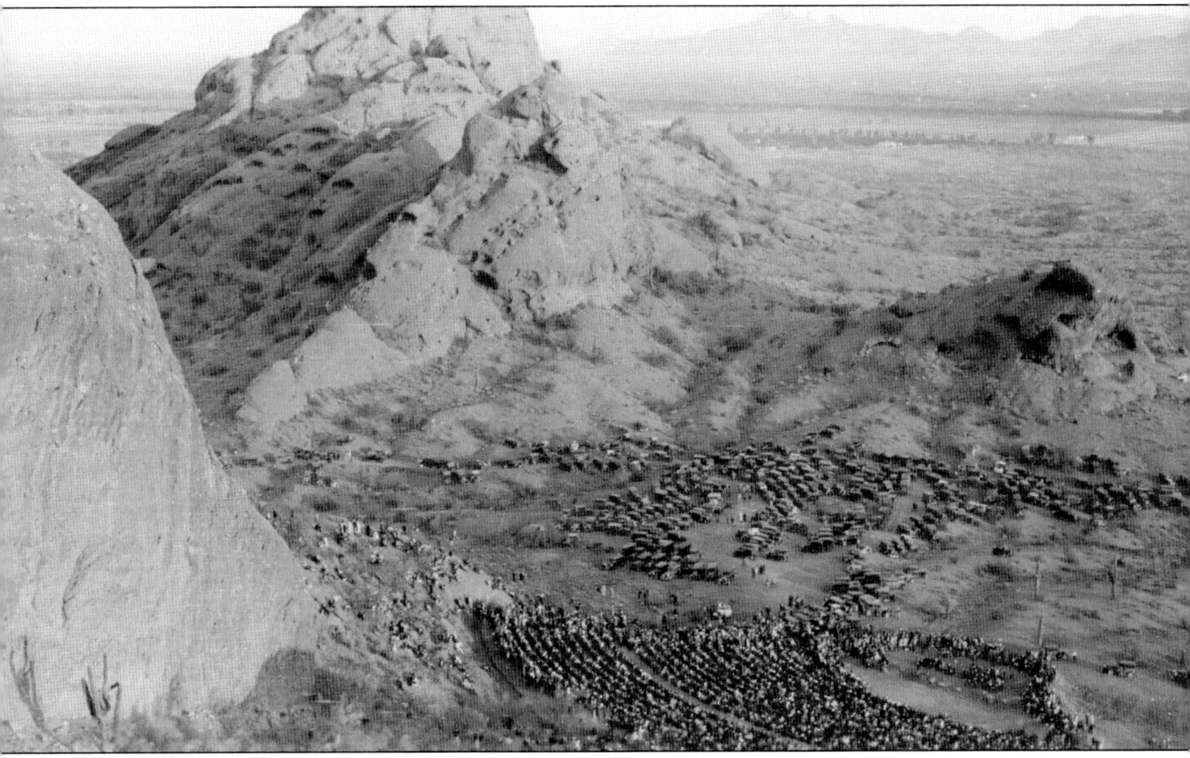

The Easter sunrise service at the Papago Park amphitheater was well attended on April 1, 1934. Today, East McDowell Road runs left to right through the area in the photograph where the cars are parked, so the amphitheater has limited usefulness. When Company 874 left, Company 1826V resumed work at the park. All of its men were veterans, mostly of World War I, but a few of the Spanish-American War. The company included men from Arizona, New Mexico, Wyoming, Colorado, Oklahoma, and Texas. Company 1826V reported six to nine African American members while occupying Camp SP-5. (NARA MD.)

Four

Northeastern Arizona
Apache, Gila, and Navajo Counties

Apache, Gila, and Navajo Counties had 19 companies, with three at Petrified Forest National Park and the rest as Forest Service companies. Unfortunately, photographs were not located for six of the companies.

In Apache County, Camp F-4 was located near Springerville but only worked during the summer of 1933. Very few records exist for this camp, and even its location is uncertain. A camp inspection report notes its work included the construction of the Escudilla fire lookout and fence and campground construction in Greenlee County's Hannagan Meadows area. Camp F-76, Greer, was also headquartered in Apache County. It was occupied for only three summer seasons, 1938–1940. Its work included constructing check dams on the Little Colorado River in Greer Valley and improving campgrounds, including Sheep's Crossing.

In Gila County, Camp F-16, Pinal Mountain (Globe), was occupied much of 1933–1942. A 1941 camp inspection report summarizes its work as constructing 39 impounding dams, improving seven springs, and building three fire lookout towers, including Signal Peak. They did a wide range of typical Forest Service projects, including building at least one ranger station. They had side camps at various times at the Boyce Thompson Arboretum, J.K. Ranch, and Parker Creek. Little is known about Camp F-36, Miami. It was only occupied the summer of 1933, and a 1934 *Arizona Republic* article summarizes its work as erosion control, stringing telephone lines, building fences and roads, and constructing fishponds at McNary. Camp F-45, Miami, was only occupied during 1933–1935. Little is known of its work, but one camp inspection report lists these projects: building and maintaining truck trails and fences, building recreational facilities, developing springs, doing erosion control and revegetation, and doing grazing surveys and plans. Camp F-77, East Verde, was occupied only the summers of 1940 and 1941. They completed FR 64, the Control Road, begun earlier by Camp F-23. Camp inspection reports credit them with constructing a 140-foot-long steel bridge and four 20-foot-long masonry bridges, developing 20 acres of recreational facilities, and building two fire lookouts, among other projects.

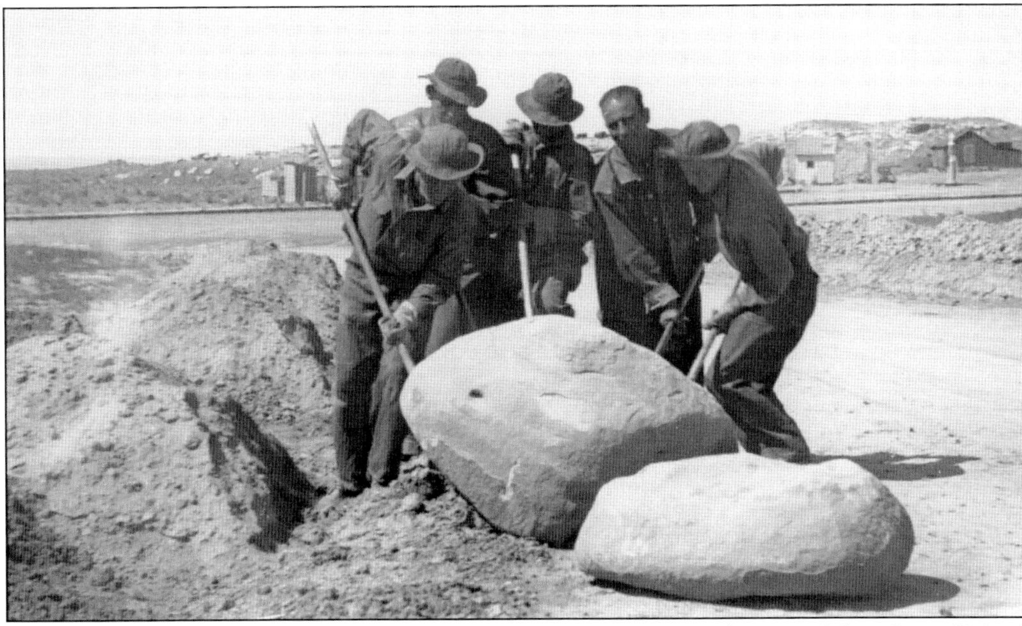

Work at Petrified Forest National Park was directed from three camps between July 1934 and March 1942, with a few breaks. They were NM-1, NM-2, and NP-8. Even before the CCC arrived, the park had tapped into other New Deal funds, such as CWA and PWA, for archeological surveys and the construction of fences, roads, bridges, and campgrounds. In this photograph from the early 1930s, enrollees construct the road near the Rainbow Forest headquarters. The enormous influx of New Deal federal monies was a "watershed" for the park, according to historian George Lubick. (PFNP.)

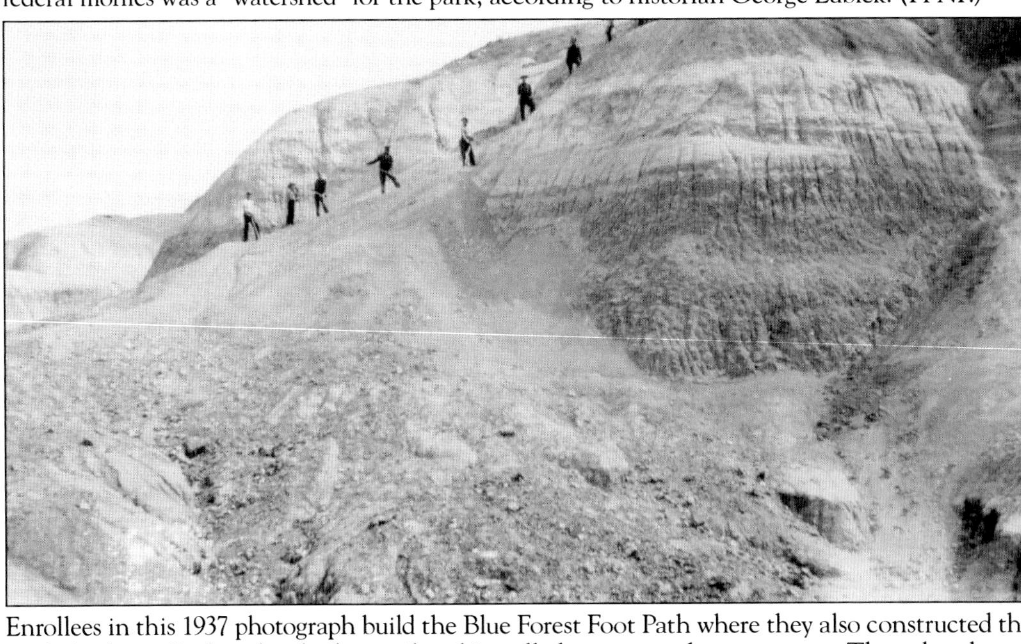

Enrollees in this 1937 photograph build the Blue Forest Foot Path where they also constructed the road. At Agate Bridge, they built a trail and installed a water and sewer system. They also cleared the Pictograph Rock Foot Trail, participated in paleontological and archeological excavations, did petrified wood surveys, and collected specimens for the park museum collection. They acted as guides for visitors 1935–1941, sometimes staffing six locations during one season. (NARA-RMR.)

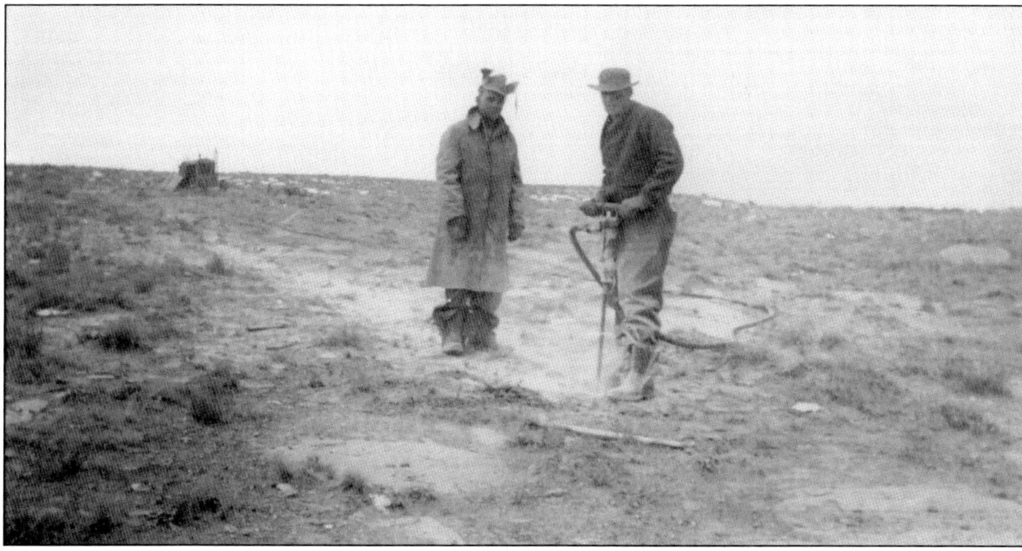

Once Petrified Forest National Park had a reliable CCC-built boundary fence, cattle from nearby ranches could not enter. Building a fence across rock was not easy, as it required drilling holes in the hard surface for the posts, as seen here in this c. 1935 photograph. Enrollees built a number of ranger residences and storage buildings that are still in use today. They also strung telephone lines, built an entrance station at Painted Desert, and did flood control work along the Rio Puerco. (PFNP.)

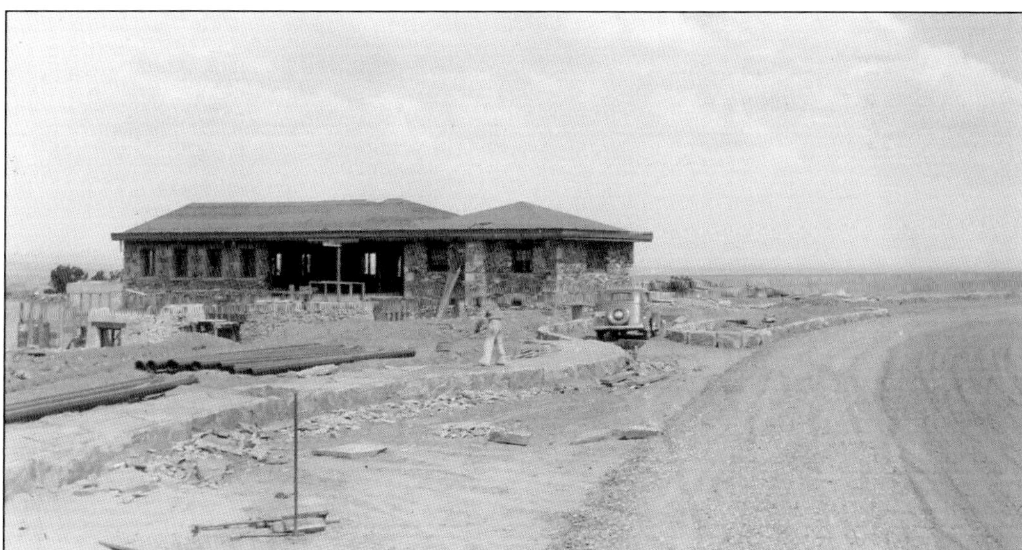

The Painted Desert Inn can only be called a masterpiece of CCC work. The complete remodel of the inn started in 1937 with a PWA grant, but it quickly turned into a CCC-dominated project. Enrollees assisted the stonemasons building the walls and finished the landscaping. Inside, enrollee work included plastering and painting walls, laying flagstone floors, and making furniture. Outside they built walks, curbs, gutters, signs, and the parking lot. (NARA MD.)

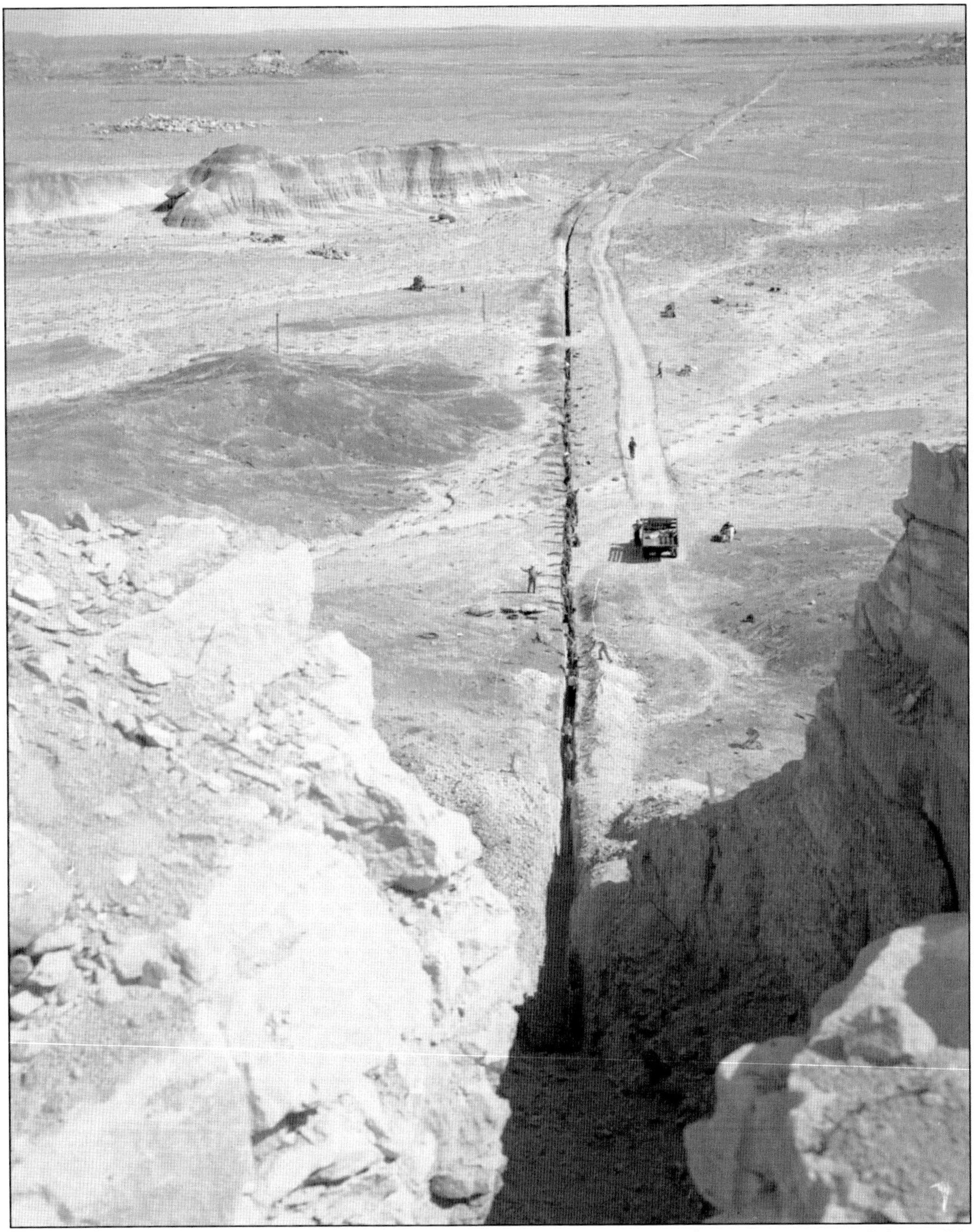

The most labor-intensive project for the Petrified National Forest was the construction of the park's 11.71-mile-long water pipeline from 1938 to 1940. It was said—at the time—to be the longest pipeline throughout the National Park system. It was connected to a CCC-built 50,000-gallon concrete reservoir. Much of the digging was done by hand with some blasting, but there were no serious injuries on this project. This photograph was taken in 1939 near Agate Bridge. From 100 to 130 enrollees were working on the pipeline by 1939. Other work included constructing water reservoirs, doing landscaping, and participating in a boundary fence survey. Much of the infrastructure work accomplished by the CCC and the New Deal is still being used today. (PFNP.)

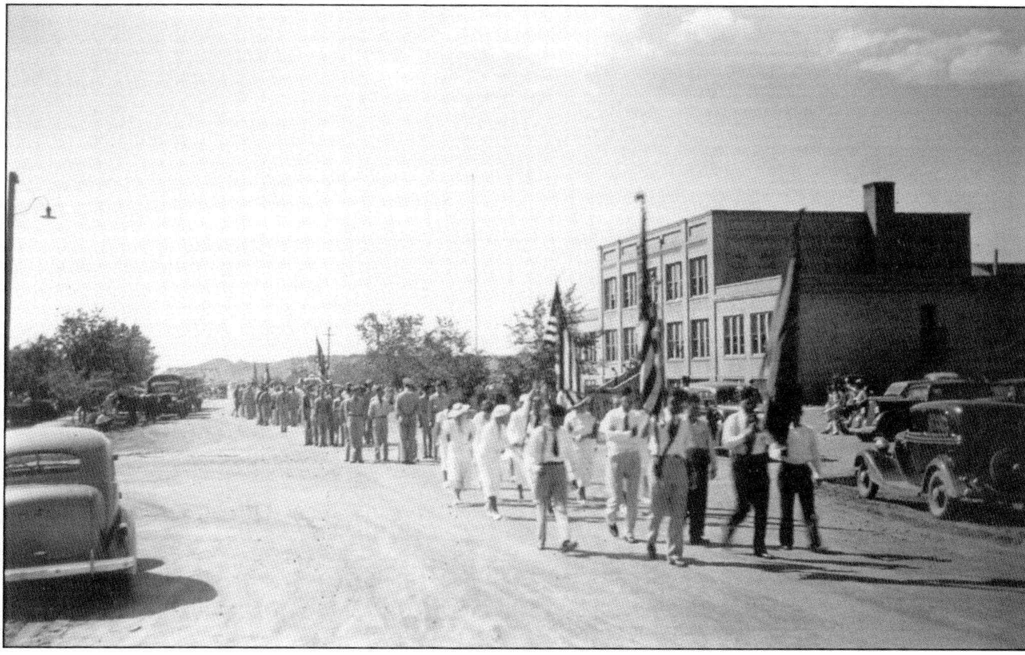

On September 17, 1937, the American Legion held a Constitution Day parade in Holbrook. Legionnaires led, followed by the American Legion Auxiliary and 100 CCC enrollees. The CCC and other New Deal programs can only be called "dramatic" in the progress of Petrified Forest from "shabby" to its status as a respected national park, says historian George Lubick in *The Petrified Forest National Park*. (NARA MD.)

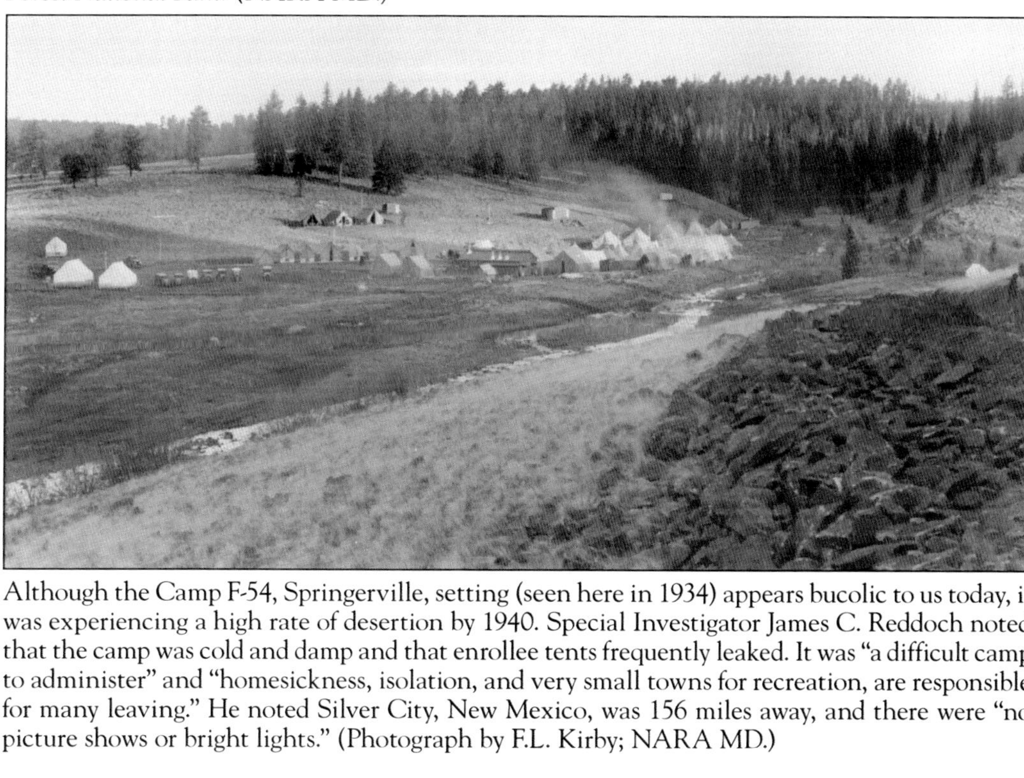

Although the Camp F-54, Springerville, setting (seen here in 1934) appears bucolic to us today, it was experiencing a high rate of desertion by 1940. Special Investigator James C. Reddoch noted that the camp was cold and damp and that enrollee tents frequently leaked. It was "a difficult camp to administer" and "homesickness, isolation, and very small towns for recreation, are responsible for many leaving." He noted Silver City, New Mexico, was 156 miles away, and there were "no picture shows or bright lights." (Photograph by F.L. Kirby; NARA MD.)

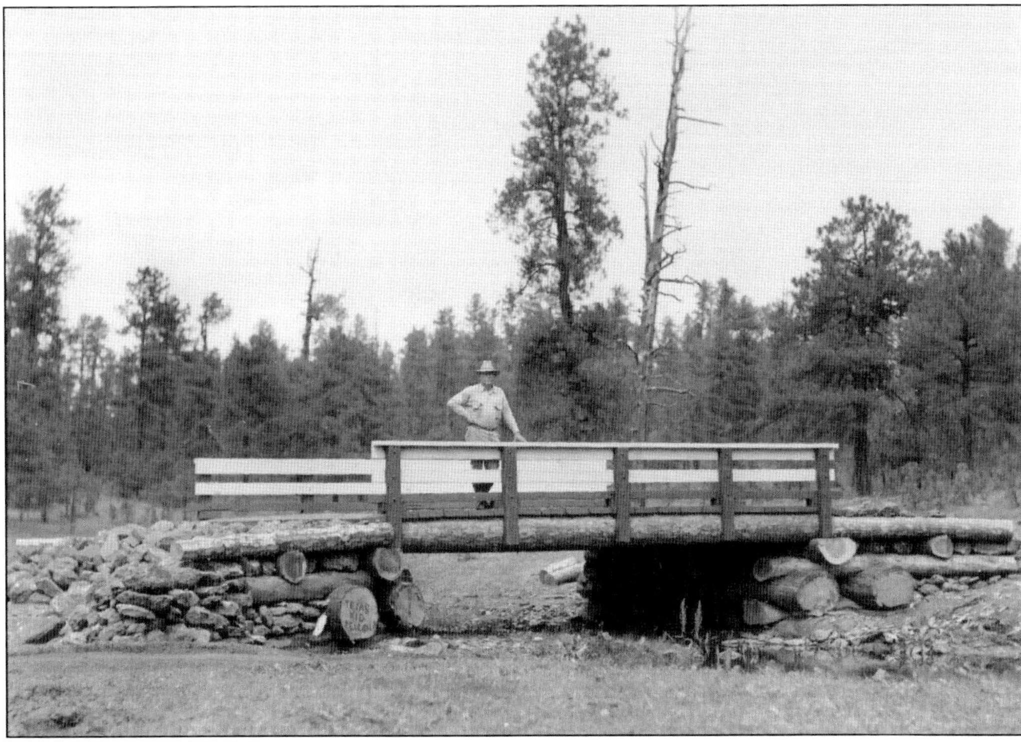

Besides building bridges like this one on the Water Canyon Truck Trail, as seen here in 1934, Camp F-54, Springerville, enrollees fought a great deal of forest fires. It was common for enrollees to be trained in basic firefighting and to drop their work projects to fight a fire. During June 1936, they fought over 40 fires. One of their major projects was constructing the Diamond Rock Road (FR 276). They also improved the Coronado Trail from a Hannagan Meadow side camp. (Photograph by F.L. Kirby; USFS, SWR.)

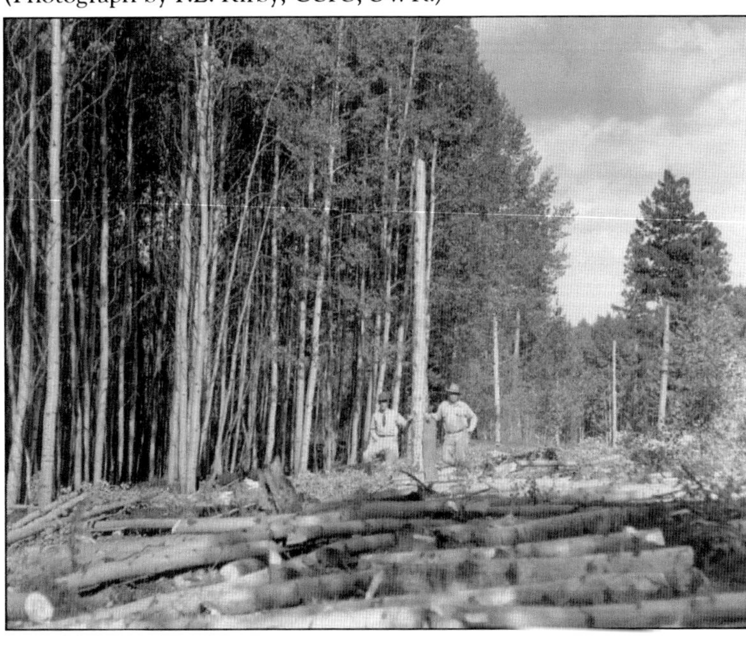

Clearing the 16-foot right-of-way for a telephone line was often not easy. Note the cut-down timber in the foreground of this 1934 photograph. Camp F-54, Springerville, enrollees staffed side camps at Big Lake and Crescent Lake. At Big Lake, they stocked fish as well as raising a dam's height and digging spillways. Out of Crescent Lake they did bridge and fence work. (Photograph by F.L. Kirby; USFS, SWR.)

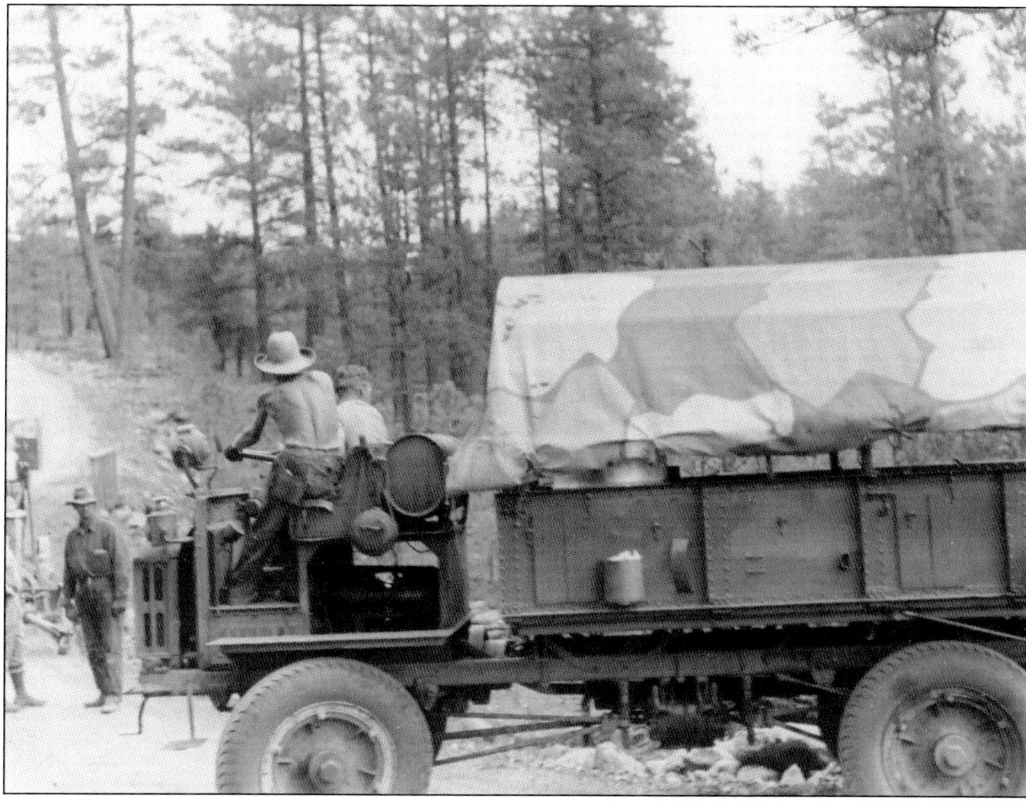

Sometimes, CCC equipment was made up of the leftovers from World War I, such as this four-wheel drive vehicle doing maintenance on the Water Canyon Truck Trail in 1934. Those Camp F-54, Springerville, enrollees who managed to deal with the camp's isolation had access to a top-notch library and recreation room. The nearby east fork of the Black River was said to have outstanding trout fishing. (JI.)

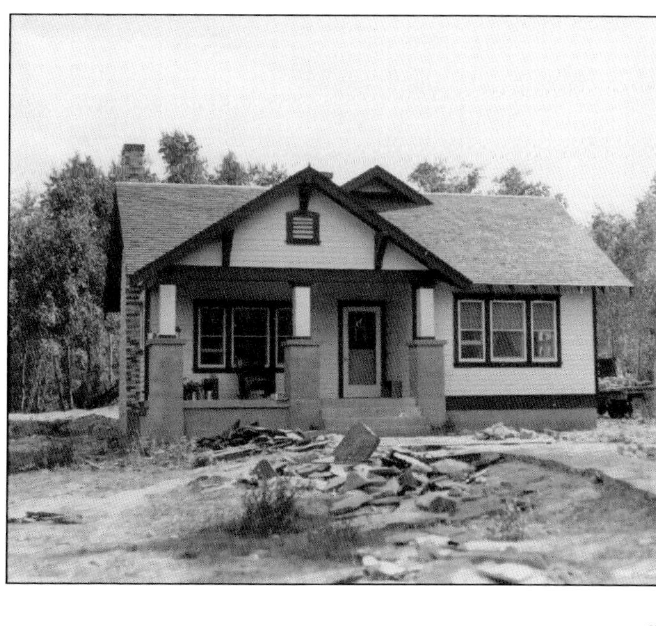

Camp F-55 was located at Alpine in Apache County and was sometimes called Three Forks Camp. It was occupied the summers of 1933 and 1934. Its work included prairie dog eradication and the construction of roads, telephone lines, and the Water Canyon Ranger Station dwelling (seen here in 1934). Alpine, at an elevation of over 8,000 feet, was said to be cold even in July. Enrollee tents were heated with stoves, and most enrollees wore the winter uniform through the summer. (Photograph by F.L. Kirby; USFS, SWR.)

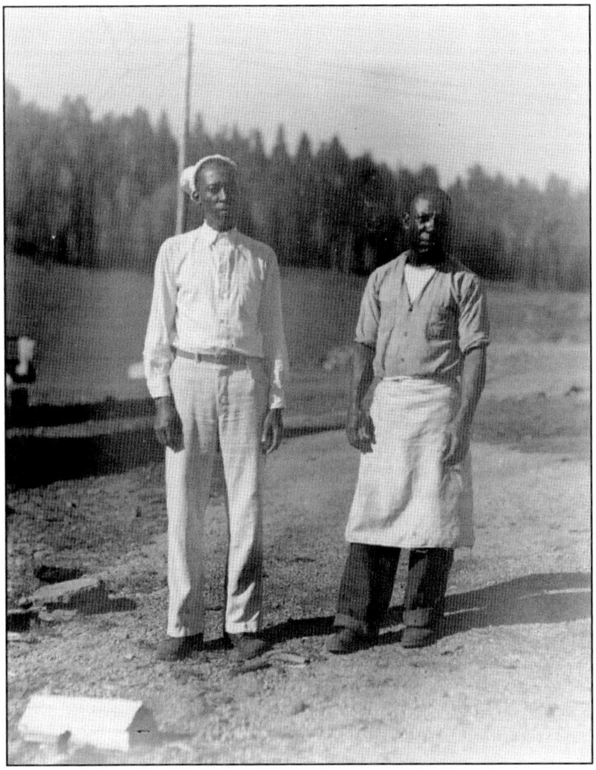

Mess cooks for Camp F-55 pose in 1934. Members of Company 1830V, these men are surely veterans of World War I. While African Americans were frequently given jobs others did not want, the role of the mess staff in any camp was critical. Enrollees' hard physical labor required a great deal of food. Special investigators, such as A.W. Stockman, noted that most enrollee sit-down strikes and refusals to work were almost always related to inadequate mess. (JI.)

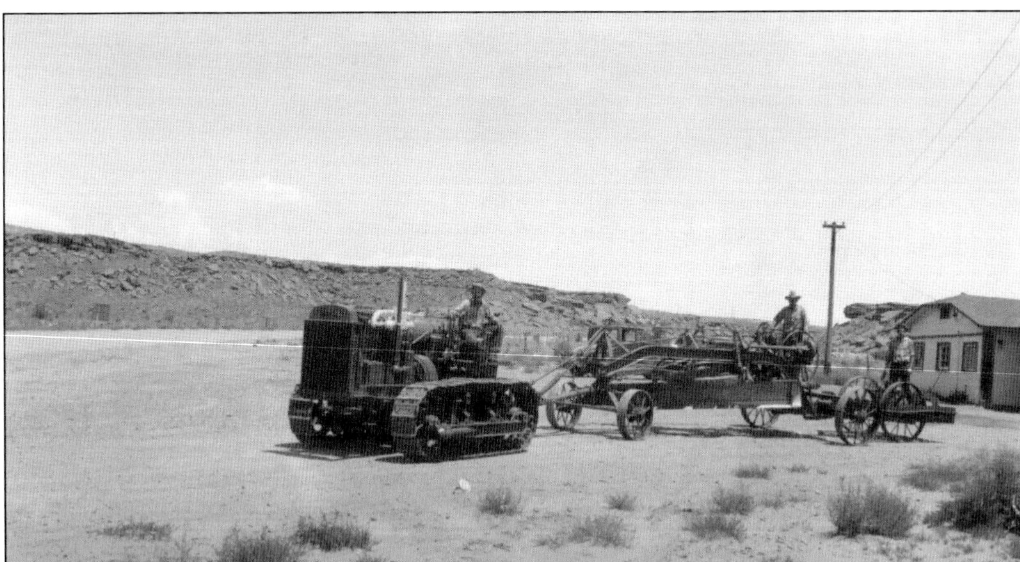

Navajo County Camp F-21, Hart Canyon, was only occupied in the summer of 1933. This photograph shows a tractor, grader, and ripper on its way to Hart Canyon in 1933. Sitgreaves National Forest Supervisor F.L. Kirby noted CCC road building made the forest "accessible for fighting fires, and thereby lowered the fire hazards." *Arizona Republic* writer L.C. Bowles said the CCC was highly successful at "building a new road through the lovely green wilderness that later and wiser generations may enjoy it." (Photograph by F.L. Kirby; USFS, SWR.)

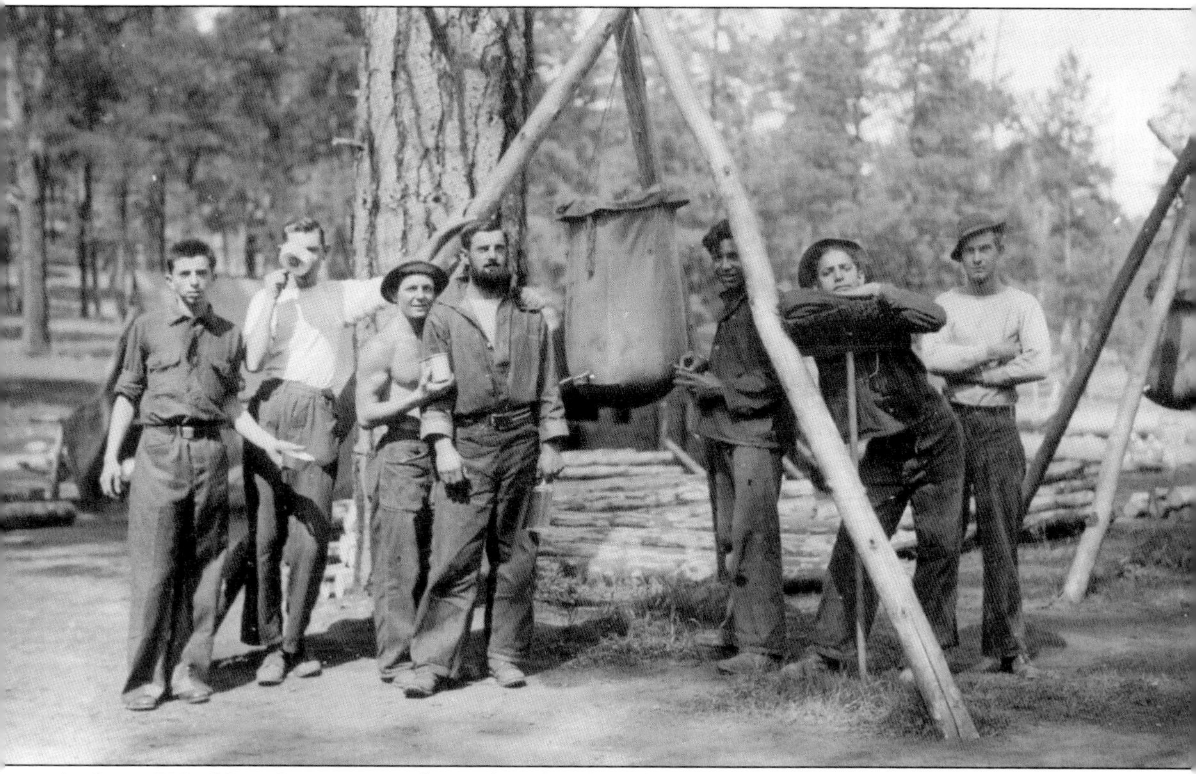

At Camp F-21, Hart Canyon, enrollees take a break at the water bag in 1933. Typically, their talk was about money, girls, cars, their next liberty trip, or their work. The enrollee on the extreme left is wearing the dress uniform so he was likely the company clerk. The others are wearing a mix of the blue denim work uniform and civilian garb. Enrollees' pants were often too short or too long, due to growth spurts or the supply room being out of the right sizes. According to Robert J. Moore in *Civilian Conservation Corps in Arizona's Rim Country*, Camp F-21 did a great deal of improvements to FR 300, which follows the Mogollon Rim. Even today this road is a pleasant drive, with expansive views. (JI.)

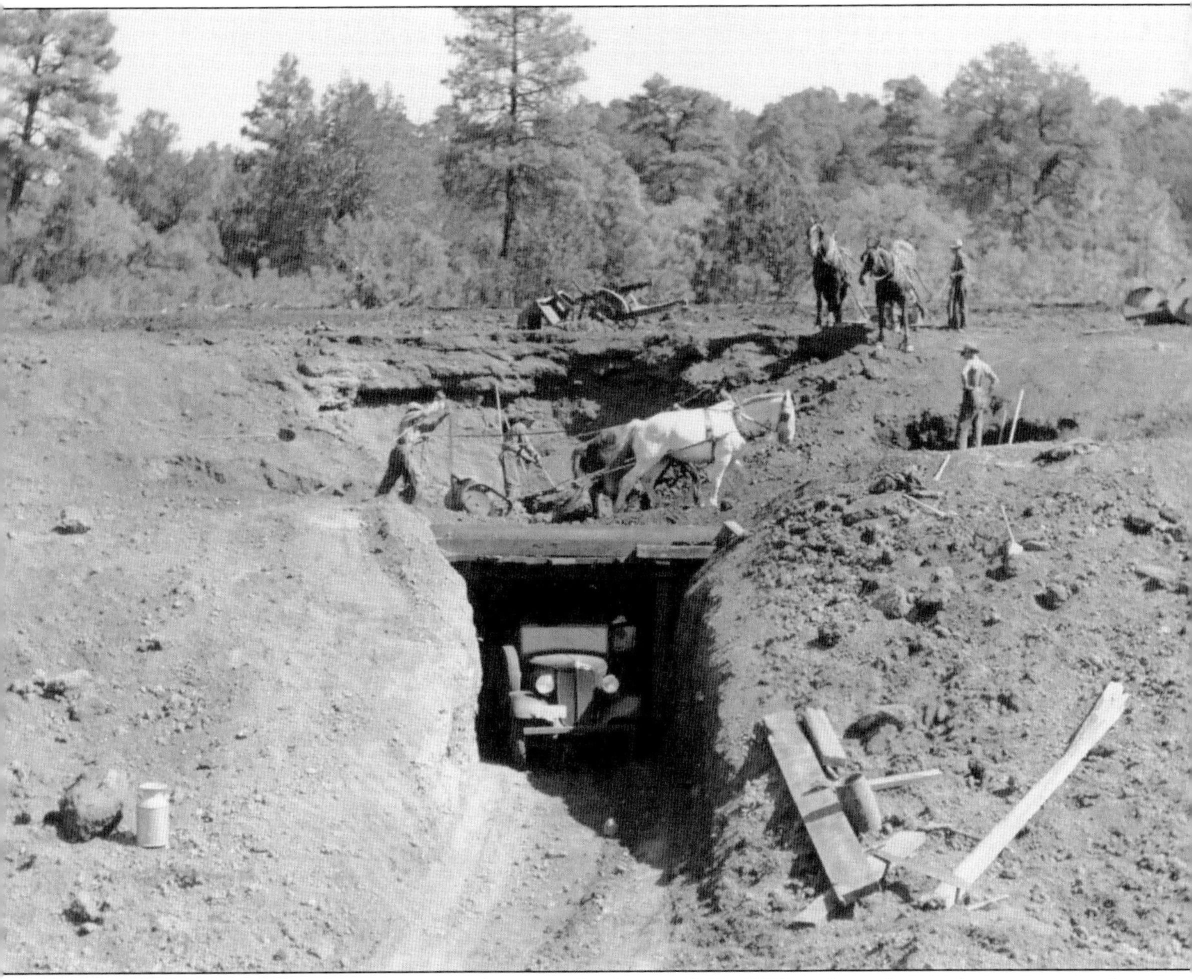

Camp F-22, Los Burros, was occupied seasonally during 1933–1938 and was located near present-day Pinetop, Arizona. Their post office was at McNary; however, McNary was a dry town. As alcohol was served in Pinetop, it was a favorite of the local loggers and enrollees. By April 1936, this camp had completed over 2,000 acres of timber stand improvement and seven miles of road. The timber stand improvement crew supplied the logs for the reconstruction of the ancient American Indian pueblo at Kinishba on the reservation near Fort Apache. This 1934 photograph shows a truck being loaded with cinders for the surfacing of the South Boundary Road. F-22 enrollees fought forest fires, eradicated twig blight, developed campgrounds at Pinetop and Lakeside, and assisted with the creation of the Lakeside ski area. (JI.)

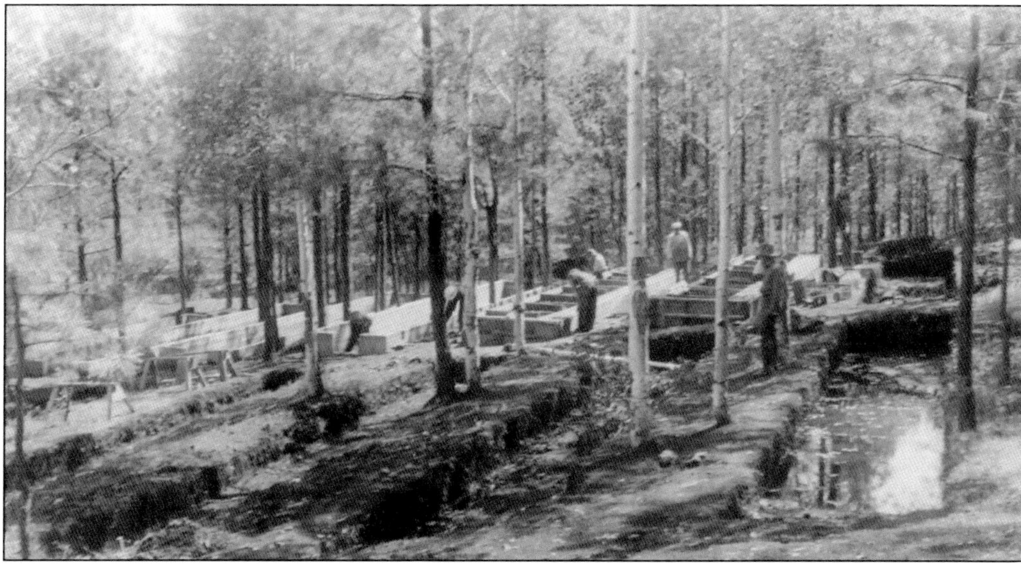

Camp F-22, Los Burros, constructed 16 fish rearing ponds (seen here in 1934) at the Pinetop Fish Hatchery. At Pinedale, they constructed a ranger station, barn, residence, and water storage tanks. It had a side camp at Willow Springs, said by enrollees to be a very desirable place to work. In 1937 and 1938, a group of enrollees from Petrified Forest National Park was housed temporarily at Los Burros, cutting logs for the remodeling of the Painted Desert Inn. (JI.)

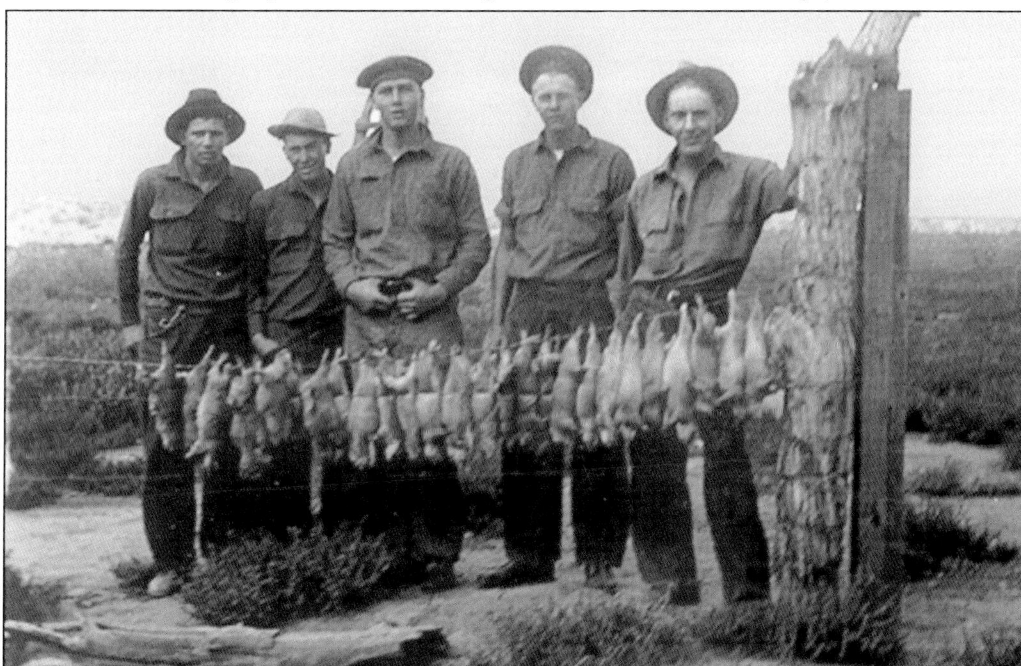

One of the tasks of Camp F-22, Los Burros, was exterminating prairie dogs. In this 1933 photograph, enrollees pose with dead prairie dogs near Clay Springs. By April 1936, prairie dog elimination had covered 47,670 acres. Early on, the indiscriminate use of poisons for rodent control was opposed by environmental groups such as Audubon Society, according to author Neil M. Maher in his *Nature's New Deal: The Civilian Conservation Corps, and the Roots of the American Environmental Movement.* (RJM.)

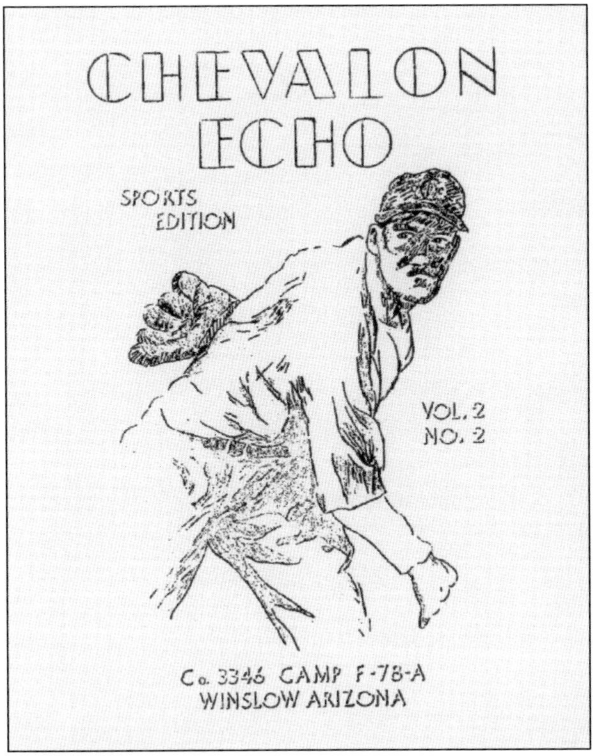

Camp F-78, Chevalon Canyon (south of Winslow), served Navajo County as well as Coconino County. It was occupied from June 1939 to November 1941. Its camp newspaper, shown here from 1940, assisted in educating enrollees. Nationwide, the CCC from 1933 to 1942 helped 110,000 men learn to read and write. This camp's work accomplishments were impressive, including a 138-foot-long steel bridge in Chevalon Canyon near Mormon Crossing, at least 10 stock tanks, the Dutch Joe fire lookout, and the Big Chevalon Campground, as well as assistance with the construction of the Mormon Crossing ski area. (RJM.)

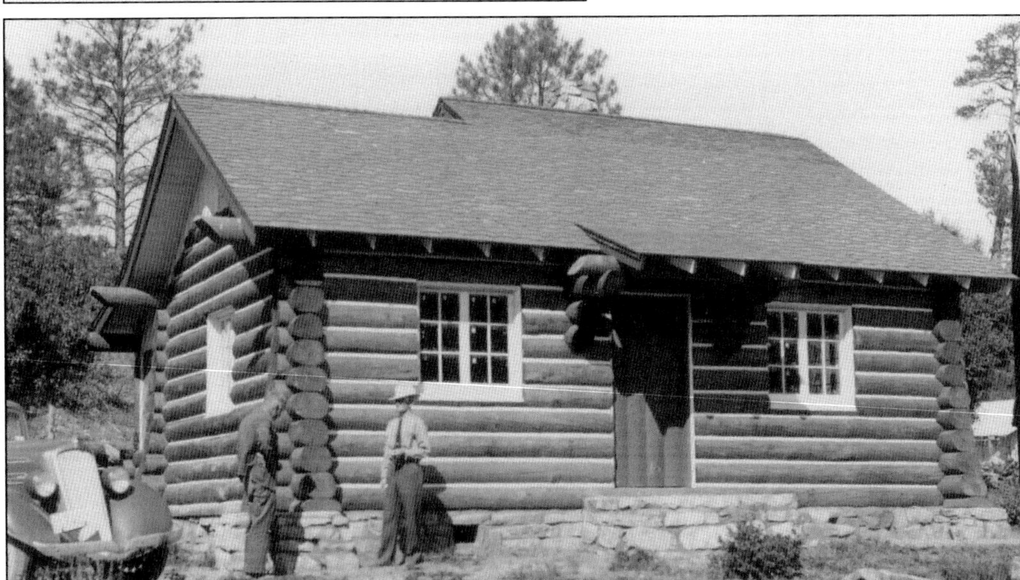

Company 807 used Camp F-23, Indian Garden (near Payson), the summers of 1933–1937. Occupied very early in the CCC program, it was established on May 24, just a day after the first companies arrived in the state. In June, Gila National Forest Supervisor T.T. Swift was quoted as saying that there was no lack of projects for the CCC and that in the Gila the priority would be replenishing the range. The photograph shows the Indian Garden log cabin in 1937. (Photograph by Chas. C. Cunningham; USFS, SWR.)

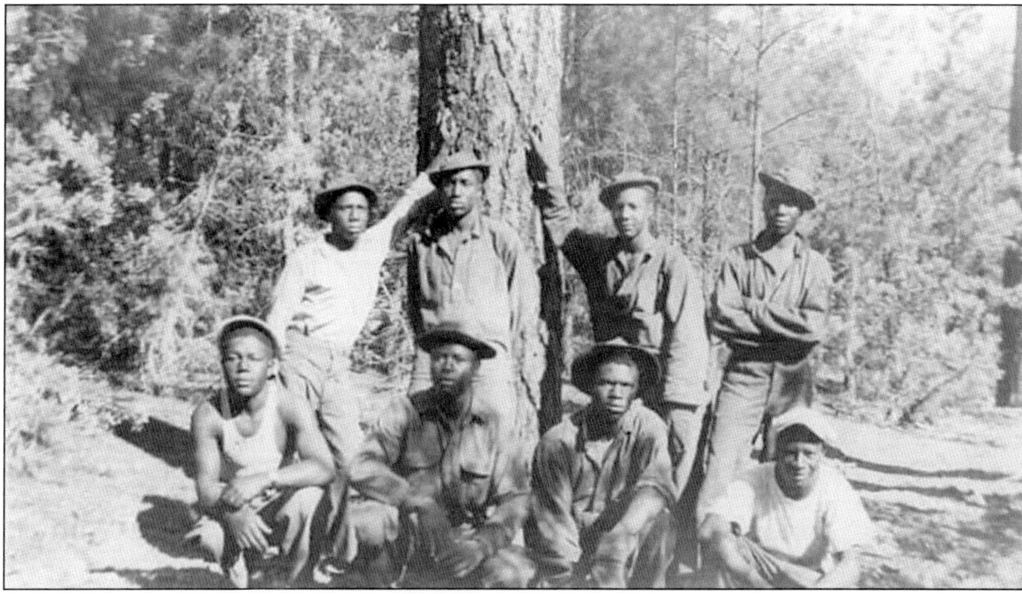

Camp F-23, Indian Garden, African American enrollees pose in 1933. The Great Depression was harder on families of color, who had higher rates of unemployment than whites. The fact that enrollees were required to send $25 home from their $30 monthly wages was a blessing to many poor families. (JI.)

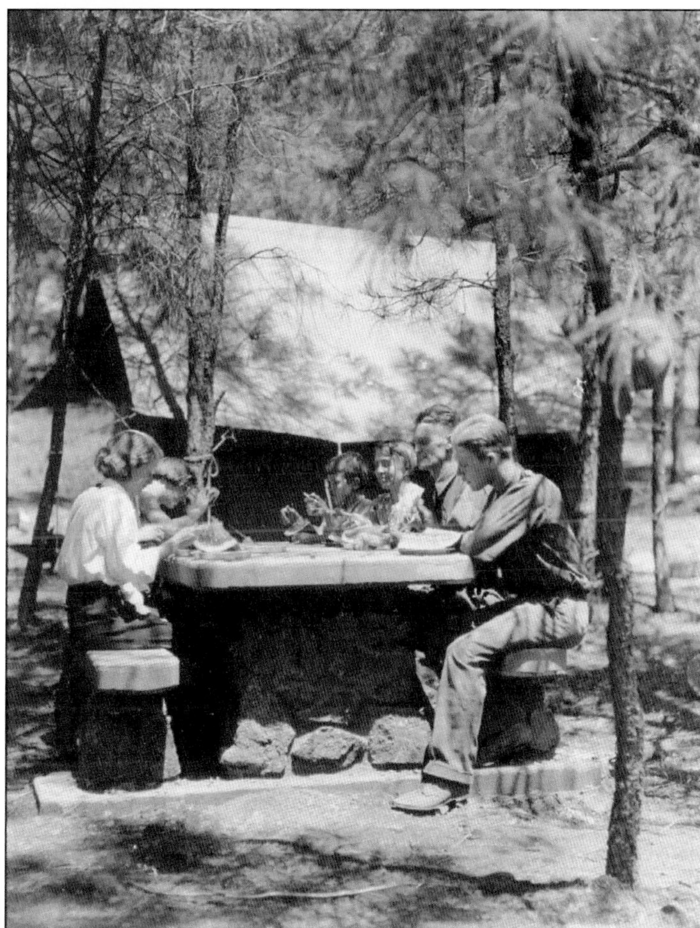

Camp F-23, Indian Garden, enrollees built the Tonto Creek Campground as seen here in 1934. They were also busy fighting fires, doing erosion control, and improving springs. They spent considerable effort in improving the Control Road (FR 64) and the Chamberlain Trail (FR 200). Their work was done from a number of side camps including one at Horton Creek. (Photograph by F.L. Kirby; USFS, SWR.)

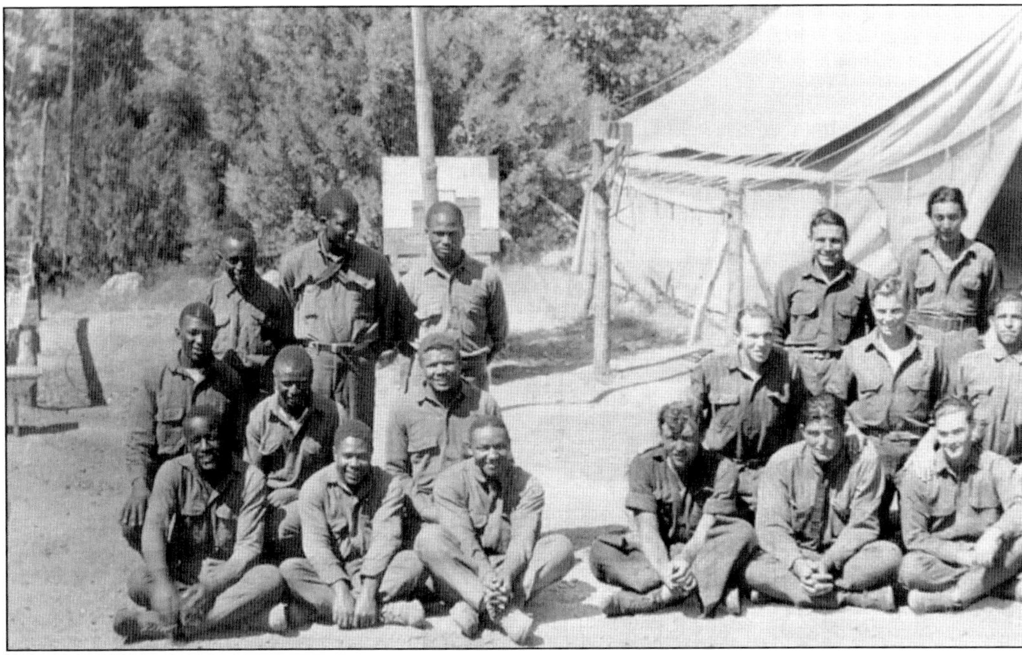

During a time of segregation, sometimes men were even segregated in photographs, as in this 1933 image of Camp F-24, Bar X (near Young). The camp was only occupied the summer of 1933 and located near Haigler Creek. It did considerable roadwork improving the Chamberlain Trail (FR 200) and improving a number of springs used by sheep men. Other work included stream improvement, forest thinning, and erosion control. (RJM.)

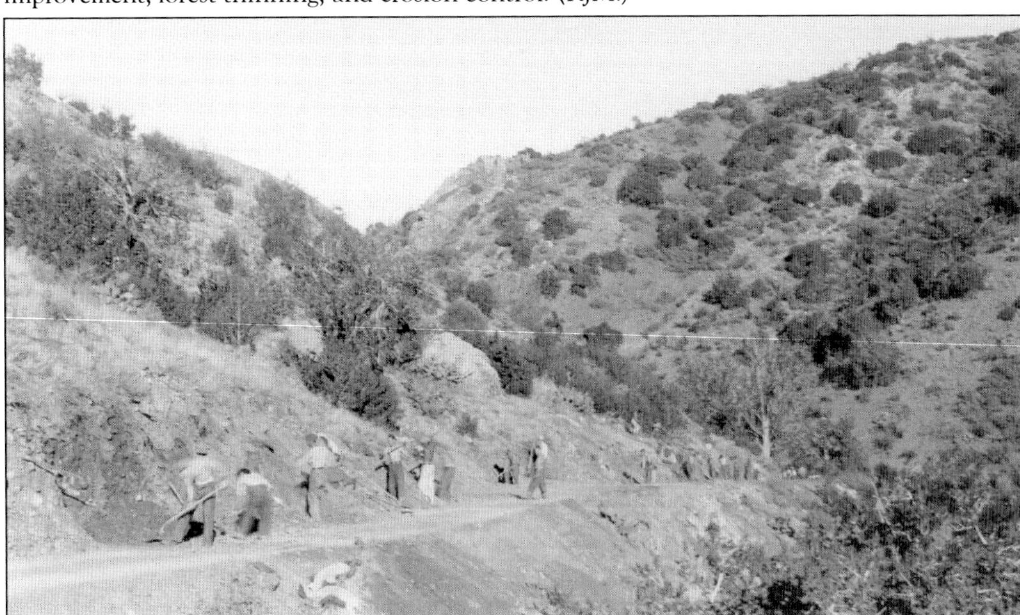

Camp F-25, Tonto Basin, was also called Sunflower and was occupied in 1933–1935. Its work included road construction, as seen here in the widening of the Slate Creek Road No. 1 in 1933. Other work included laying out and maintaining truck trails, stringing telephone lines, performing erosion control, and building a fire lookout, ranger station, and associated buildings. (JI.)

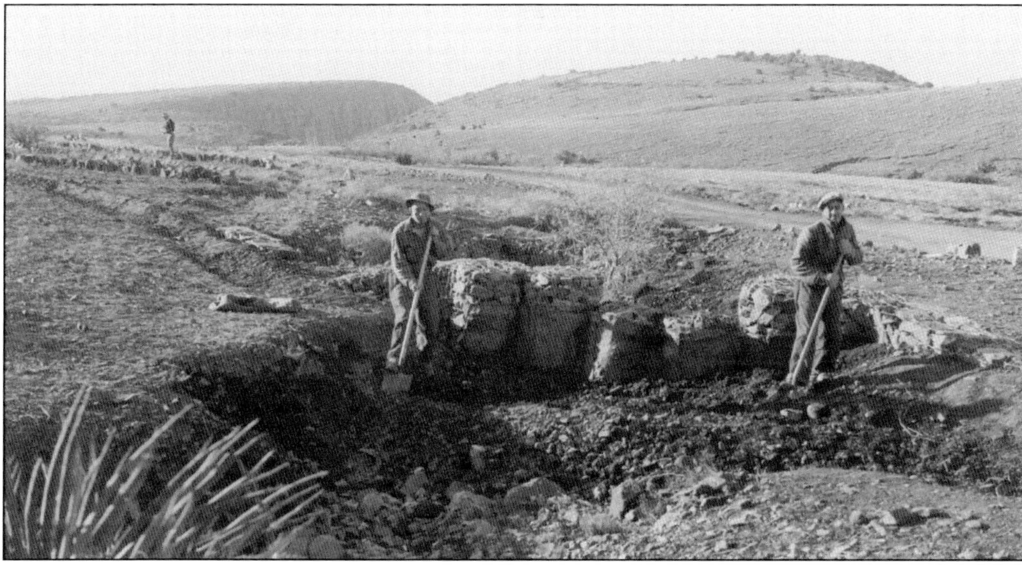

Camp F-29, A Cross (near Globe), was occupied the winter seasons of 1933–1938 and did considerable erosion-control work, as seen in this 1935 photograph. Note the contour dams in the background. In March 1935, cooperating with Camps F-23 and F-25, they completed a 65-mile-long telephone line from Payson to Globe to be used exclusively for emergencies such as forest fires. Other work included working on the Chamberlain Trail, the Conor Canyon Stock Trail, and the Natural Drainage and Pocket Roads. (NARA MD.)

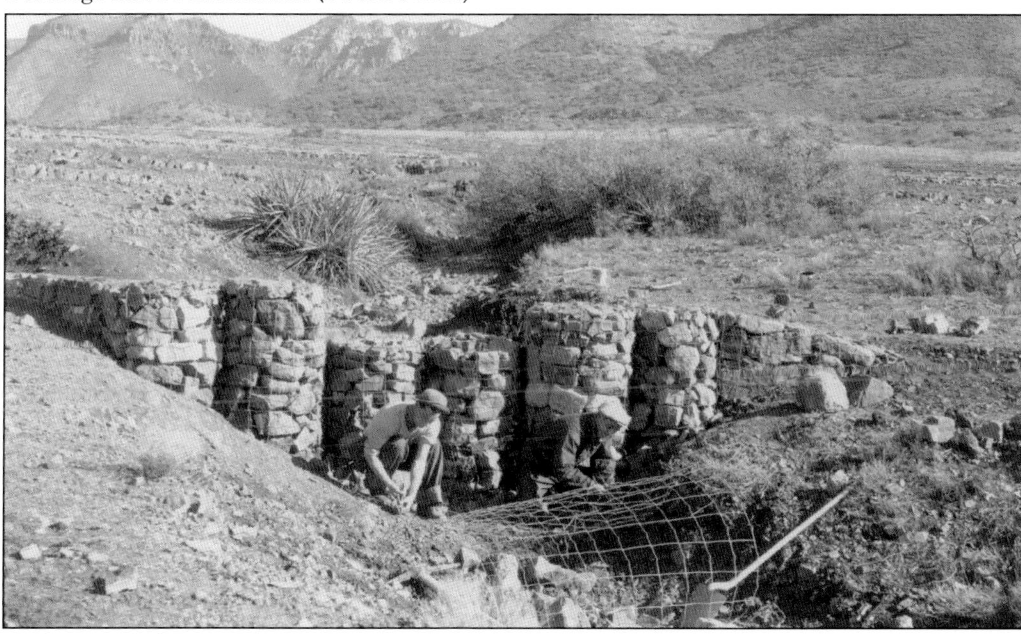

In this 1935 photograph, Camp F-29, A Cross, men use wire to make cylinder-basket erosion-control dams. Note the contour dams in the background. Other work included spring development and construction of a ranger station and its associated dwellings. Truck trail work included the A Cross Tonto Truck Trail from Tin Ranch to Cactus Butte Saddle and the Pleasant Valley Road to Tin Ranch. They also worked experimental plots at the Parker Creek Ranger Experimental Station. (NARA MD.)

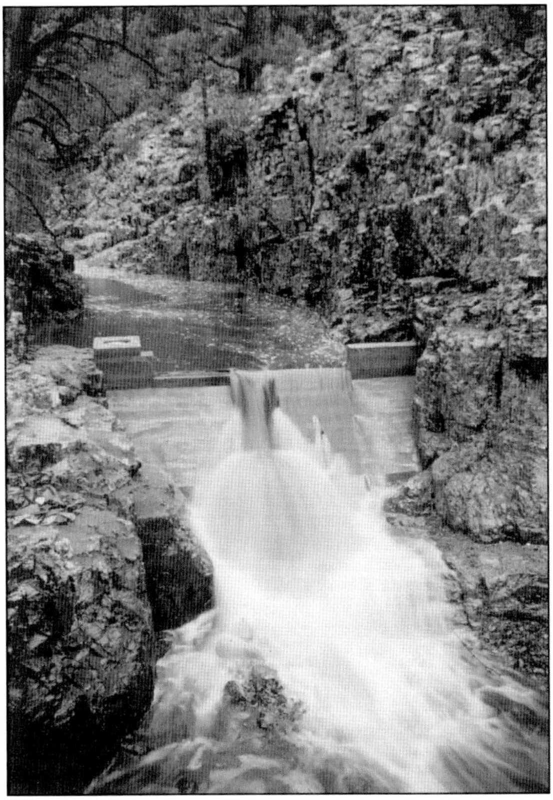

Camp F-29, A Cross, work included constructing dams on Pocket and Parker Creeks. This photograph, taken in 1935, shows a dam and weir construction done by F-29, but the location is unknown. Like most CCC camps, F-29 had an ongoing program to improve the enrollees' education. The November 24, 1936, issue of their camp newspaper, the *A-Cross Bull*, noted that of 169 men in the camp there were 47 men at grade 1–6 level, 62 at grade 7–8, 57 at grade 9–12, and two at grade 13. This was typical of most Arizona camps. (TNF.)

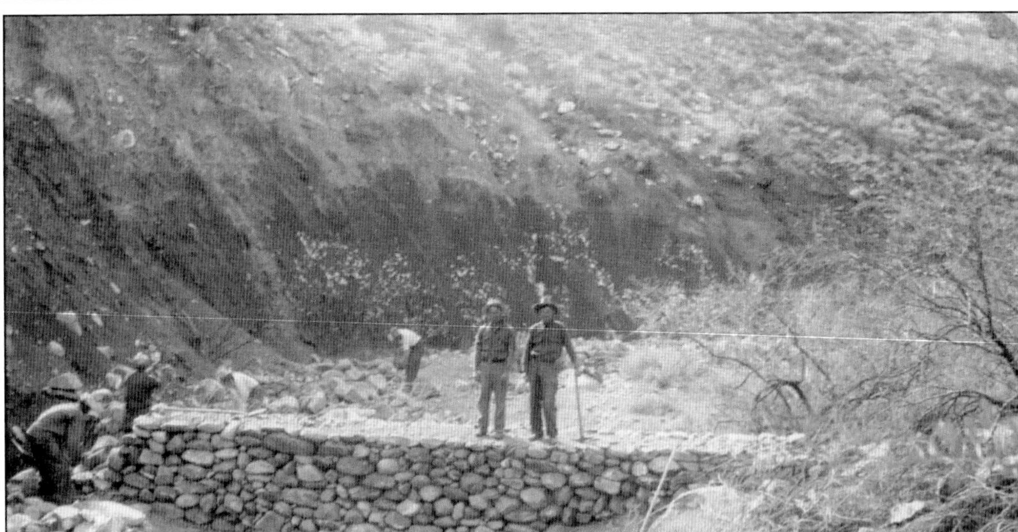

Camp F-38 was also called Tonto Basin, but its location is unknown. Company 807 occupied it only during the winters of 1933–1934 and 1934–1935. Its work included the construction of a ranger station and erosion-control work, as seen in this 1935 photograph. A March 1935 camp inspection report lauded them for the "very sturdy" 800-foot-long telephone line that stretched across Roosevelt Lake. While enrollees learned job skills, they were trained "to become better citizens," according to Tonto National Forest Supervisor T.T. Swift. (Photograph by F.L. Kirby; USFS, SWR.)

Five

Northern Arizona
Coconino County and Grand Canyon National Park

Coconino County is over 18,000 square miles in area, making it larger than nine states. The CCC worked in every part of this county except the North Kaibab National Forest.

No place in Coconino County was affected more by the CCC than Grand Canyon National Park, where as many as four companies of 200 men were working simultaneously. The park benefited more from the CCC than any other single institution in Arizona. Here, the enrollees built roads, trails, and buildings.

The enrollees gained much from their experience. Company 818 enrollee Manuel Fraijo said, "If it hadn't been for the CCC camps, I would have ended up a drunk or in jail." Nick Duncan, another Company 818 enrollee and a decorated World War II veteran, said that the CCC gave him "confidence in myself which I never had before." The fact that enrollees sent home $25 a month to their poor families "was a lifesaver," said Company 818 enrollee R.D. "Bo" Moorehead. The enrollees had fun as well. Joseph Stone recalled liberty trips into Flagstaff and going to dances at Northern Arizona University, where a bootlegger sold "white lightning" to enrollees.

The Coconino National Forest also profited greatly, almost always having two camps during the CCC era. Coconino camps stretched from Schultz Pass north of Flagstaff to Pivot Rock 75 miles south on the Mogollon Rim. The first projects in the Coconino were resource oriented—such as road, fence, and telephone line construction—but gradually, recreational projects were initiated. Flagstaff's Snowbowl ski area and the road leading to it were CCC projects. If not for the CCC, the Snowbowl would likely not exist today.

The Coconino National Forest was the only Arizona agency to be part of the CCC Artists Program. Under this 1934–1937 program, hundreds of artists lived at CCC camps and documented their work with paintings and drawings. Company 821 enrollee Creston F. Baumgartner completed at least eight paintings for this program, but only photographs of two of them have survived.

The county's northernmost community of Fredonia hosted camp G-170, where enrollee work included fences, roads, corrals, and telephone lines. Unfortunately, none of their photographs were located in archives.

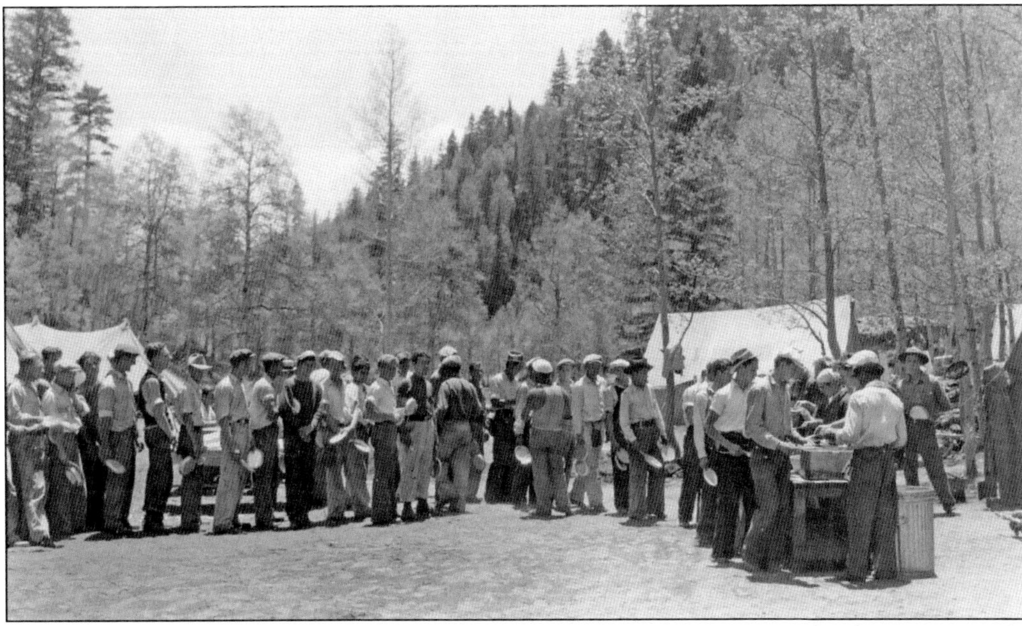

Enrollees line up for food at Grand Canyon North Rim in summer 1933. The first camp on the South Rim was occupied May 29, 1933, and the North Rim camp was opened the following day. The men have not yet received their uniforms. South Rim Company 819 enrollee George Cox said in the beginning enrollees ate out of mess kits and had to sit on the ground. When the wind blew, the red dust would get into their milk, and pretty soon they were drinking red milk. (GCNP.)

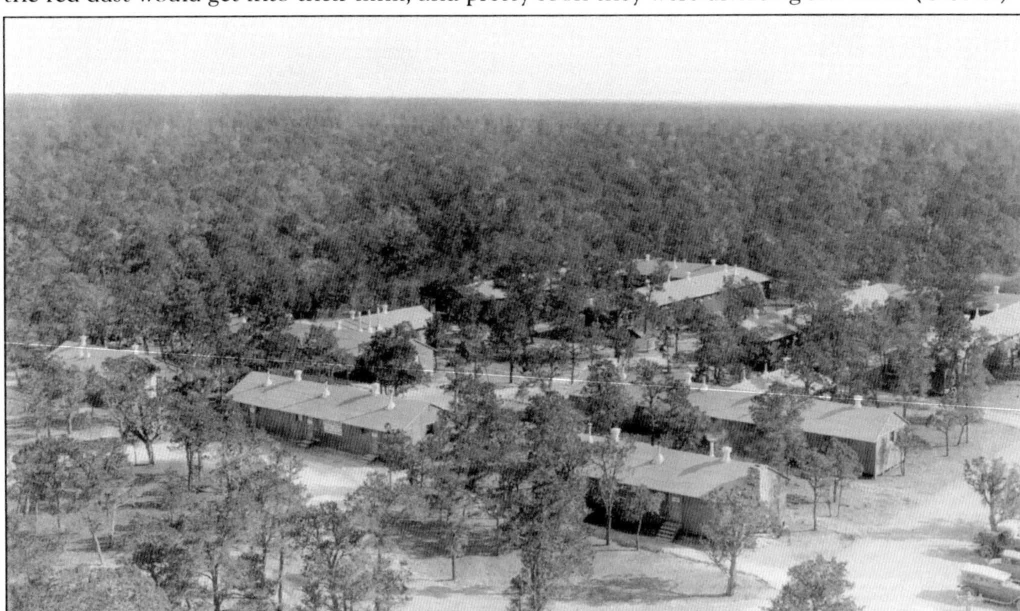

While South Rim (pictured here around 1936) and Desert View enrollees slept in barracks, enrollees on the North Rim and at the canyon bottom at Phantom Ranch slept in tents. Company 818 moved seasonally, working on the North Rim during summer months and at Phantom Ranch during winter months. The South Rim hosted Companies 819, 847, and 4814. Desert View hosted Companies 2543 and 2833. (GCNP.)

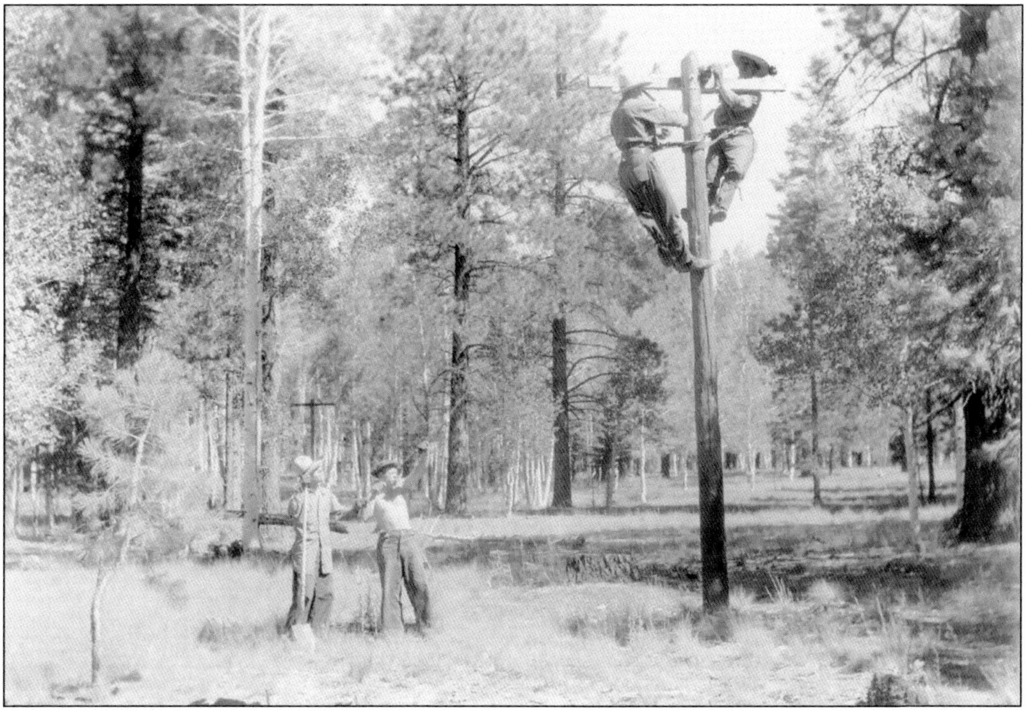

Grand Canyon North Rim enrollees constructed numerous telephone lines, such as this one pictured around 1935. The North Rim hosted Companies 818, 2833, and 3318 during the summer seasons of 1933–1940. Work included building fences, stringing the trans-canyon telephone line, repairing the North Kaibab Trail, constructing warehouses and residences, laying pipelines, developing springs to benefit wildlife, cleaning roadsides, building tree towers for fire observation, and constructing the Lodge parking lot and stone wall. North Rim CCC companies fielded outstanding boxing and baseball teams. (GCNP.)

Camp NP-3 at Phantom Ranch at the bottom of Grand Canyon, seen in this c. 1935 photograph, was considered one of the most isolated in the country. Company 818 occupied this camp during the winters of 1933–1935. Enrollees enjoyed volleyball and wrestling as well as evening movies under the stars on their "main street." Enrollees were from Arizona, Texas, or Oklahoma. Today, the site of Camp NP-3 is the Phantom Ranch Bright Angel Campground. (GCNP.)

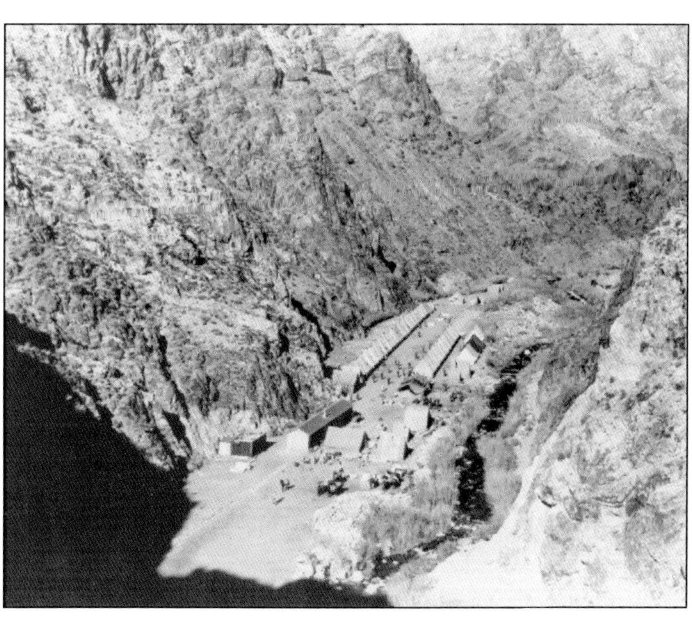

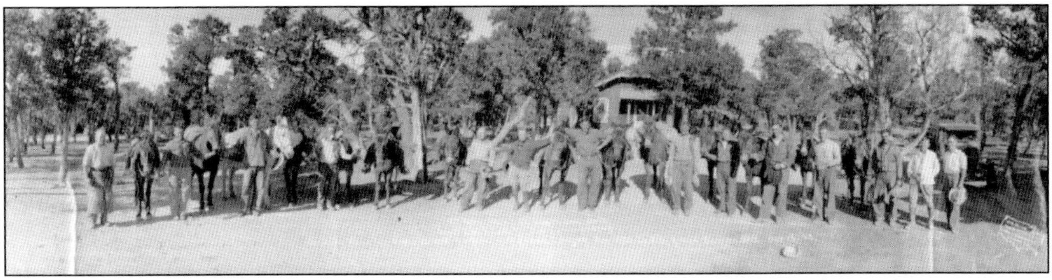

The Seventh Pack Train poses on the South Rim on October 13, 1933. This military-run unit from Fort Huachuca supplied Camp NP-3 at the canyon bottom, without missing a scheduled run between October 1933 and May 1936. Five days a week, 20 mules, each carrying 200 pounds, averaged 30,000 pounds weekly. According to Company 818 enrollee Louis Purvis, everything for the camp but water was hauled in. Food, mail, and work necessities such as blasting powder, shovels, gasoline, tools, and wheelbarrows came by mule. During the winter, extra mules carrying coal were added. (Fort Huachuca Museum.)

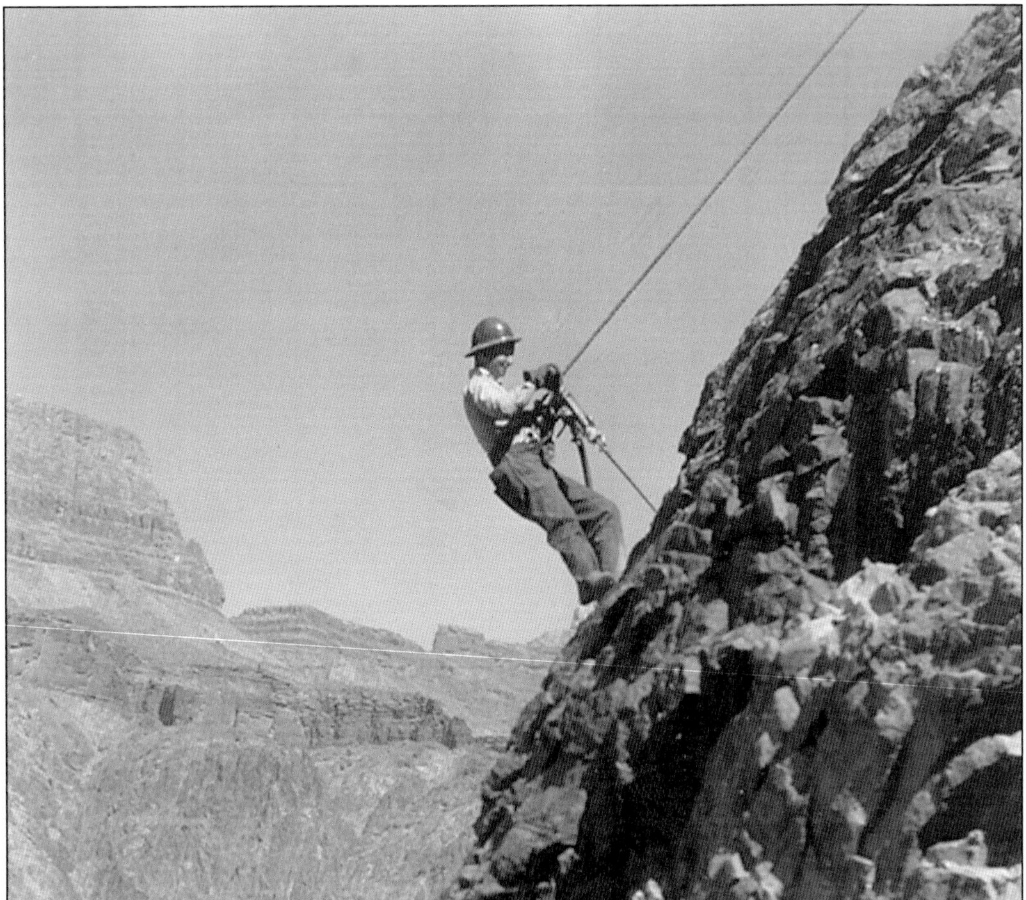

Construction of the Colorado River Trail frequently required rappelling off steep cliffs. The two-mile-long trail began December 1933, was completed January 1936, and required 40,000 pounds of blasting powder. Blasted from hard granite and schist, it is conservatively estimated to have taken 13,800 man-days to complete. This dangerous work resulted in a number of injuries but no enrollee deaths. (GCNP)

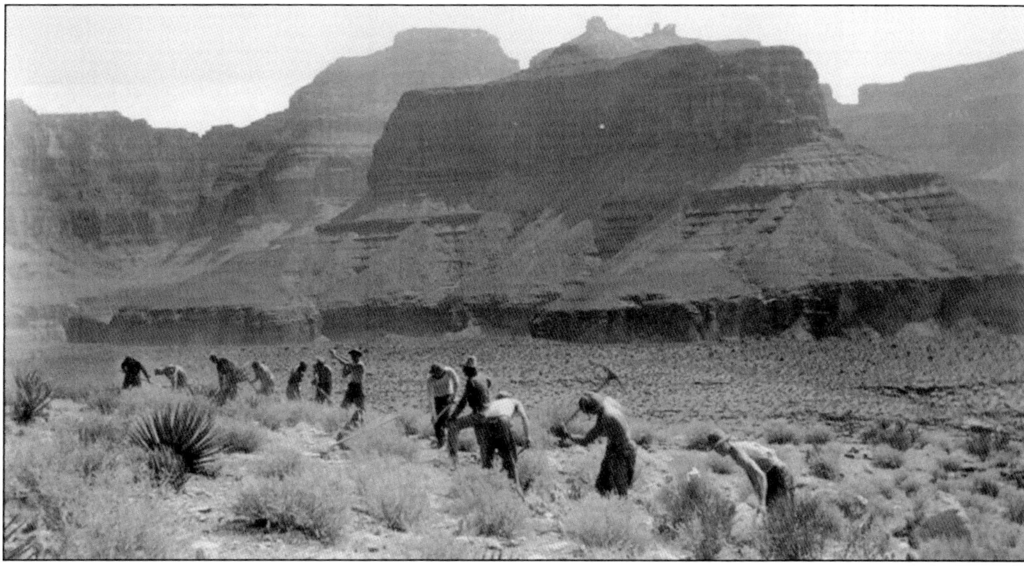

Enrollees constructed the Clear Creek Trail across the Tonto Plateau. This nine-mile-long trail begins near Phantom Ranch and goes east into the Clear Creek drainage. It was started November 1933 and completed May 1935. It required 10,000 pounds of blasting powder, and part of the work was carried out from a spike camp of tents six miles from Phantom Ranch. Enrollees also constructed the Ribbon Falls Trail. Many enrollees who learned to handle explosives in the CCC used those skills while serving in World War II. (GCNP.)

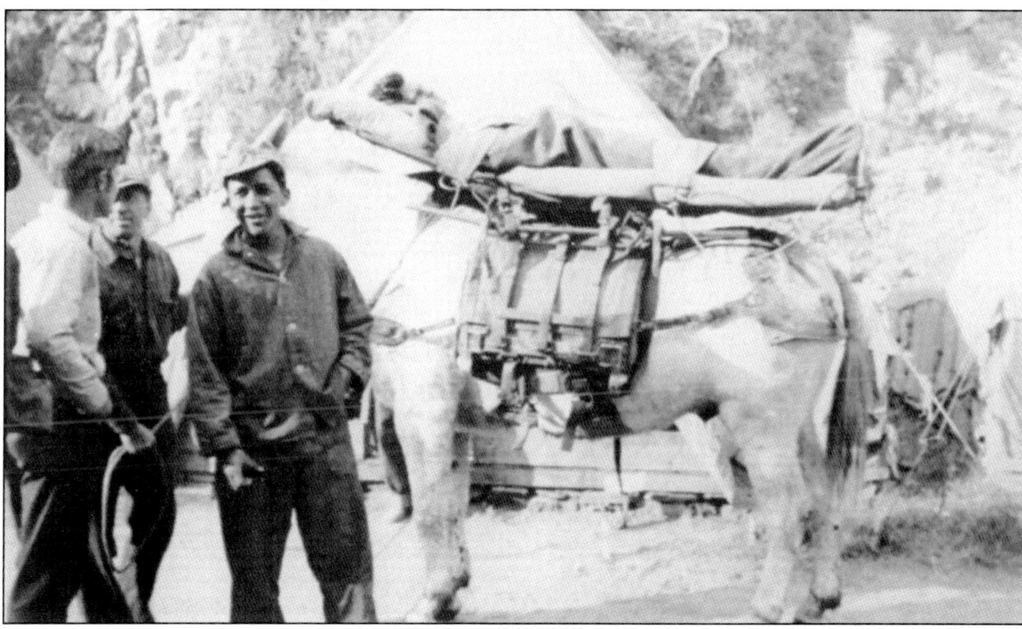

The Army camp officers emphasized safety, and the CCC hired experienced hard rock miners as trail construction supervisors. Two Fred Harvey cabins were rented: one for an operating room and one for a four-bed hospital. The mule litter in this 1936 photograph was created for CCC use. During the three seasons at Grand Canyon bottom, only 34 men were evacuated to the rim. The ride to the South Rim Hospital lasted four hours, and one enrollee described it as "a mixture between riding a ship in a heavy storm and an automobile running on flat tires." (GCNP.)

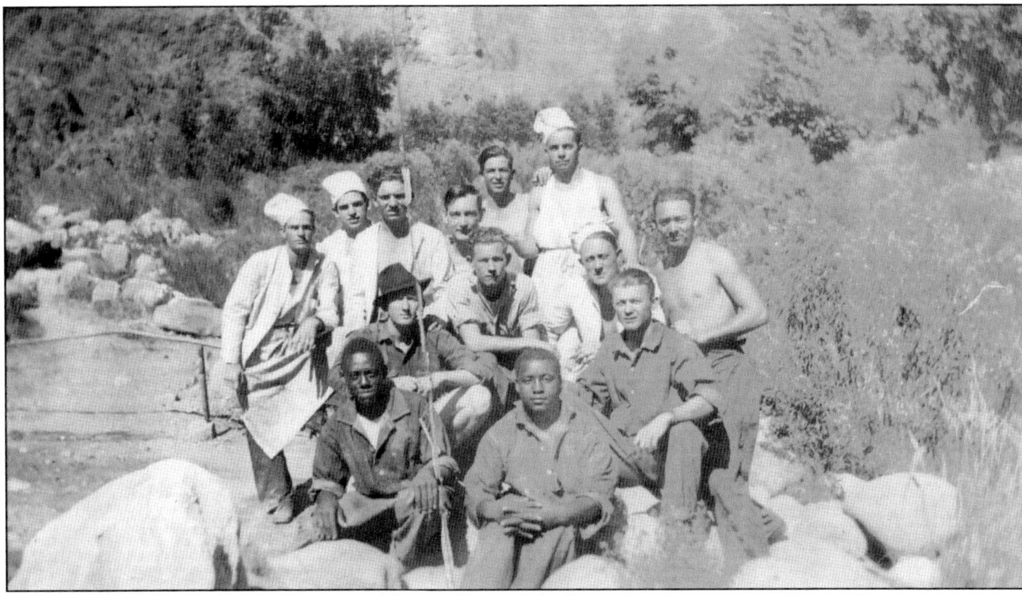

John B. Scott, an African American enrollee, took this photograph in 1935 and titled it *Kitchen Crew*. The United States as a whole—and most CCC companies—was segregated, relegating African American enrollees to cooking and domestic work. However, Company 818 often had African American enrollees doing the same work as white enrollees. Scott, once he reached the status of seasoned trail worker, was often a mentor to new enrollees. On one occasion, he saved a new enrollee's life by pulling him away from an impending rock fall. (GCNP, John B. Scott Collection.)

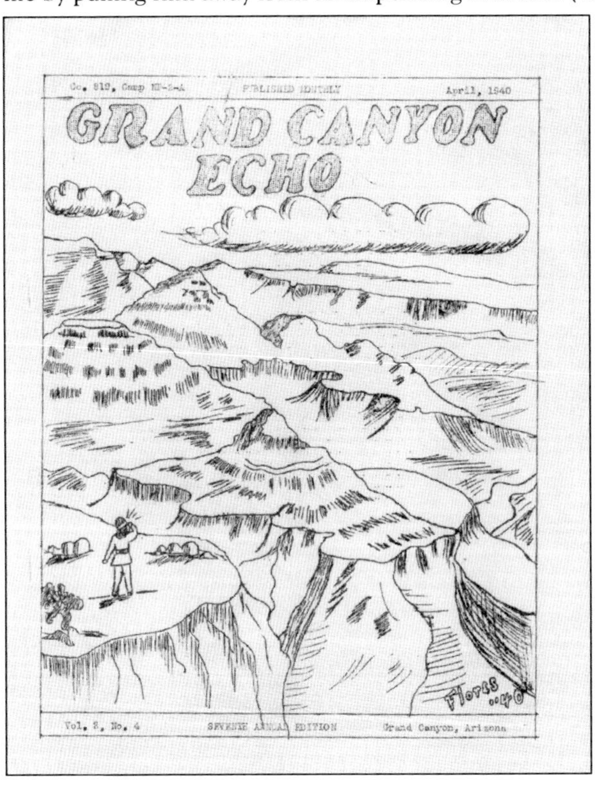

From 1936 to 1940, Company 819 at the South Rim Camp NP-2 published a monthly mimeographed newspaper as part of the camp journalism class. Most Grand Canyon newspapers contained a list of the newspaper staff, an editorial, camp news, work news, sports, cartoons, gossip, and frequently a page or more of jokes. These newspapers provide a clear picture of what was on the minds of the enrollees and leaders. (GCNP.)

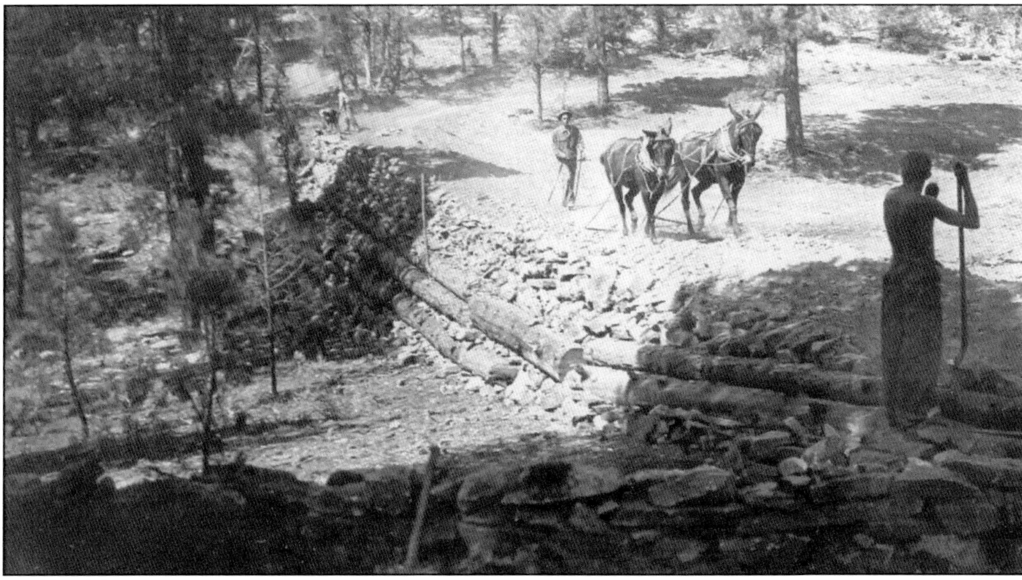

Some of the first CCC projects on the South Rim were 15 tanks, or reservoirs, located from east of Desert View all the way to Great Thumb. They were used for wildlife and firefighting. The CCC constructed Deer Tank No. 1 in 1933. Other South Rim projects were participating with other companies to string the trans-canyon telephone line that went from rim to rim via Phantom Ranch, building the Bright Angel Trail's resthouses and the rustic rim stone wall in the village, and improving the Bright Angel Trail. (GCNP.)

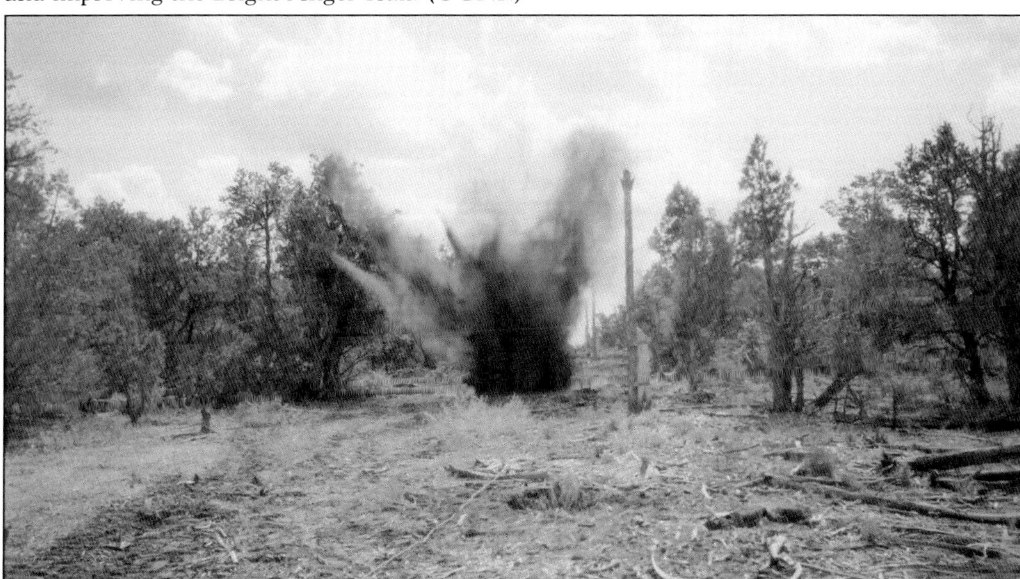

Clearing truck trails often required blasting tree stumps, as shown in this 1938 photograph. This work, most likely along Grand Canyon National Park's south boundary toward Pasture Wash, opened that area for future use. Other CCC endeavors included a reliable telephone line to Desert View, fences along the park's south boundary, and the Shoshone Point picnic area. Enrollees staffed park visitor centers, assisted with rescues, and plowed snow off roads and sidewalks during the winter. (GCNP.)

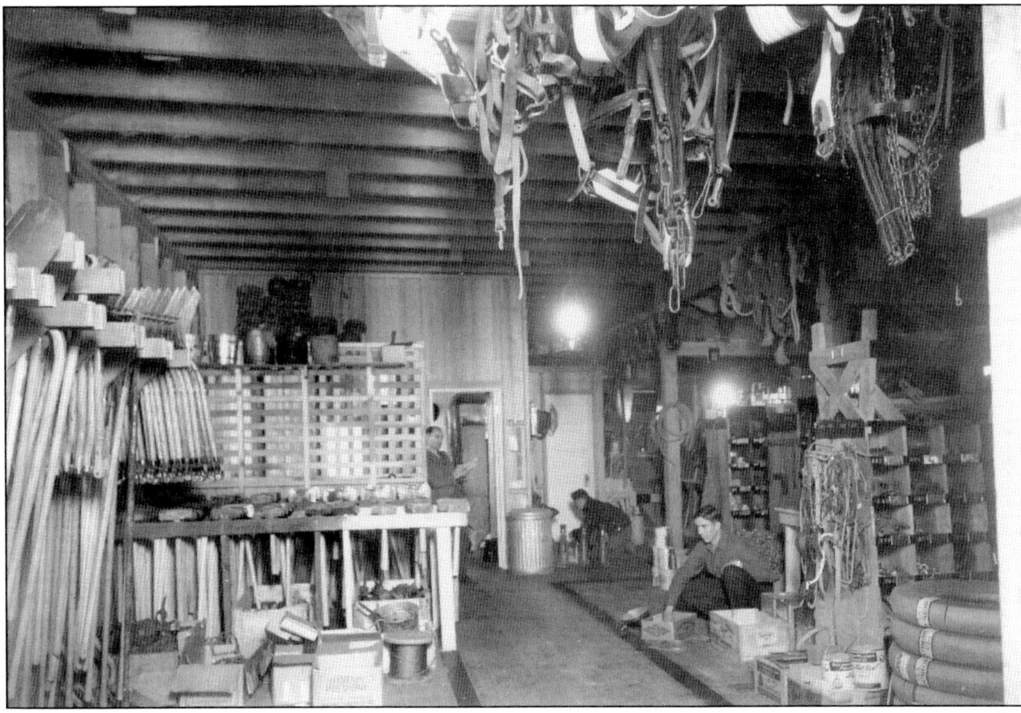

An extensive supply network such as this South Rim CCC warehouse in 1936 was required to accomplish the hundreds of CCC projects. At Grand Canyon's North and South Rims, enrollees completed extensive improvements in infrastructure, such as pipelines, fences, telephone lines, sidewalks, warehouses, parking lots, rim viewpoint guardrails, signs, power lines, and sewage lines. (GCNP.)

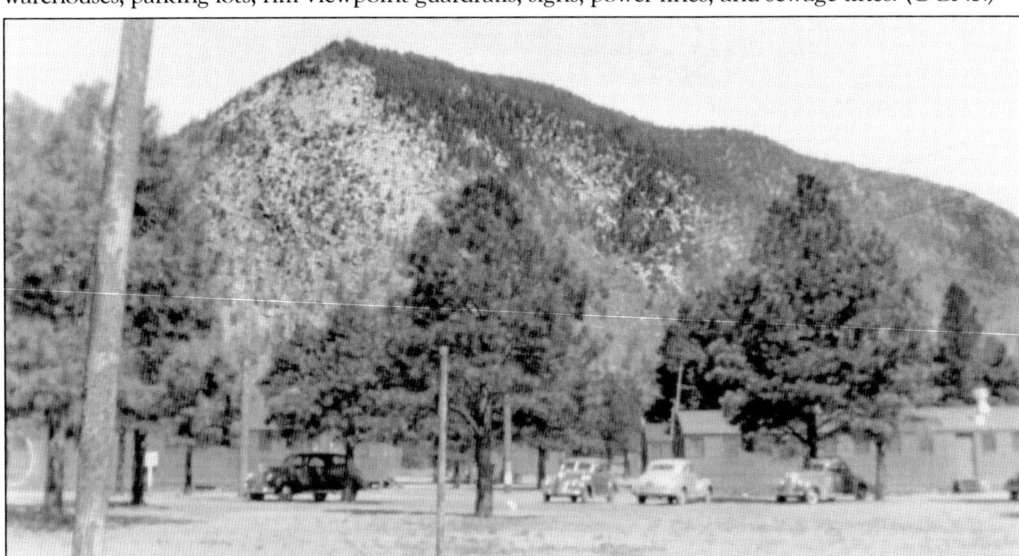

Enrollees from Pennsylvania staffed Camp NP-12, Mount Elden, seen here in 1941, part of the time. This camp did work at Sunset Crater, Walnut Canyon, and Wupatki National Monuments in 1938–1942. In October 1941, when an Army Air Corps B-18 bomber crashed on nearby Agassiz Peak, enrollees assisted in the body recoveries as well as in disassembling the wreckage. They also assisted the US Forest Service with firefighting. (KNF.)

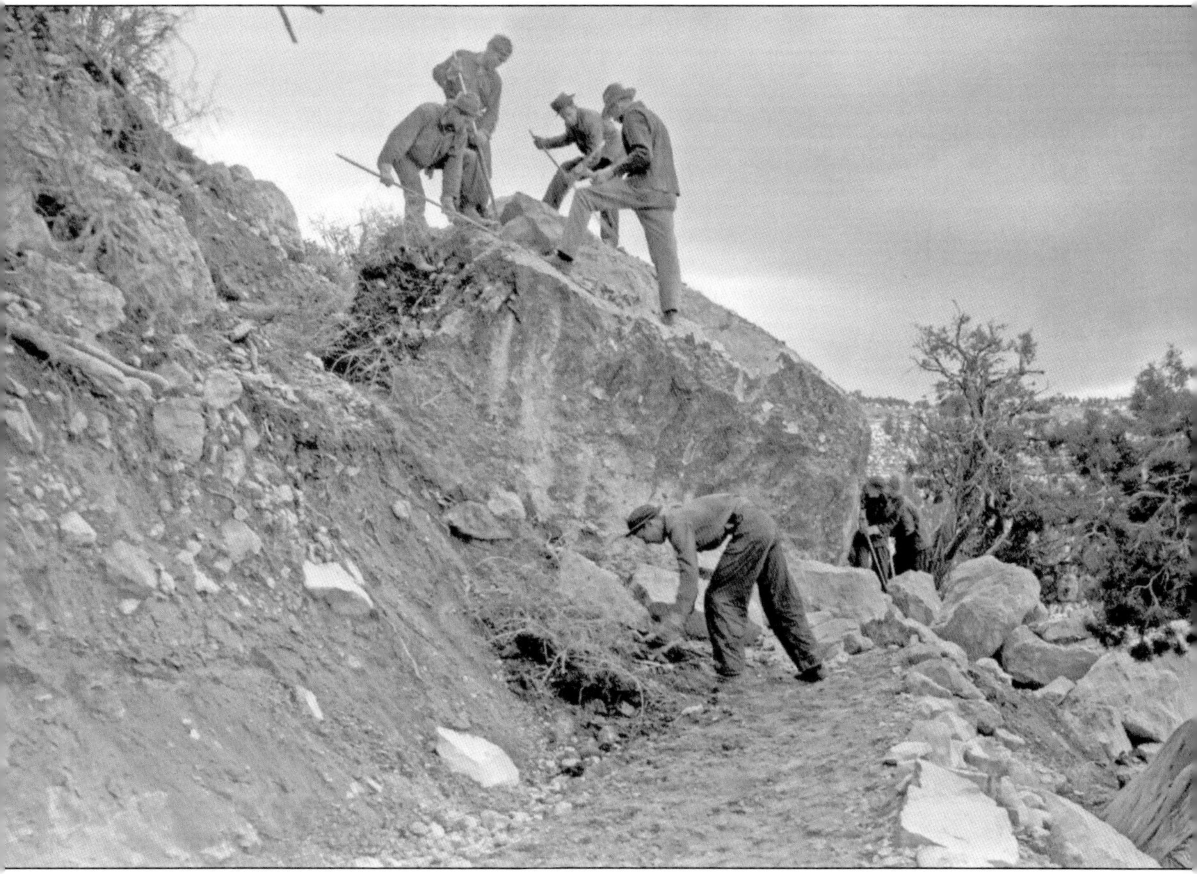

Enrollees begin the process of removing a boulder on the South Kaibab Trail here in 1936. The boulder will be blasted into smaller pieces that can be shoved off the trail. The boys did considerable trail maintenance on South Rim trails, including shoveling snow during winter months. They rerouted and widened parts of the Bright Angel Trail as well as obliterated the earlier abandoned trail alignment. On the North Rim, they did considerable trail maintenance on the North Kaibab Trail. Their most lasting work was in the Inner Canyon, where they constructed the Colorado River Trail, Ribbon Falls Trail, and the Clear Creek Trail. (GCNP.)

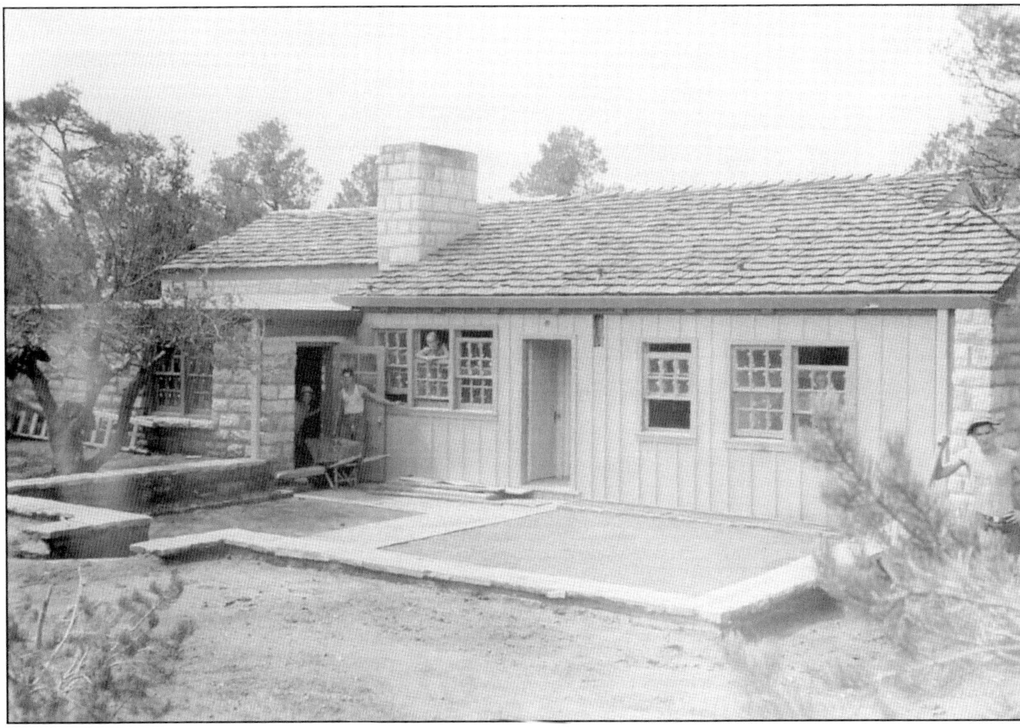

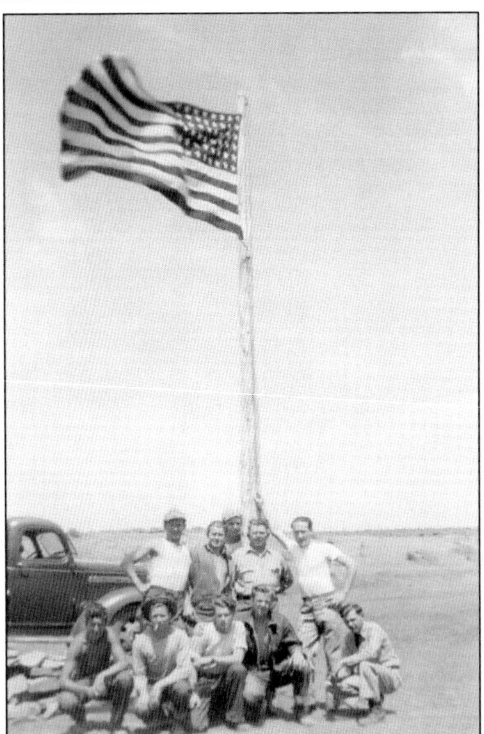

The CCC constructed this Walnut Canyon residence in 1940. At Walnut Canyon, enrollee work included the building of two new stone residences, an administration building (visitor center), and a restroom building; improvement of the Island Trail; construction of fences; maintenance of roads; firefighting; and staffing of the visitor center. They completed a 6.5-mile-long water pipeline from Mount Elden that totaled 13,584 man-days. (Photograph by Paul Beaubien; FMM.)

A group of enrollees pose by the flagpole around 1940 at the Old Heiser Camp near Wupatki National Monument. At Wupatki, their work included a new water system, new residences, and an administration building (visitor center). These stone buildings were made from native stone and designed to be unobtrusive and look like ruins. Heiser Spring had insufficient water to support a full-size camp, so this was always a spike (side) camp. (FMM.)

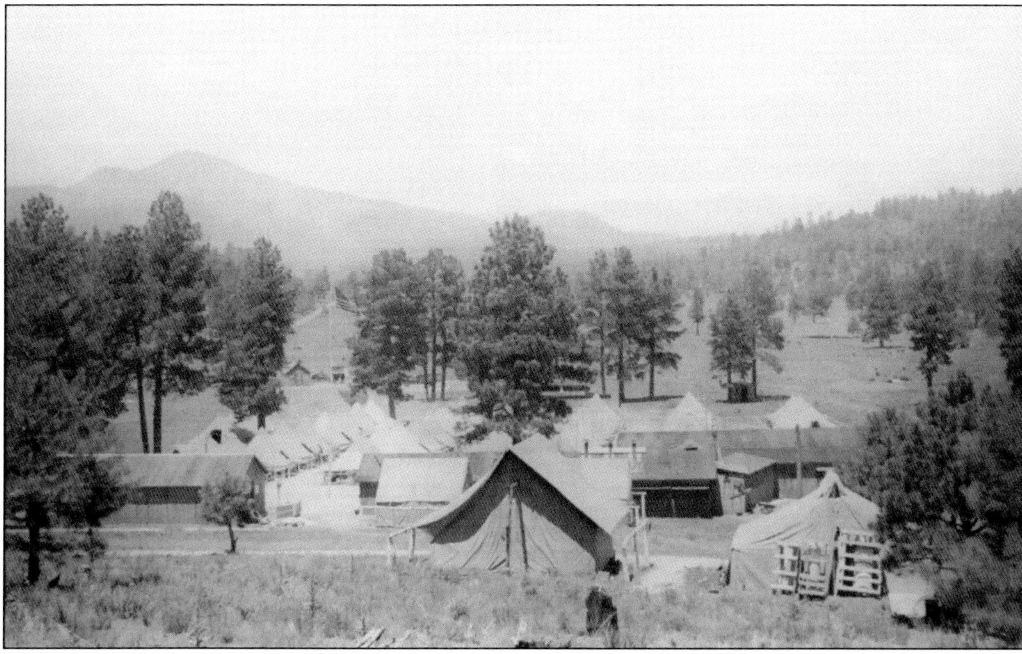

Company 1838, as well as two companies of Pennsylvania boys, staffed Camp F-28 south of Williams, seen here in 1935. The Williams camp was occupied summers 1933–1940. It was a favorite of enrollees because of the friendly way the town and newspaper treated them. Its largest project was completing the road from Williams to Perkinsville. Other projects included building fences, erecting the White Horse and Kennedy Dams, building water reservoirs (tanks), making campgrounds, and constructing the Bill Williams Fire Lookout. (JI.)

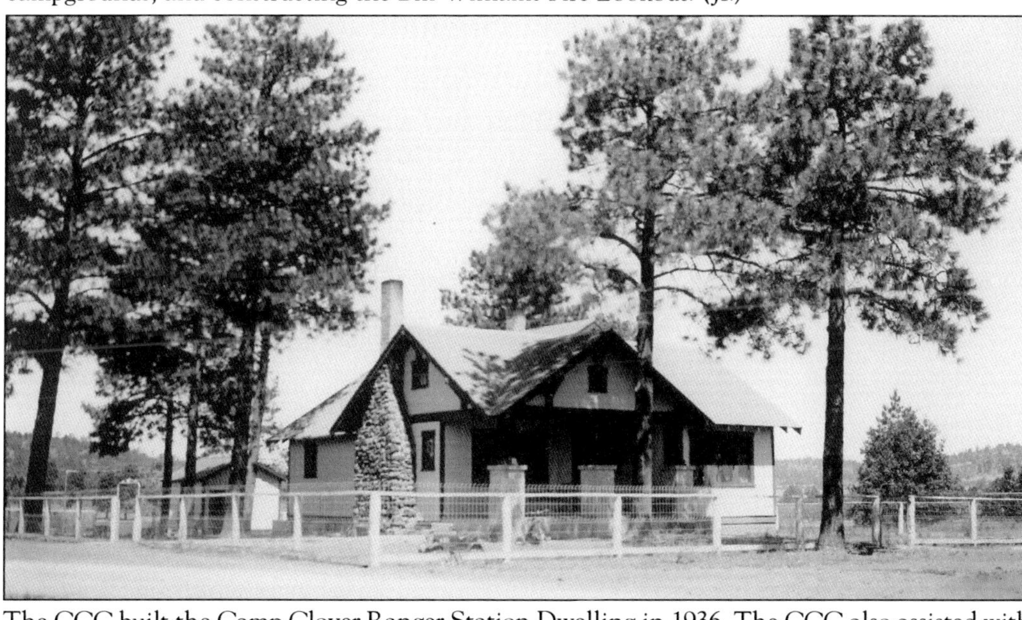

The CCC built the Camp Clover Ranger Station Dwelling in 1936. The CCC also assisted with a ranger station and barn at Camp Clover and had one other camp in the Kaibab National Forest at Bellemont, but it closed after five months' occupancy. It was said to be located near Hill Spring, now within the Navajo Army Depot. (Photograph by Richard H. Lewis; USFS, SWR.)

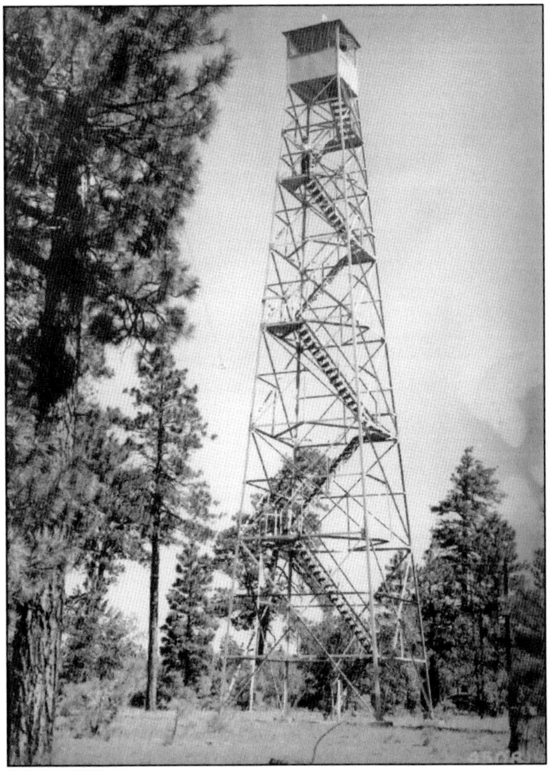

Enrollees constructed the Grandview Fire Lookout seen here in 1948. Enrollees also completed a two-room cabin for the fire lookouts. Camp F-28, Williams, enrollees spent considerable time fighting forest fires from both the main JD Dam Camp and a spike camp at Spring Valley. During this time the Forest Service had a policy of quickly suppressing all forest fires. Nationwide, the CCC assisted this policy by constructing fire towers, telephone lines, and truck trails. (Photograph by Edgar Perry; USFS, SWR.)

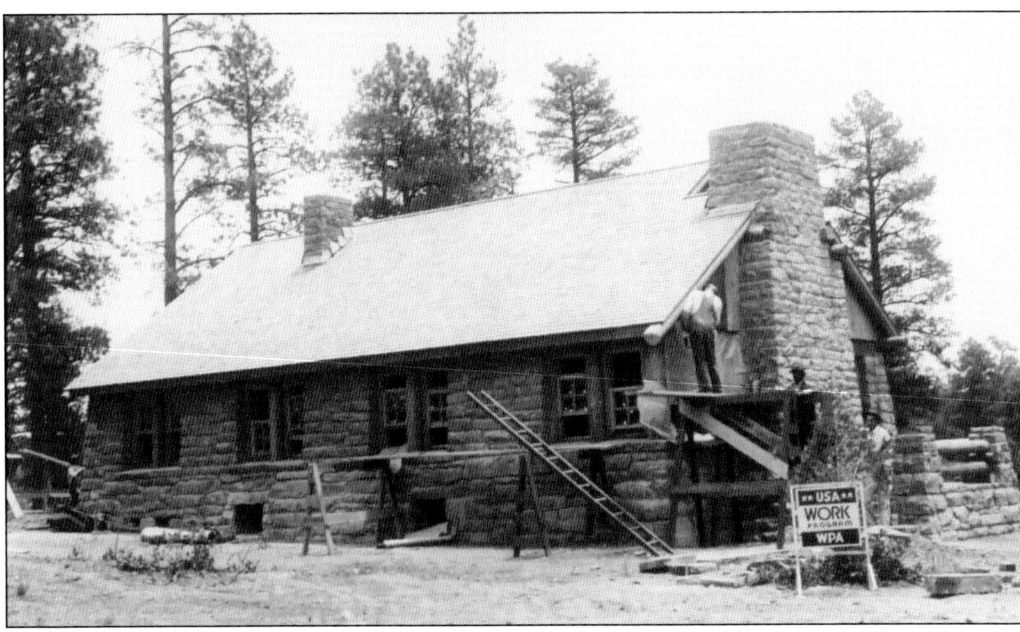

The Moqui Ranger Station was constructed in 1940. The six rustic stone buildings were apparently a WPA project, with possible CCC assistance. Buildings include a ranger residence, a seed house, a pump house, a barn, a garage, and a ranger office. The construction is from locally quarried sandstone along with wood logs. All the buildings are well preserved today, and they are considered outstanding examples of Forest Service rustic architecture. (KNF.)

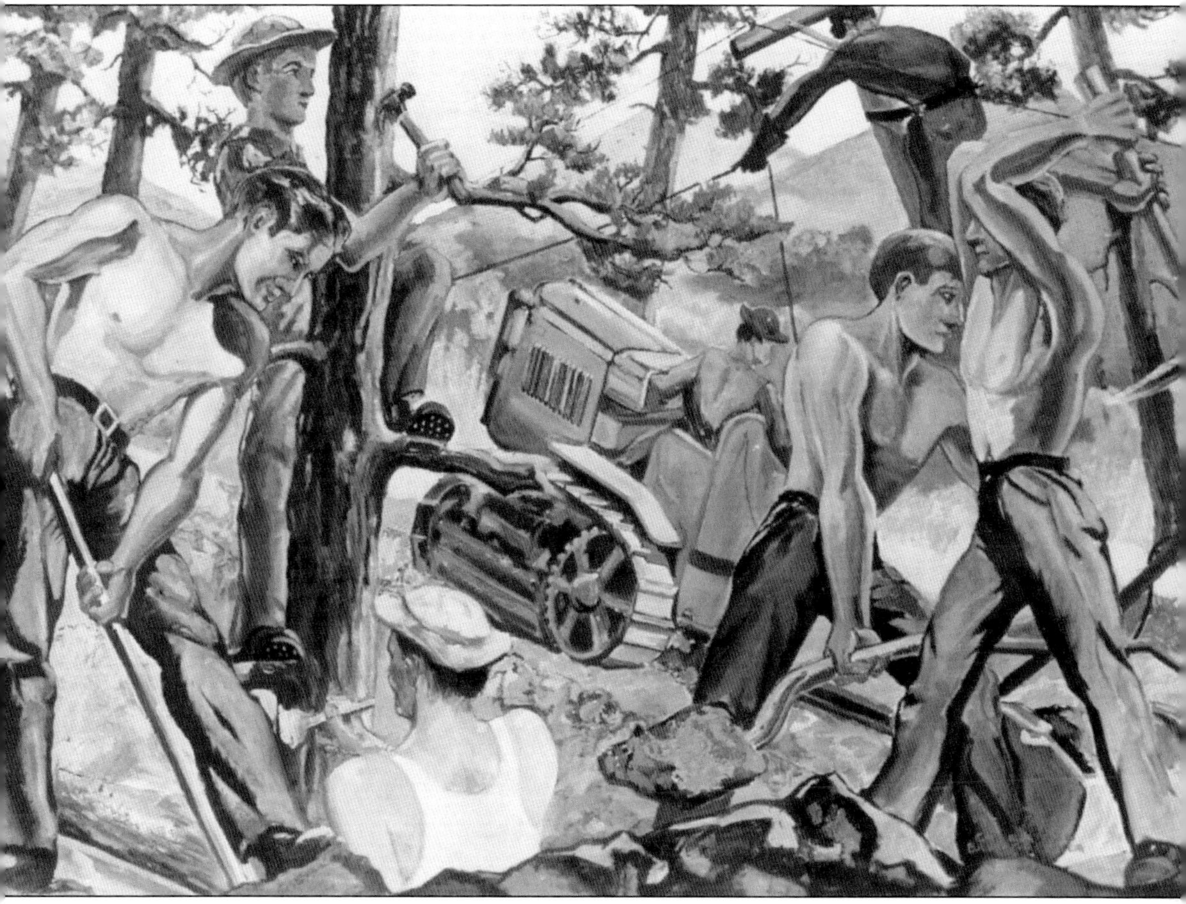

Creston F. Baumgartner, the only Arizona participant in the national CCC Artists Program, titled this painting *Four Different Crews*. Baumgartner (1908–1984) was a member of Company 821 in the Coconino National Forest, where he made paintings, created Forest Service signs, and assisted with the camp newspapers. The painting location is the Schultz Pass camp, and the enrollees are representative of work crews doing roadside cleanup, road building, telephone line stringing, and porcupine extermination. Baumgartner did at least eight paintings as a CCC artist, but none are in federal government hands today. Before entering the CCC, Baumgartner participated in the CWA Artists Program, where he painted a mural of flowers and cactus in the Arizona Capitol Building. (NARA MD.)

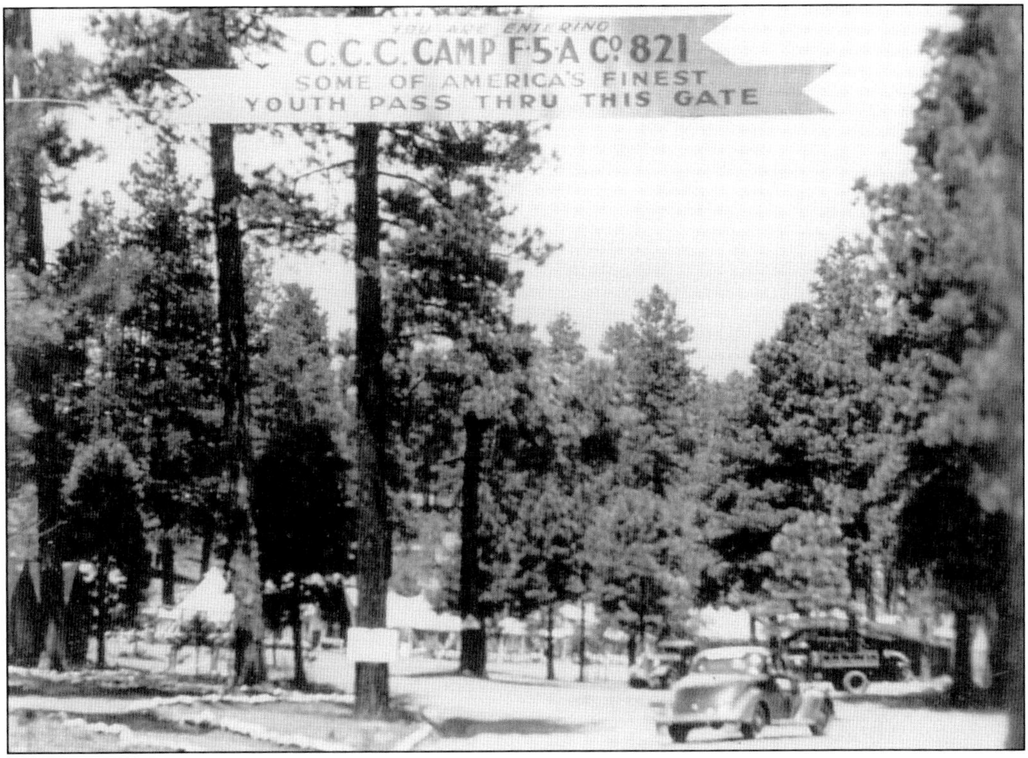

Camp F-5, Schultz Pass, pictured around 1934, was occupied in summers 1933–1939. It was located just outside the city of Flagstaff. This was one of the first camps to be occupied in northern Arizona, opening on May 28, 1933. An enrollee described the unloading of their baggage in a grove of pine trees: "There were no buildings, no company street, no headquarters . . . in fact the only thing to see in Camp now is one little lonesome water faucet." Their most demanding project was construction of the Schultz Pass Road. (JI.)

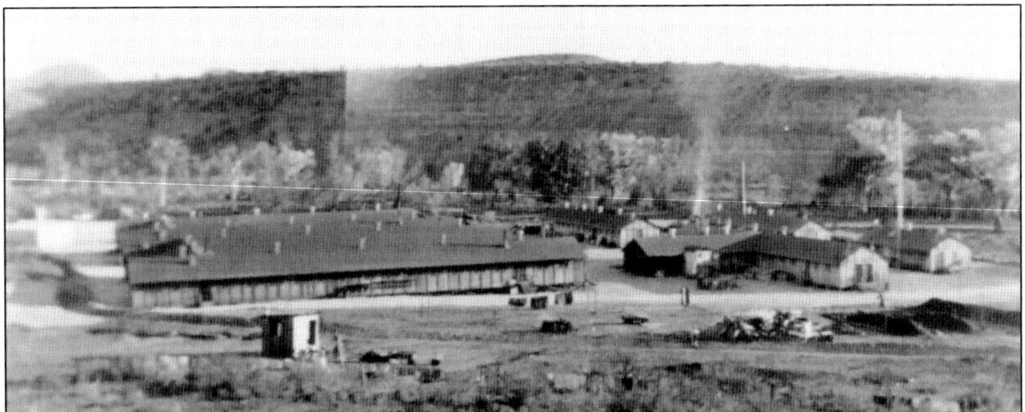

Camp F-35, Clear Creek, is in this c. 1940 photograph. Enrollees who worked the summer months at Schultz Pass or Mormon Lake spent their winter seasons at Sedona, Clear Creek, Beaver Creek, or Verde No. 1. During the 1930s, Sedona was a center for Hollywood movie making. In 1940, 17-year-old Pennsylvania enrollee Bill Dean worked at the Clear Creek camp and was thrilled to get autographs of his western cowboy heroes Tom Mix, Ken Maynard, and Buck Jones on his days off in Sedona. (JI; RJM.)

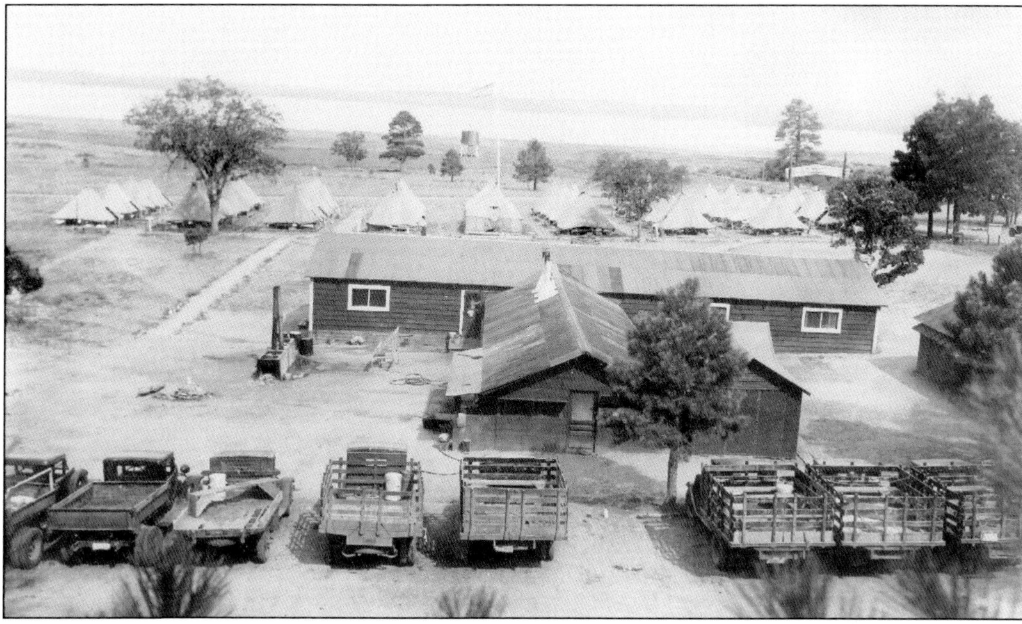

Camp F-6, Double Springs, was located at Mormon Lake, seen here in 1936. This camp was occupied in the warmer seasons 1933–1936 and then was used as a side camp of Camp F-75, Pivot Rock, during the summers 1937–1942. Enrollee work included constructing campgrounds, roads, fences, and telephone lines; fighting forest fires; developing springs; performing road maintenance; and plugging sinkholes in Lake Mary. (CNF.)

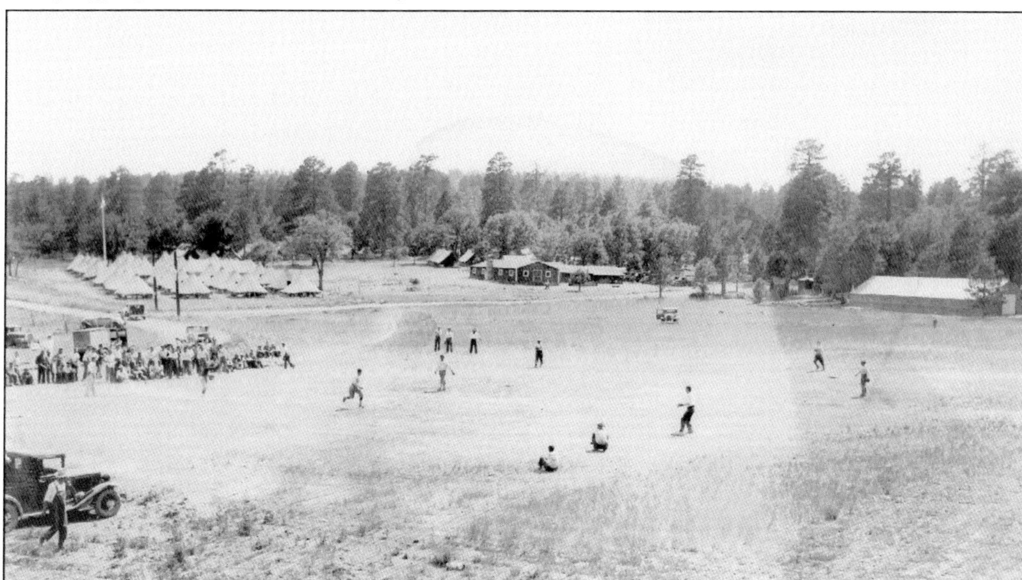

Enrollees are enjoying baseball at Camp F-6, Double Springs, in 1936. Baseball was the enrollees' favorite sport, followed closely by boxing and football. Most camps had a recreation hall, where billiards was popular. Often the hall had a radio, and sometimes even a record player. Many camps had a library, which often subscribed to enrollees' hometown newspapers. Many enrollees looked forward to a weekend liberty trip to a nearby town to hang out at the local drugstore soda bar. Some used these trips to obtain alcohol, which was prohibited in camp. (CNF.)

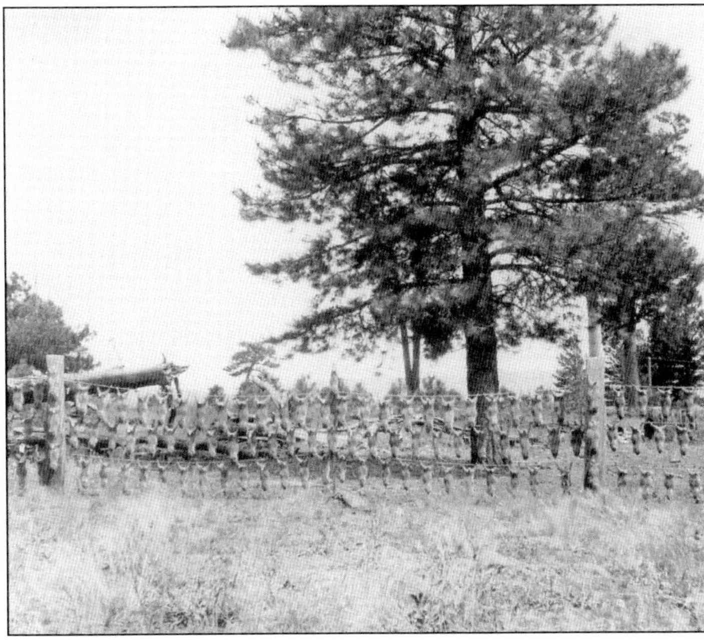

Camp F-6, Double Springs, did a great deal of prairie dog extermination as well as extermination of other rodents and porcupines. Prairie dogs were considered a nuisance, as livestock could put a foot in a prairie dog hole and get injured. In the early 1930s, hundreds of quarts of poison were put out. Porcupines were killed with poisonous bait and .22 rifles, as a porcupine eating the bark completely around the tree (girdling it) could make the tree less valuable for timber sale. (CNF.)

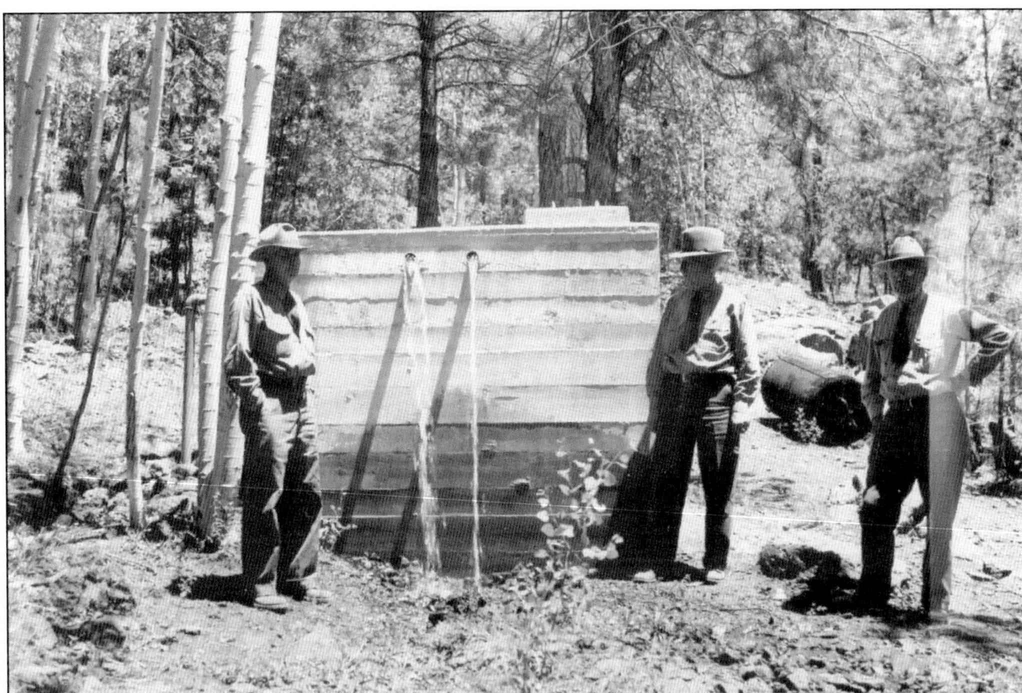

This 1941 photograph shows range water development at an unknown location in the Coconino National Forest. Typically, work crews would dig or even blast earth and rock to get to the spring's source in hopes of increasing the spring flow and then pipe the spring to a reservoir such as this one. Water was frequently rationed from the reservoir to give a more even flow of the spring between wet and dry times of the year. Those that were improved in the forest included John Lee, Double, Wallace, Navajo, Winsor, Hance, Black, and Griffith Springs. (NARA MD.)

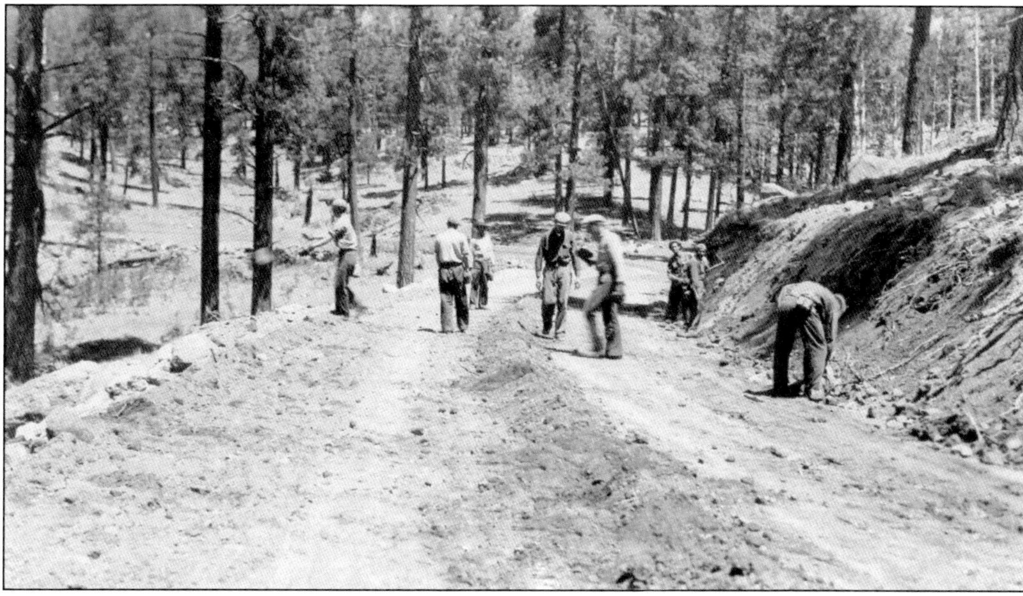

Camp F-5, Flagstaff, enrollees are improving a road here in 1936. Considerable resources were put into upgrading Forest Service roads to standard. Frequently, widening roads required considerable blasting of rock. Enrollee Alan Wilkerson, interviewed by Flagstaff author Jane Jackson, called the unimproved roads "simple" and "more pathways than anything." He believed the purpose of upgrading the roads was "to enable firefighters to get in and control fires." Wilkerson, 17 years old and a grade school dropout, was a great fan of Zane Gray novels, so coming to the Coconino National Forest was "real exciting." (CNF.)

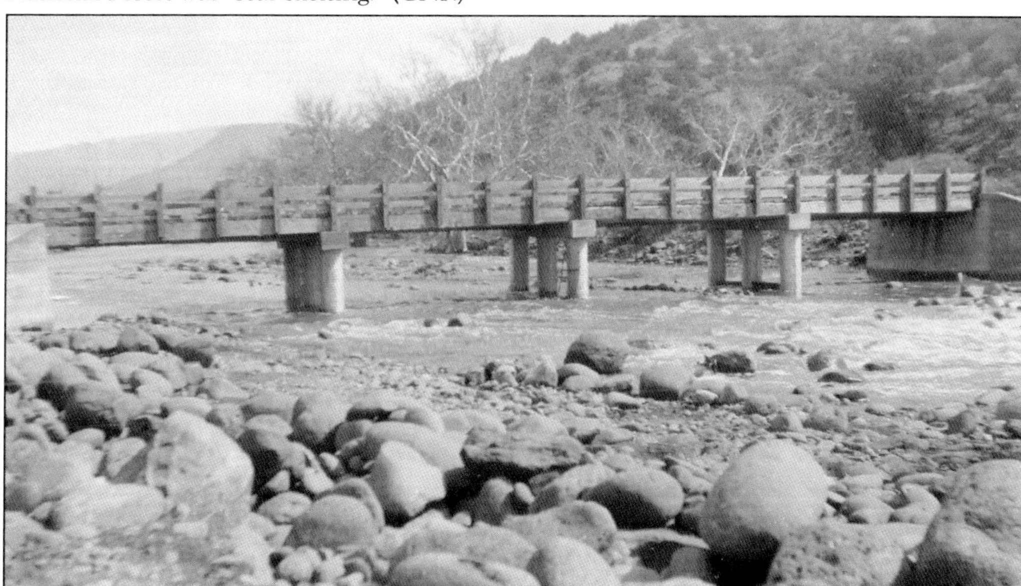

In addition to constructing many roads and truck trails, enrollees built several bridges. The CCC stretched this bridge over Dry Beaver Creek south of Oak Creek in 1936. Present-day State Route 179 has bypassed the bridge, but in 2013 the abutments appeared quite sturdy. Other CCC-built bridges included ones at Munds Park, Beaver Creek, Walker Creek, Red Tank Wash, and Schnebly Hill Road. (Photograph by Emil Geffert; USFS, SWR.)

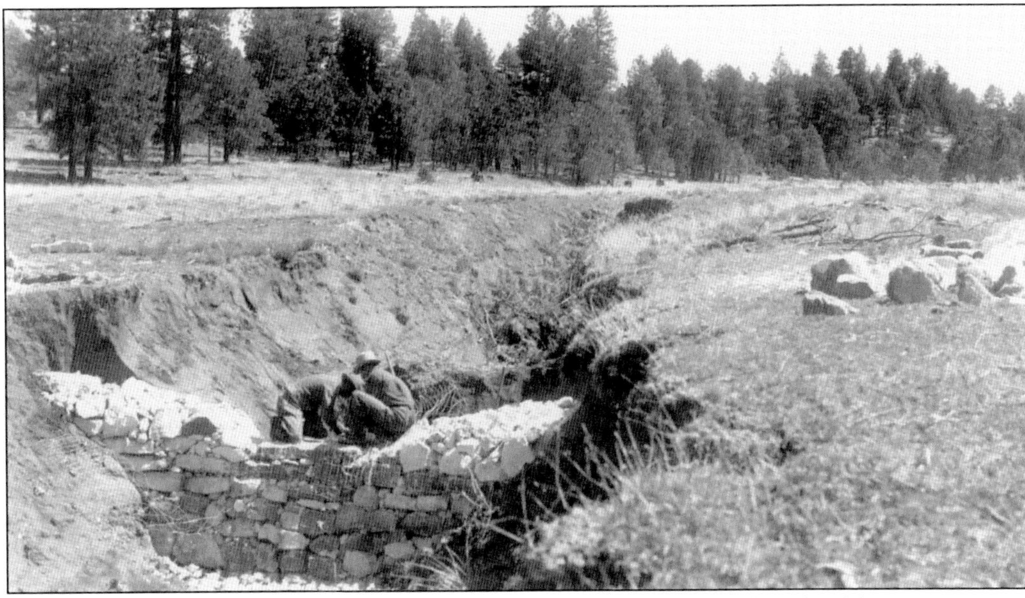

Decades of timber harvesting and overgrazing resulted in the demise of much of the native grasses and the loss of topsoil. Camp F-5, Schultz Pass, enrollees constructed erosion-control dams such as these, pictured around 1936. Although these projects were quite labor intensive, many of these erosion-control features are still functioning. (CNF.)

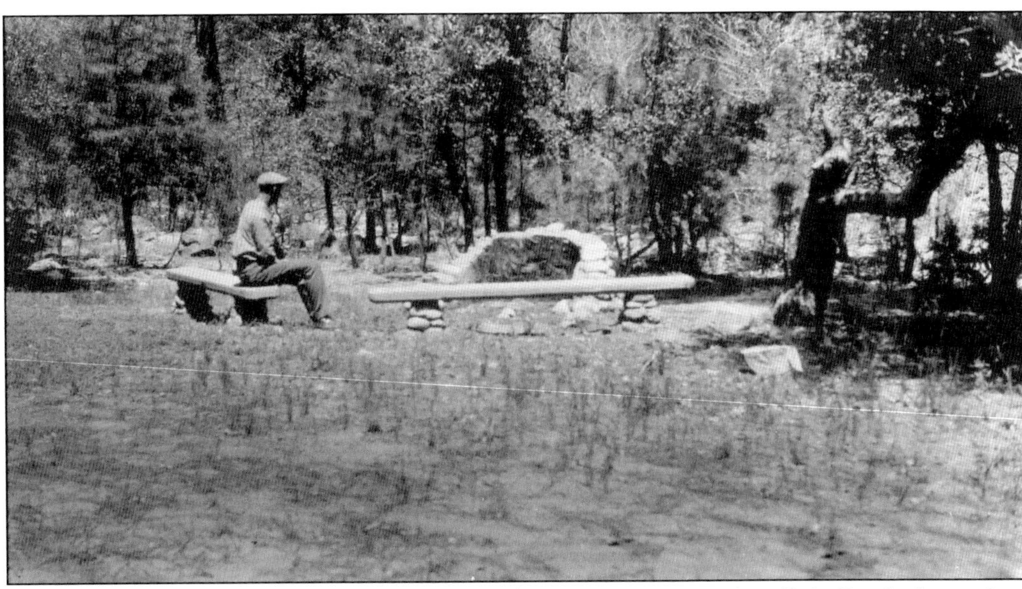

The CCC constructed this open fireplace in the Purtymen area near Oak Creek shown here in 1934. When the CCC first began work in Arizona national forests, most of the work was oriented toward resources such as fence, road, and telephone line placement and fire suppression. Gradually, more CCC work was oriented to recreation. Coconino National Forest campground improvements included Pine Tree Flat, Lake Mary, Stoneman Lake, Banjo Bill, and Kit Carson, while picnic ground improvements included the Oak Creek Canyon vista and Schnebly Hill. (Photograph by John D. Jones; USFS, SWR.)

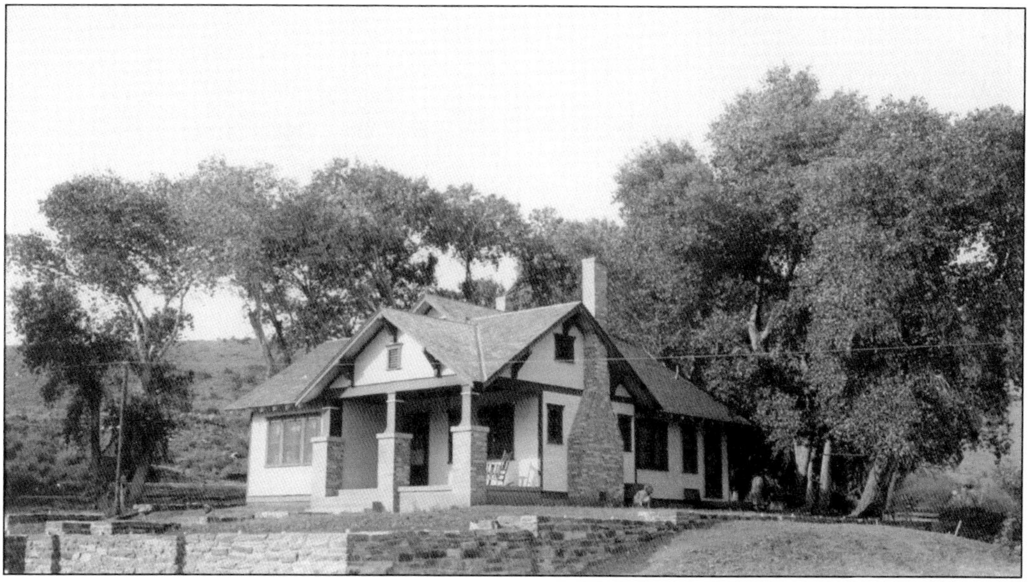

CCC enrollees constructed the Beaver Creek Ranger Station Dwelling seen here in 1936 and assisted in the construction of its associated barn-garage. Enrollees also built the ranger station barns at Sedona and Clear Creek. They constructed or assisted in the construction of fire lookout towers at Lee Butte, Deadman, and Hutch Mountain. (Photograph by Richard H. Lewis; USFS, SWR.)

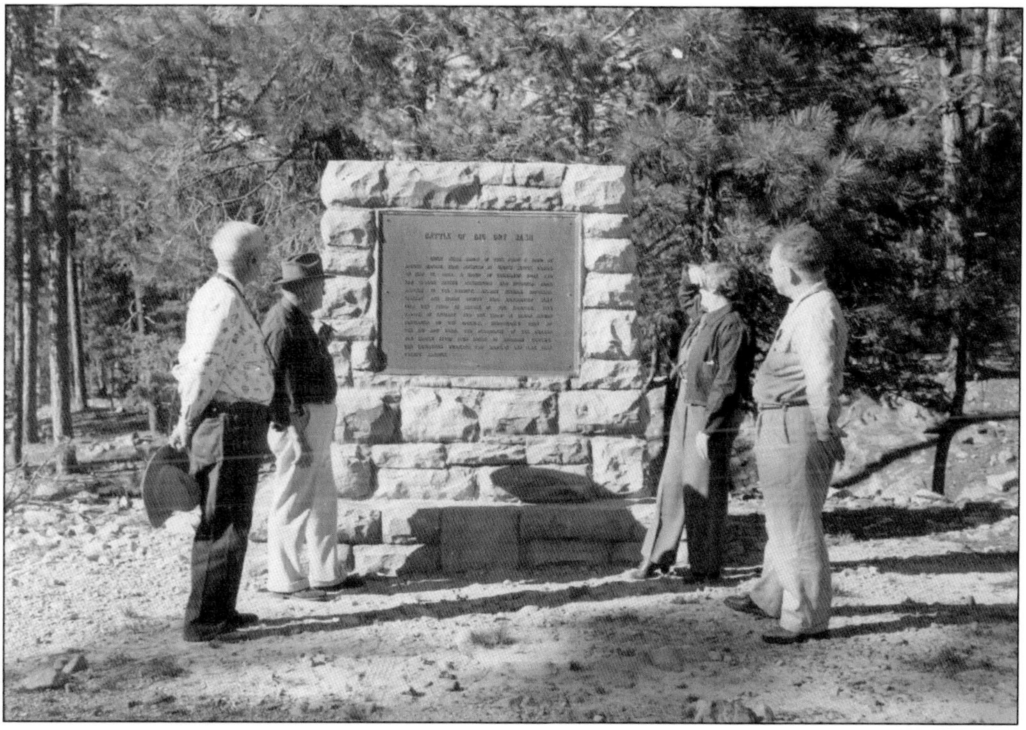

This monument to the Battle of Big Dry Wash, seen here in 1941, was CCC constructed. Enrollees from Camps F-6, Double Springs, and F-75, Pivot Rock, 1935–1938, erected two monuments to the last battle between the US military and the Apaches. The battle was fought between the White Mountain Apaches and the US Calvary in 1882. (Photograph by F.L. Kirby; USFS, SWR.)

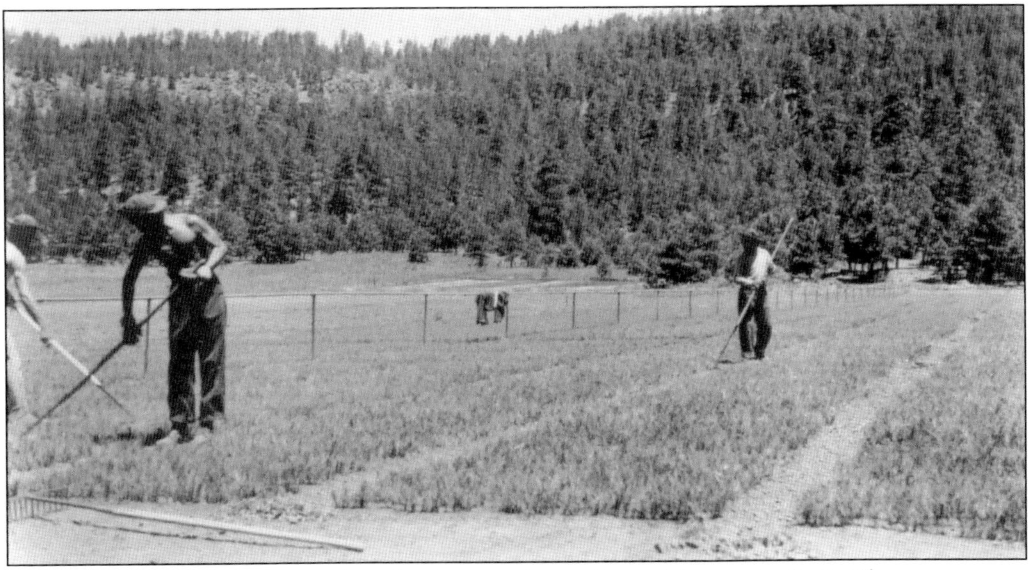

Camp F-75 enrollees are at work at the Leroux Spring Forest Nursery in 1941. The nursery was run completely by the CCC, beginning with its inception in 1934. Water was supplied from Little Leroux Spring. Work included gathering pinecones, planting the seeds, tending and watering the seeds, and preparing the seedlings for transplanting. Millions of seedlings from this nursery were planted in the Coconino National Forest. Enrollees also did considerable work at the nearby US Forest Service Fort Valley Experimental Station. (Photograph by John D. Guthrie; US Forest Service, Fort Valley Experimental Station.)

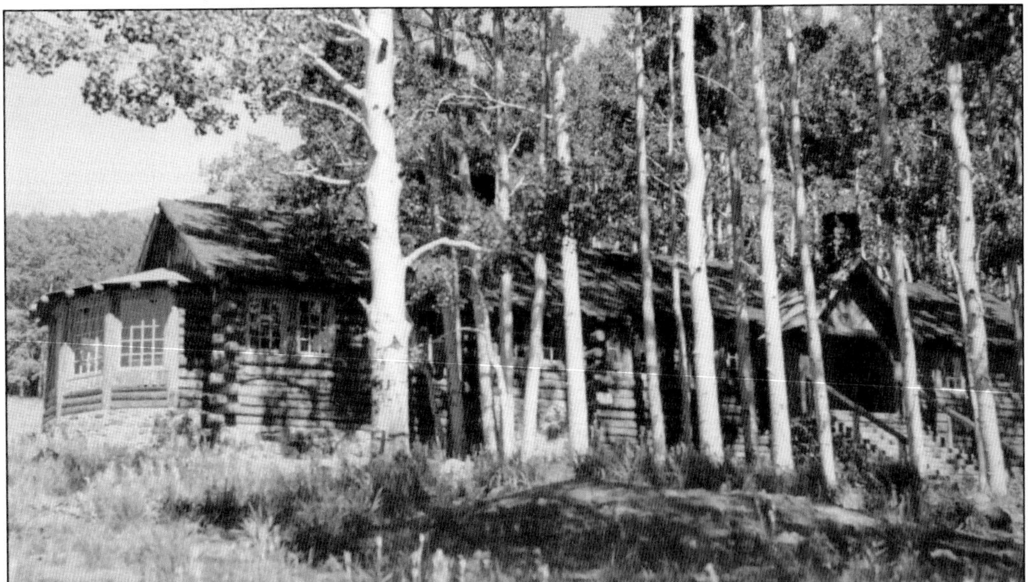

The Snowbowl Ski Lodge is pictured here in 1948. Beginning in 1939, enrollees did substantial work building the seven-mile-long road up the mountain to the ski area, a 400-car parking lot, the first lodge, and the first ski runs, and carving rustic log signs for the ski area. As many as 200 enrollees worked on the road at one time, and frequently they worked double shifts, starting at 5:00 a.m. and working until 9:00 p.m. The present-day Snowbowl would not exist if not for the CCC work and Forest Service planning. (Photograph by E.L. Perry; USFS, SWR.)

Six

East-Central Arizona
Mohave and Yavapai Counties

Present-day Mohave County covers an area of 13,470 square miles, making it the fifth-largest county in the United States. A very large portion of the county is federal government land, which made it excellent potential for CCC work. Part of the county is located north of the Colorado River. The area north of the river is called the Arizona Strip. It is very thinly populated, and its residents are more culturally and economically linked to Utah and Nevada than to Arizona. Because of the lack of an acceptable water source and medical facilities in the western part of the Strip, the first camp to serve the area was Camp DG-45, located at St. George, Utah. This camp, occupied from October 1935 to August 1939, spent much of its energy completing the first reliable road from St. George to Wolf Hole, Arizona. Other grazing camps on the Arizona Strip included those at Pipe Spring, Short Creek, Antelope Valley, and Fredonia.

South of the Colorado River in Mohave County, grazing camps were located at Round Valley and Kingman. The camps supervised by the National Park Service at Hualapai Mountain Park did major work, while the camp at Parker Dam was short-lived.

Today, Yavapai County covers 8,128 square miles with nearly half of it federally controlled, which also made it an excellent area for CCC work. Here, grazing camps were located at Yava and Congress Junction. The camps' work included road, fence, telephone line, and stock tank construction; well drilling; spring development; and erosion-control projects. A short-lived Soil Conservation Service camp was located at the John A. Thompson Ranch. Its work included construction of check dams and water spreaders to limit the loss of soil. The Prescott National Forest benefited greatly from the CCC, with camps operating from May 1933 to July 1942. Camp locations included Groom Creek, Thumb Butte, Prescott Fairgrounds, Walnut Creek, Lynx Creek, Verde No. 1, and Mayer.

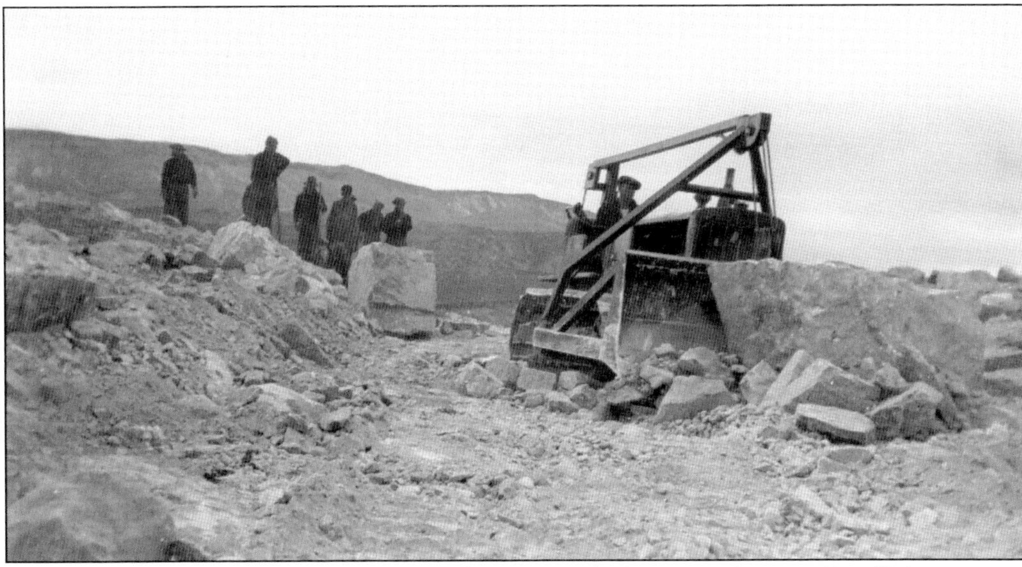

The first priority of Camp DG-45 (Division of Grazing, today known as Bureau of Land Management) was improvement of the road between St. George, Utah, and Wolf Hole, Arizona. This 30-mile-long "road" was said to be only a primitive trail and "narrow, crooked and tortuous." While much work was done by hand labor and teams of horses, bulldozers and air compressors were necessary for the more difficult sections. This 1938 photograph illustrates some of the final work after blasting occurred. (NARA-RMR.)

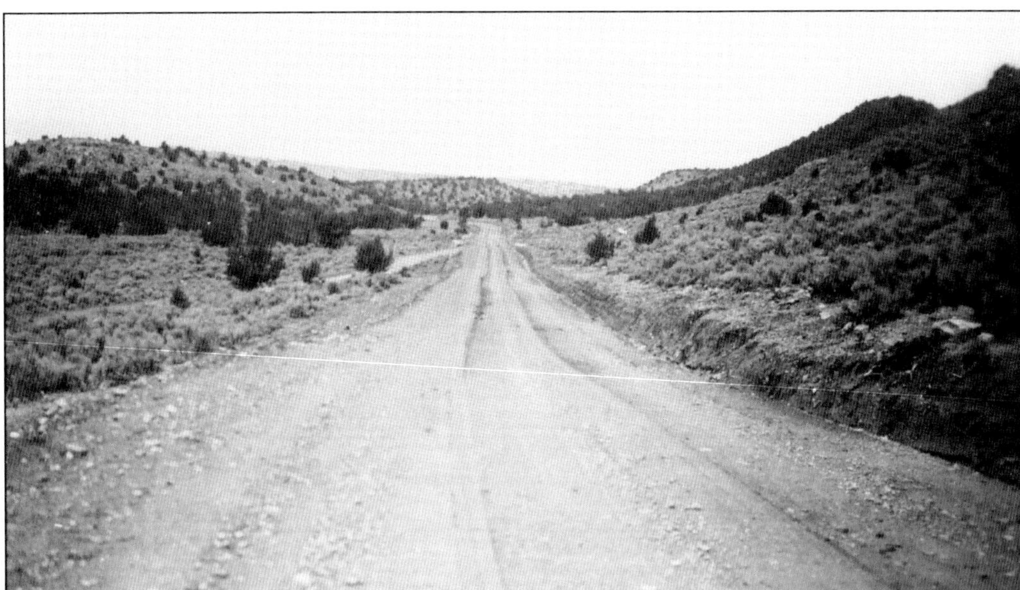

The completed Wolf Hole Road looked like this in 1937. Not only did the local newspaper, *Washington County News*, report camp activities regularly, but also the St. George Chamber of Commerce supported the camp financially by paying the rent for the camp land and buildings. Camp sports teams frequently played teams at St. George and other nearby communities and camps. Some of the enrollees even married local girls. (NARA-RMR.)

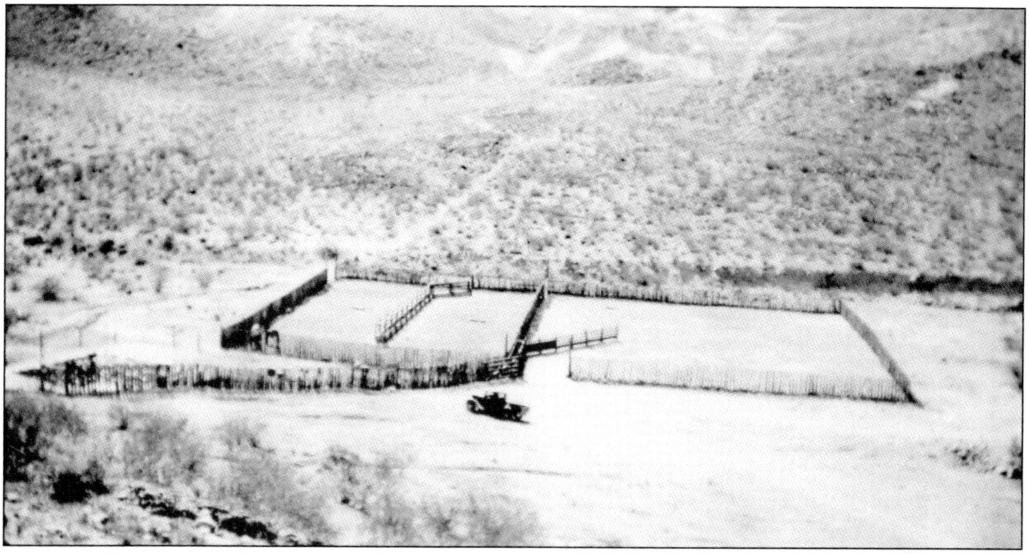

Local ranchers grazed thousands of sheep and cattle in the area south of St. George as far as Mount Trumbull. Enrollees developed Mokaac Spring (pictured here in 1936), located midway between Wolf Hole and St. George, by building a springhouse with concrete water troughs and corrals. In 2012, the springhouse and corrals still appeared quite sturdy. Other work included constructing fences, eradicating weeds, doing range surveys, fighting range fires, building truck trails, and constructing stock reservoirs such as Apex, Stateline, and Ellis Larson. (NARA-RMR.)

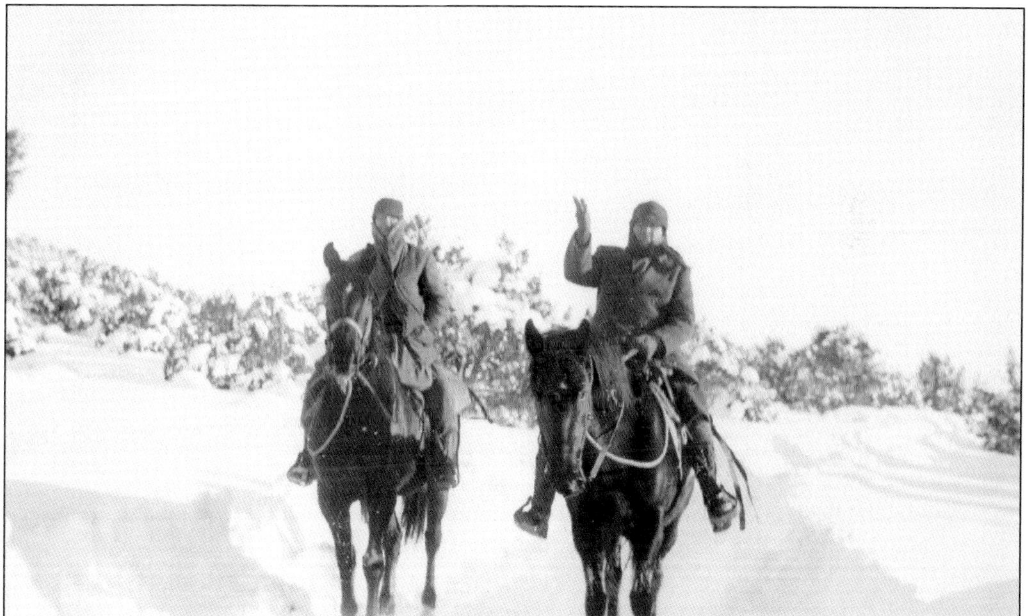

The winter of 1936–1937 was especially brutal across southern Utah and northern Arizona. At St. George, the snow was 30 inches deep and temperatures reached over 20 degrees below zero for extended periods. Thirty-five men and 20,000 to 30,000 sheep around Wolf Hole and Mount Trumbull were said to be stranded and running short on food. In this photograph taken around January 1937, sheep owners Joe and Rutger Atkin testify to the depth of the snow along the Wolf Hole Road. (NARA-RMR.)

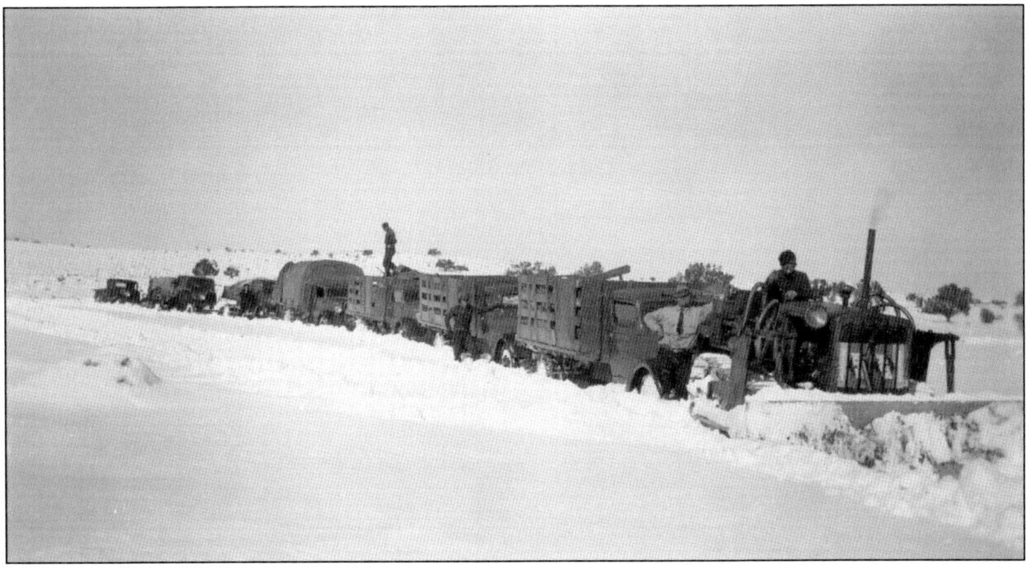

On January 7, 1937, a CCC caravan of one Caterpillar and eight trucks left St. George. On January 15, they arrived at their destination of Little Tank some 52 miles south. Twelve tons of grain and feed were unloaded for the 25,000 head of livestock in the area. Because of mechanical difficulties with the "Cat," they returned to St. George, plowing new snow as they went. (NARA-RMR.)

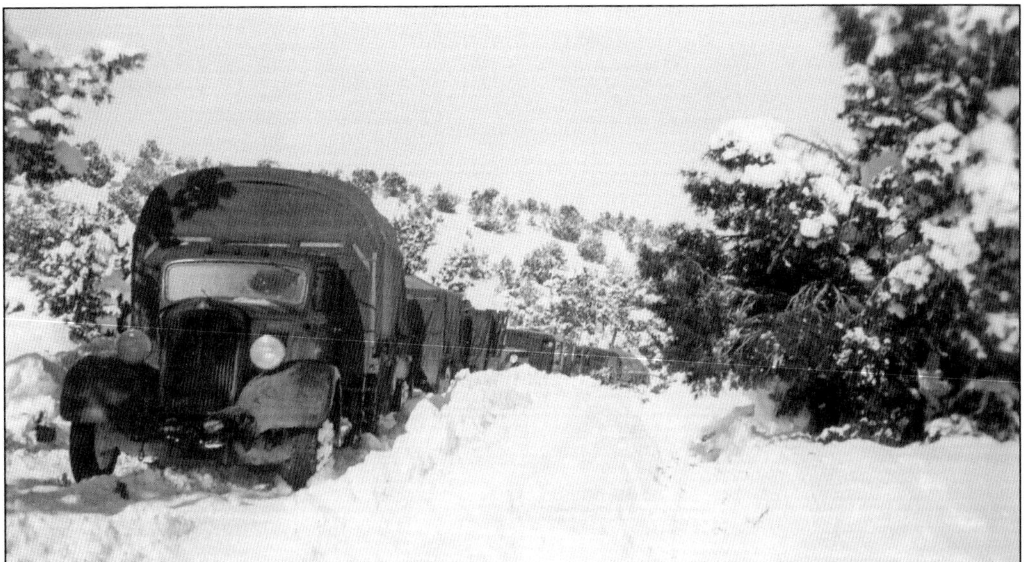

On January 22, 1937, a second caravan of two Caterpillars and 22 trucks and pickups left St. George, but going was harder as new snow had fallen. The Cats worked in relays day and night and arrived at Little Tank six days later. They began the distribution of 40 tons of feed, and the Cats worked for a week plowing roads to isolated sheep herds. On February 5, the caravan reached Mount Trumbull and returned to St. George. Direct relief was given to over 30,000 head of livestock. (NARA-RMR.)

Rancher Roy Lundren poses around January 1937 before starting on a 40-mile-long ski trip from Little Tank to his isolated sheep herd. Lundren slept out in the snow two of his four nights away and nearly died of exposure. His trip was said to be "successful." (NARA-RMR.)

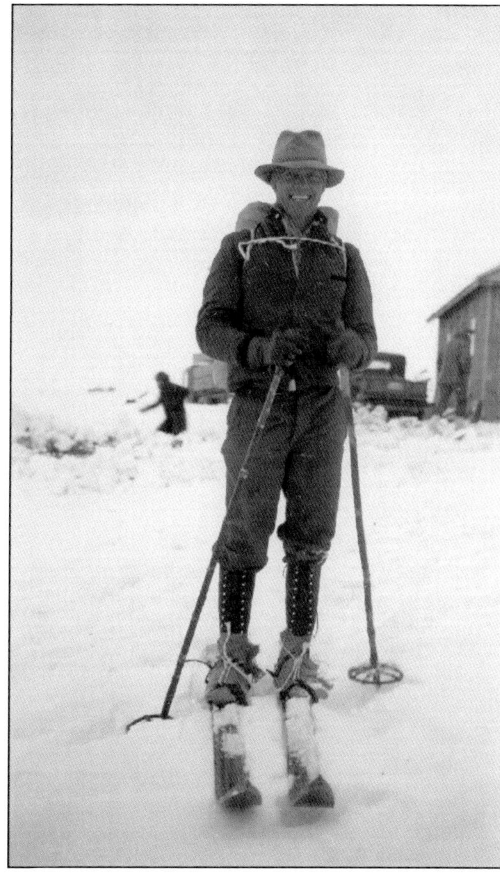

Camp DG-44, Pipe Spring National Monument (shown here in 1936), was occupied from October 1935 to October 1939. During the blizzards of 1936–1937, Pipe Spring was cut off from the outside world between December 18 and late January. Enrollees, frequently working day and night, drove tractors and trucks to bring relief to isolated stockmen and livestock. Even though this camp was located inside the national monument, most of its work was oriented to grazing outside the monument. (NARA-RMR.)

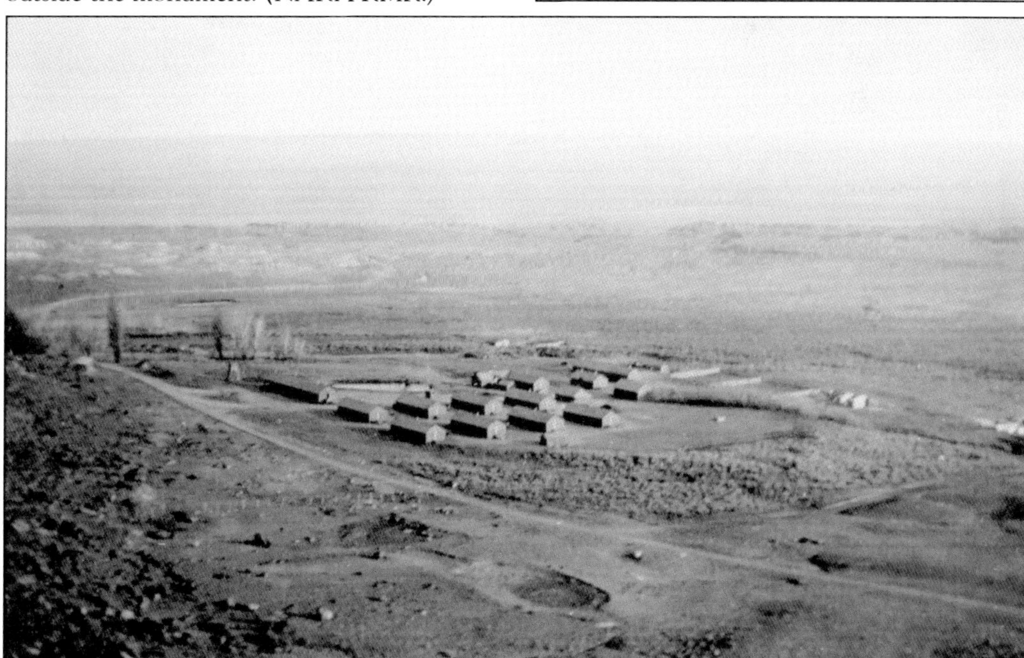

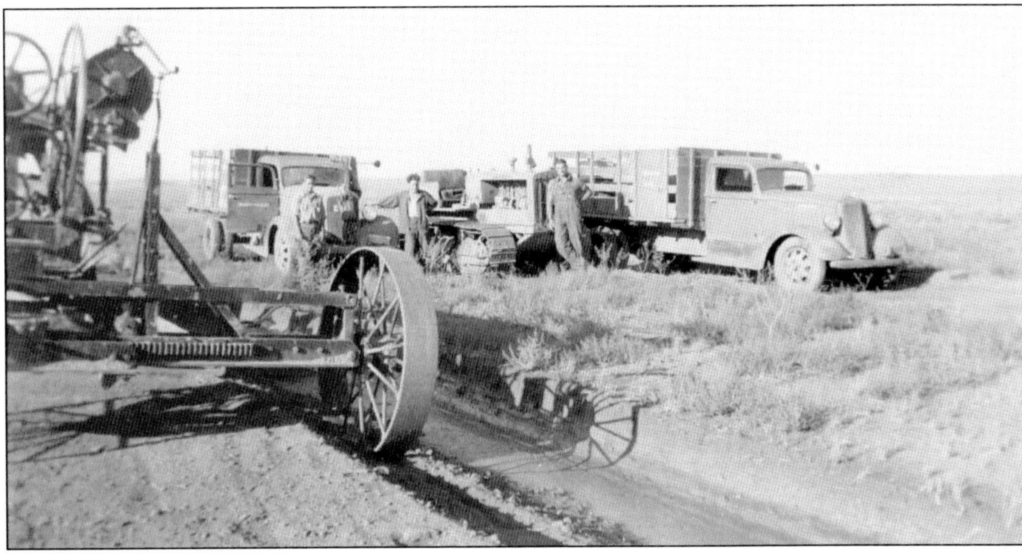

Camp DG-44 enrollees spent considerable time completely rebuilding the road from Fredonia to Mount Trumbull. Ranchers commented that the new road cut their driving time to Mount Trumbull by two hours. Work inside Pipe Spring National Monument included construction of roads, ditches, and a parking lot. They also planted trees; did landscaping; constructed a campground; and built a drinking fountain, a horse watering trough, and picnic tables. (NARA-RMR.)

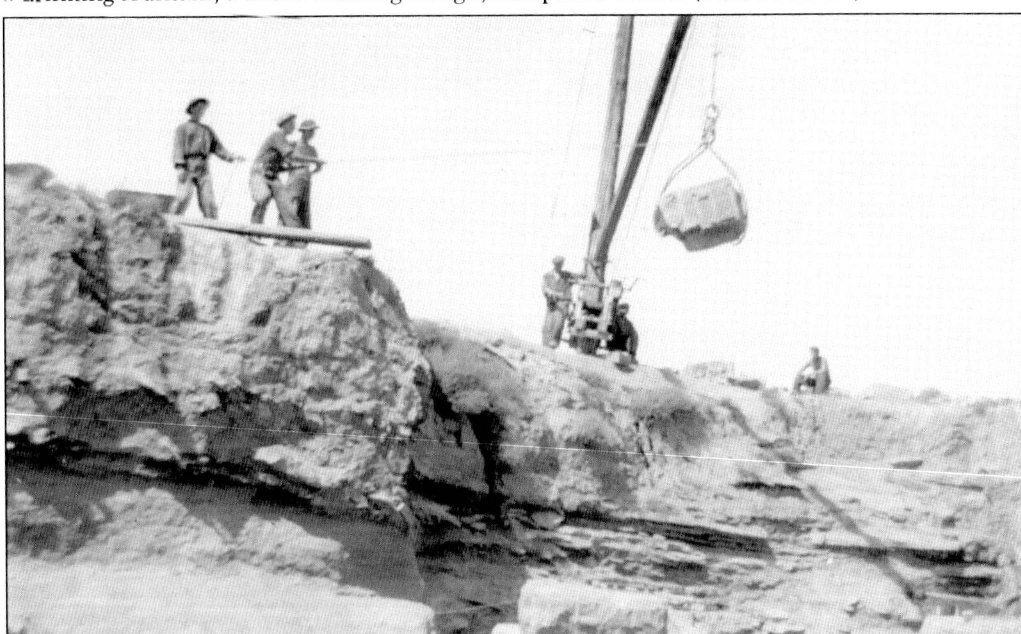

The Bull Rush Bridge was under construction here in 1937, with enrollees lowering rock for the bridge abutments using a hoist equipped with a gear drum and hand brake. Besides the Bull Rush Bridge, Camp DG-44 enrollees constructed a bridge across the Cottonwood Wash on the nearby Kaibab Indian Reservation. Other work included the construction of fences, cattle guards, truck trails, stock driveways, corrals, and stock reservoirs such as Sunset Tank and Johnson Run Reservoir. (NARA-RMR.)

When the Bull Rush Bridge was completed in 1938, it was described as a two-span timber truss bridge with each span measuring 38 feet. Beams for the bridge were as large as 10-by-12 inches and were made from a single tree. A small quarry was opened nearby for the 400 rock slabs used in construction. In 2012, the bridge was closed to all traffic and only one span remained, but much of the CCC work appeared sturdy. (NARA-RMR.)

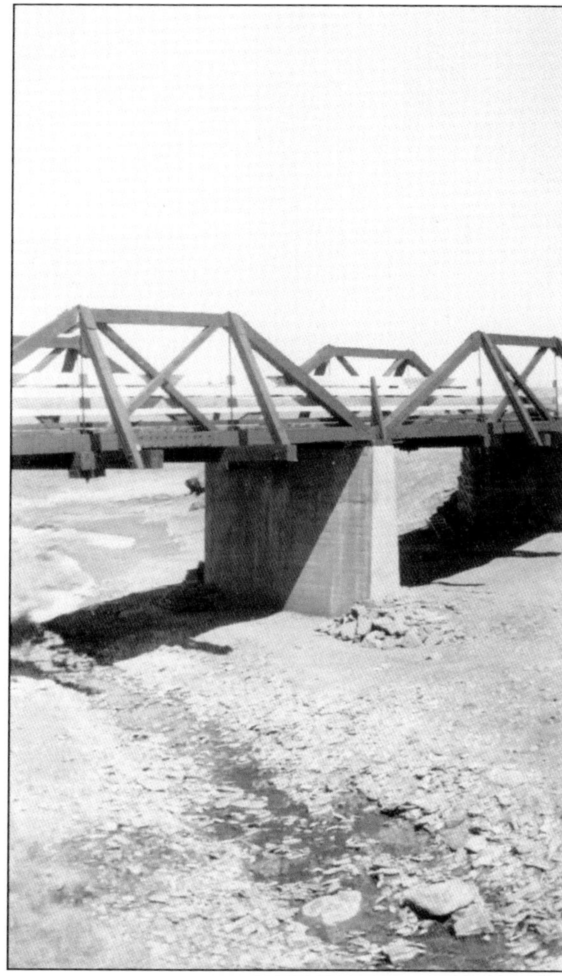

A Camp DG-44 post-cutting crew poses in 1936. This camp completed hundreds of miles of fences, and some were still being used in 2012. A November 1936 report noted that 16,000–18,000 posts were on hand for work through the coming winter. Because the work projects covered a large area, spike (side) camps, frequently consisting of 20–30 men, were located at House Rock, Hack Canyon, and Mount Trumbull. (NARA-RMR.)

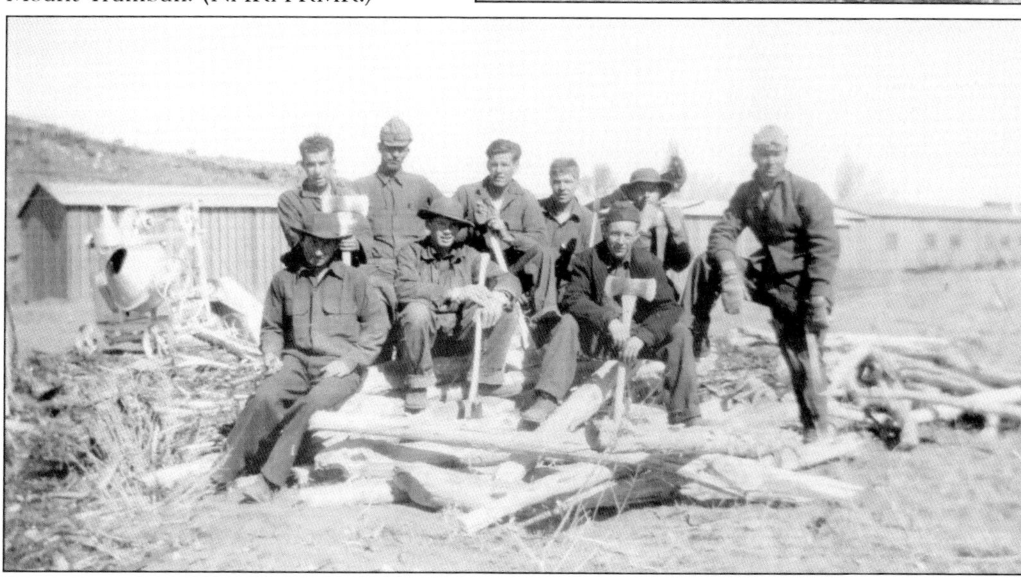

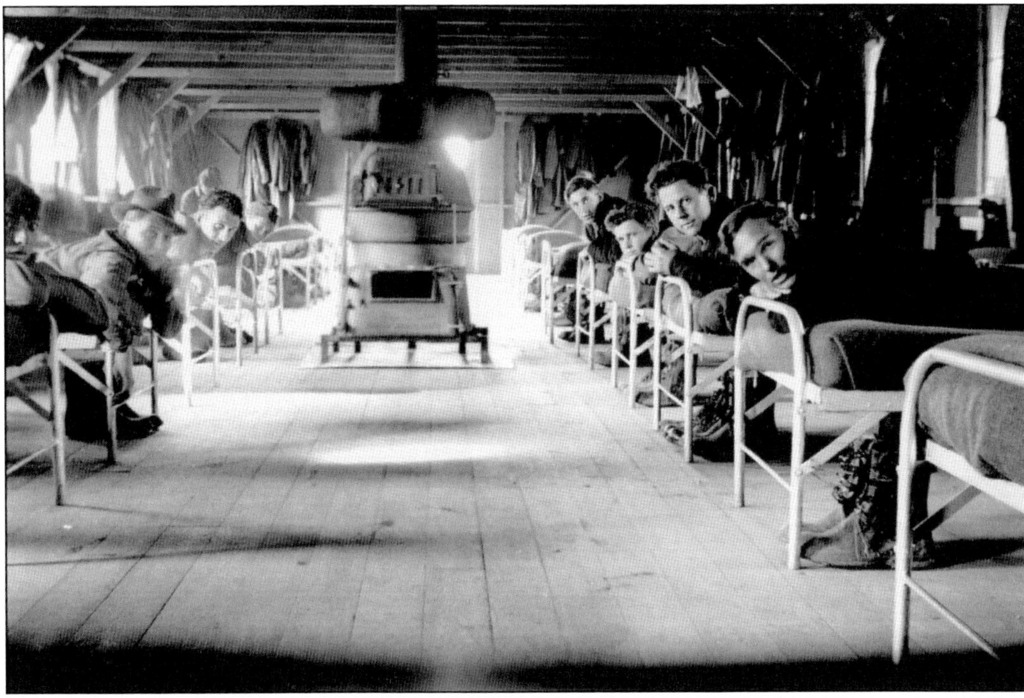

Camp DG-44 enrollees pose inside their barracks in 1935. Barracks buildings generally had sleeping space for 50 and could be disassembled and moved by truck or railway. Each morning, the enrollees would have barracks inspection. Recreation for enrollees at this camp included a swimming pool, baseball diamond, and trips into Fredonia and Kanab. The enrollees held dances at the camp and attended dances in Kanab. (PSNM.)

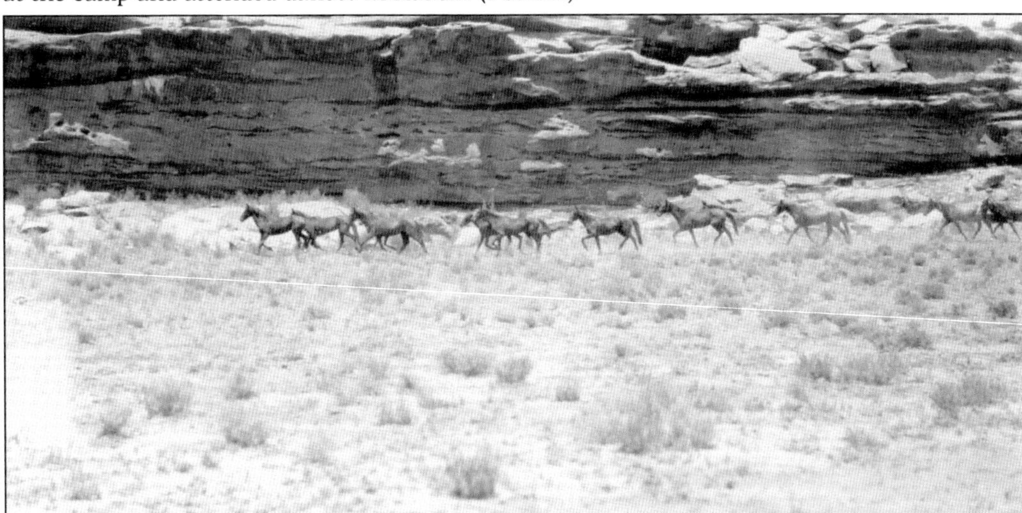

In 1937, Camp DG-44 participated in a roundup of wild horses. Seventy-five horsemen aided by two aircraft began a sweep across the open range 40 miles away. Enrollees had previously constructed a two-mile-long fence that served to funnel the horses into a sturdy corral. Four hundred horses, it was said, were trapped and eliminated from the range. The camp report for the period stated, "When it is considered that a wild horse will use as much range as two head of cattle, this work was of very beneficial value." (NARA-RMR.)

Hamilton Draper, DG-44 camp superintendent, poses in 1938. Draper went on to become one of the special investigators who reported directly to CCC Director Robert Fechner. Other investigators were E.W. Samuell, James C. Reddoch, A.W. Stockman, and M.J. Bowen. They inspected western camps regularly and often were ordered to investigate an allegation of impropriety, an enrollee death, or an enrollee letter to his congressman. (NARA-RMR.)

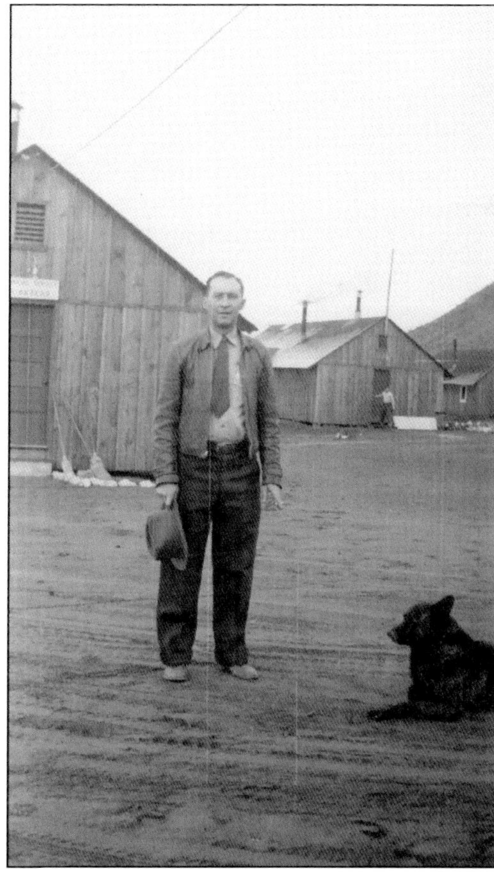

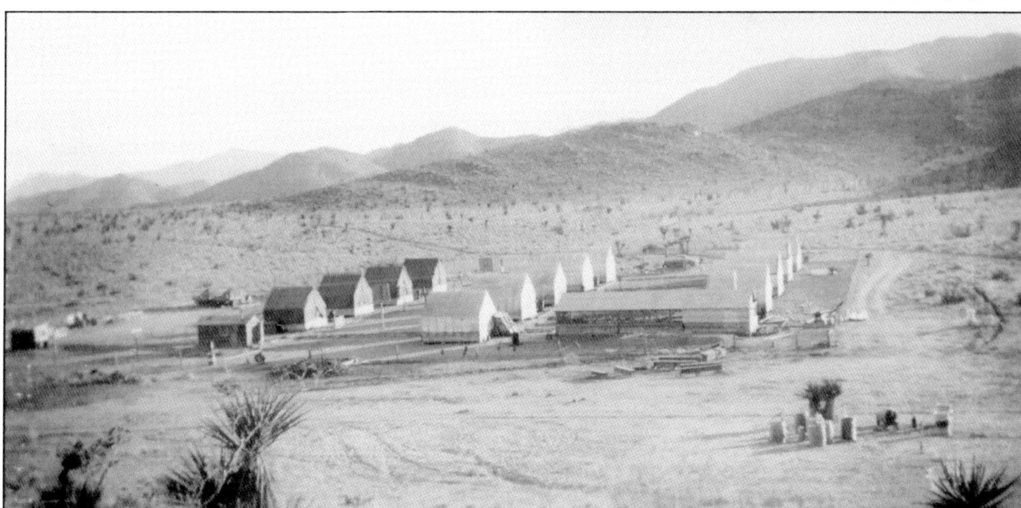

Camp DG-46, Round Valley, was located 16.8 miles southeast of Kingman and occupied from August 1935 to June 1939. Much of the camp's work was carried out by spike (side) camps such as the one at Hualapai Valley pictured here in 1937. Other spike camps were located at Francis Creek, Buck and Doe (near Peach Springs), and Rock Creek. This camp appears to have had a busy social schedule, with dances in Kingman and Wikieup. (NARA-RMR.)

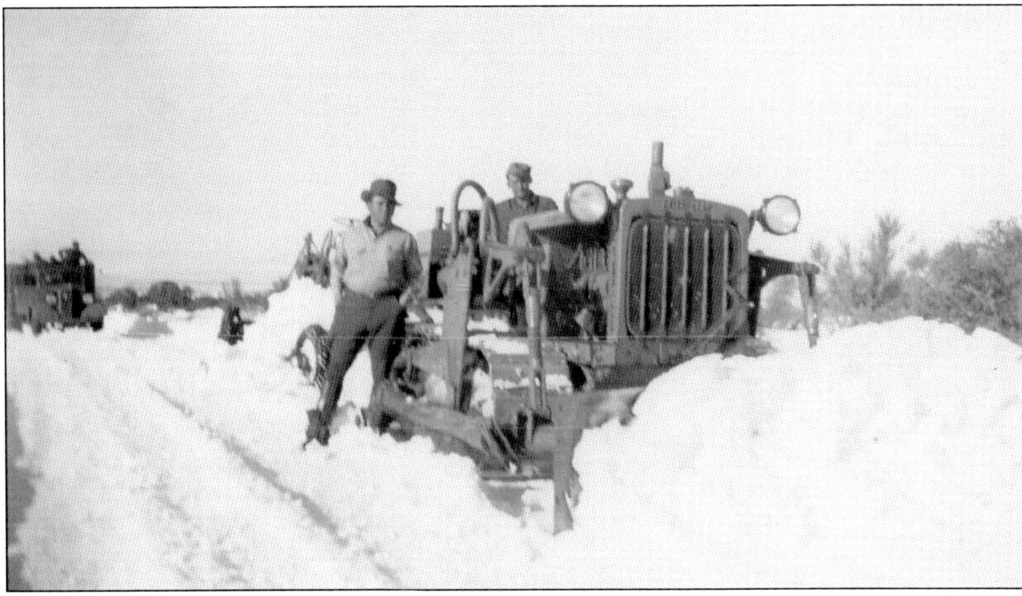

When the blizzards of 1936–1937 hit, the Round Valley camp was affected immediately. One hundred enrollees working at Hualapai Mountain Park were moved temporarily to Round Valley after receiving four feet of snow. Enrollees at the Francis Creek Spike Camp were also affected, and its personnel moved back to the main camps. In this photograph from around January 1937, enrollees are going to the rescue of 26 people who were stranded at the Democrat Mine for 20 days. (BLM.)

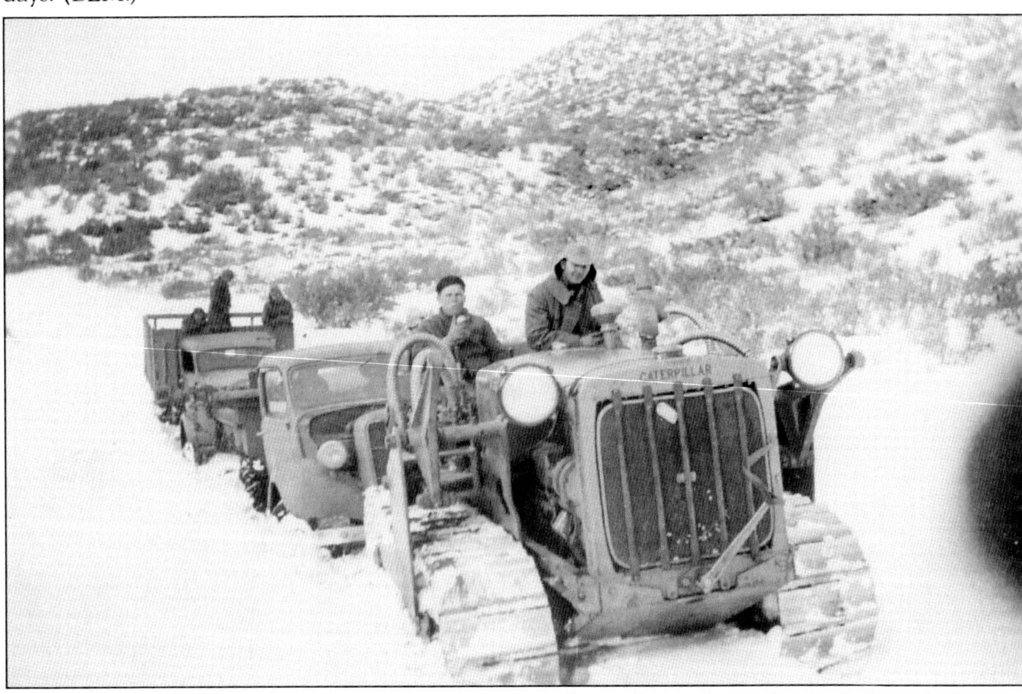

In this c. January 1937 photograph, the CCC Caterpillar pulls trucks to the Cofer Ranch. Rescues were also recorded going to the Tungston Mine and the Day family, opening the road to the Bartmus Ranch, and bringing relief to 800 sheep of the Arizona Livestock Company. (BLM.)

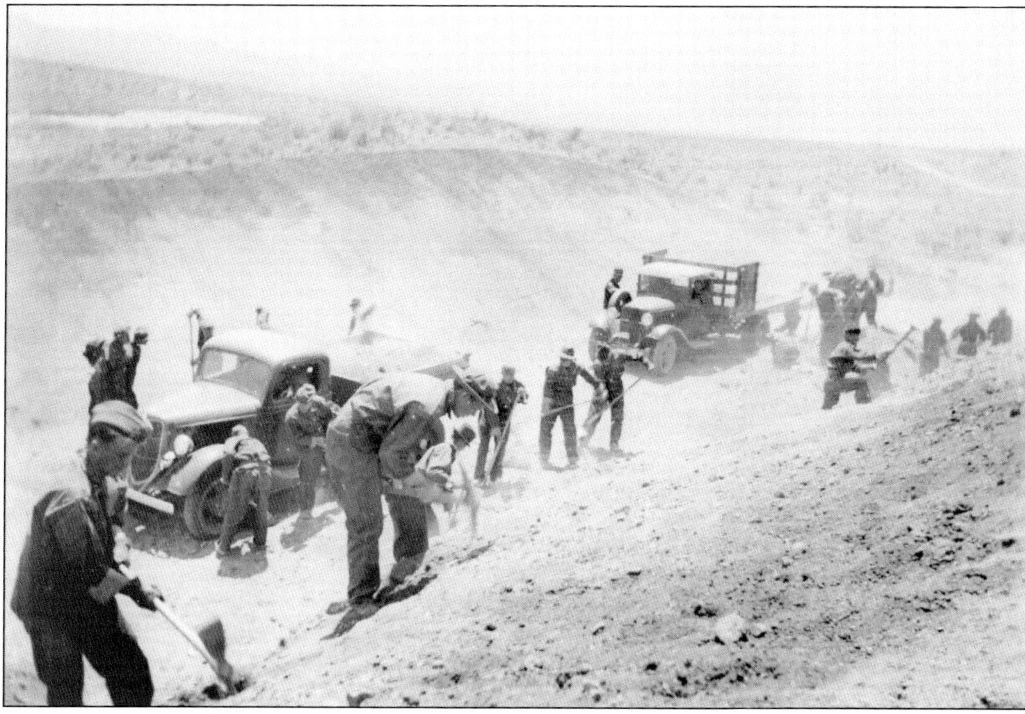

Camp DG-46 enrollees did a great deal of road improvements, such as this sloping on the Round Valley–Hackberry Truck Trail in 1937. Other road maintenance included the Big Sandy, Round Valley–Kingman, and Round Valley–Wikieup Roads. Stock reservoir tanks included Bishop and Bacon, while wells drilled included Upshaw and Neal. Many springs were developed, including Neal and Valley Springs. Enrollees strung telephone lines, built fences, killed poisonous plants, exterminated rodents, and fought range fires. (NARA-RMR.)

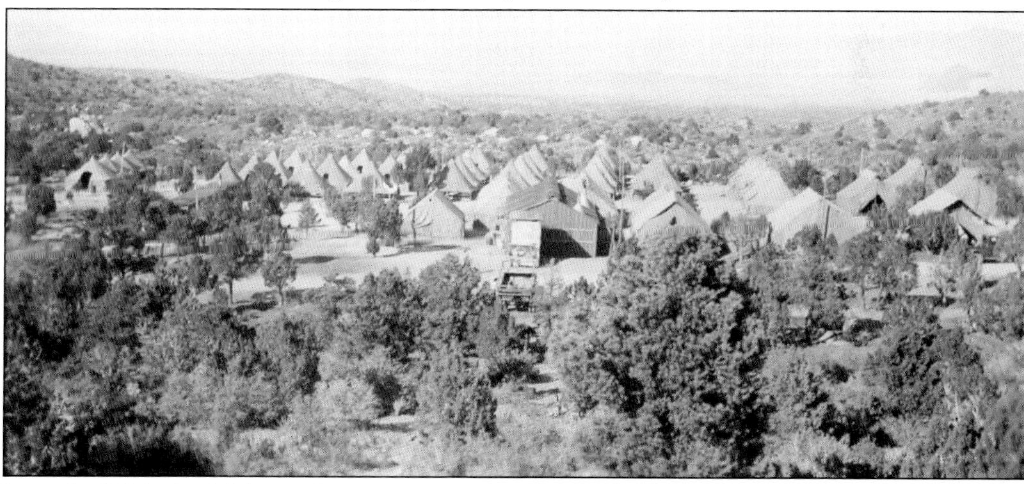

In early 1934, the Mohave County commissioners applied for two CCC camps to develop a county park in the Hualapai Mountains south of Kingman. The local chamber of commerce and newspaper were quick to support the effort. Camps SP-8 and SP-9 worked in 1934, 1935–1939, and 1940. This photograph is believed to be SP-8 in September 1934. Enrollee Randall Legler recalled not being accepted in Kingman at first, as some bars had signs saying "no dogs or CCCs allowed." (NARA MD.)

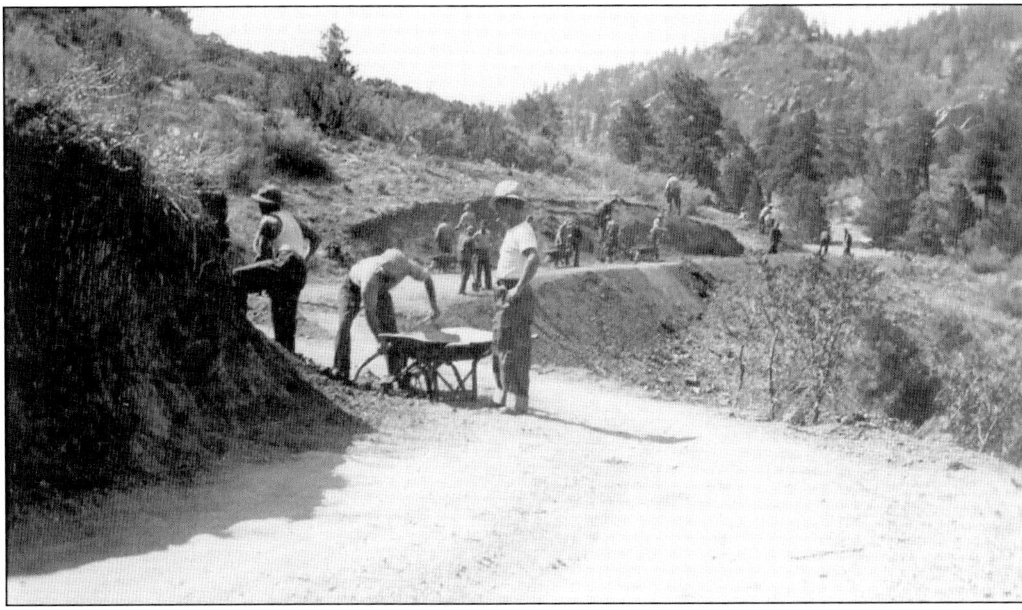

One of the first CCC projects at the county park in the Hualapai Mountains (seen here in a c. 1934 photograph) was improving the road from Kingman to the park, frequently with hand tools only. Other early projects including building fire breaks, the Aspen Springs Trail, the ranger station, a water system, and picnic and trail shelters. Later work included stringing a telephone line from town to the park, clearing a trail to Potato Patch, fighting fires, constructing parking lots, and doing land surveys. (NARA MD.)

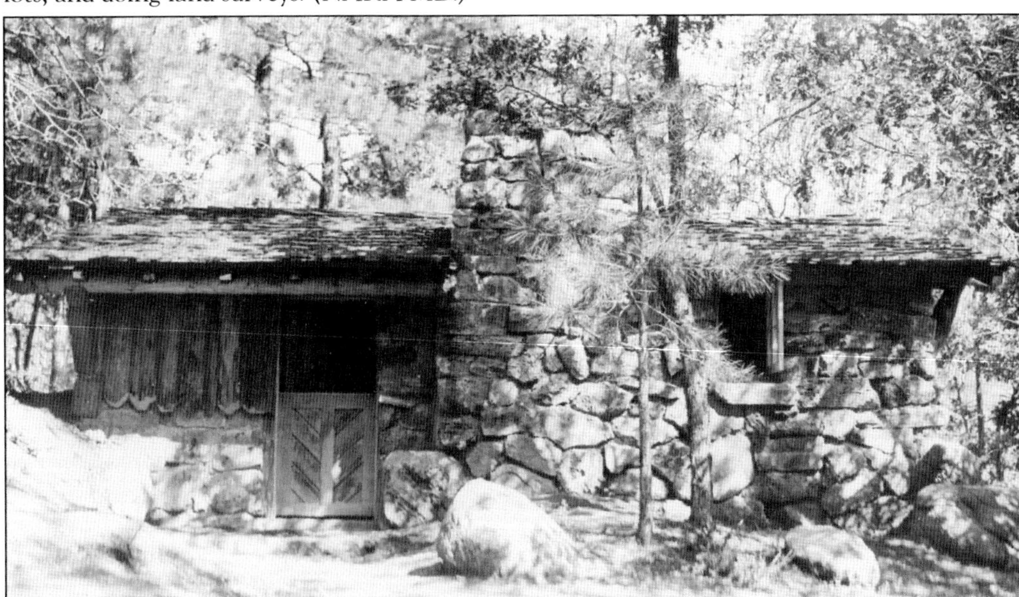

Beginning in 1936, the CCC completed a new water system, including a 50,000-gallon reservoir, and built cabins such as this one in 1937 in the county park in the Hualapai Mountains south of Kingman. Some of the enrollees worked as park guides while others constructed Swiss-Alpine–style picnic shelters and a new comfort station. The CCC built at least four of the parks' cabins. (NARA MD.)

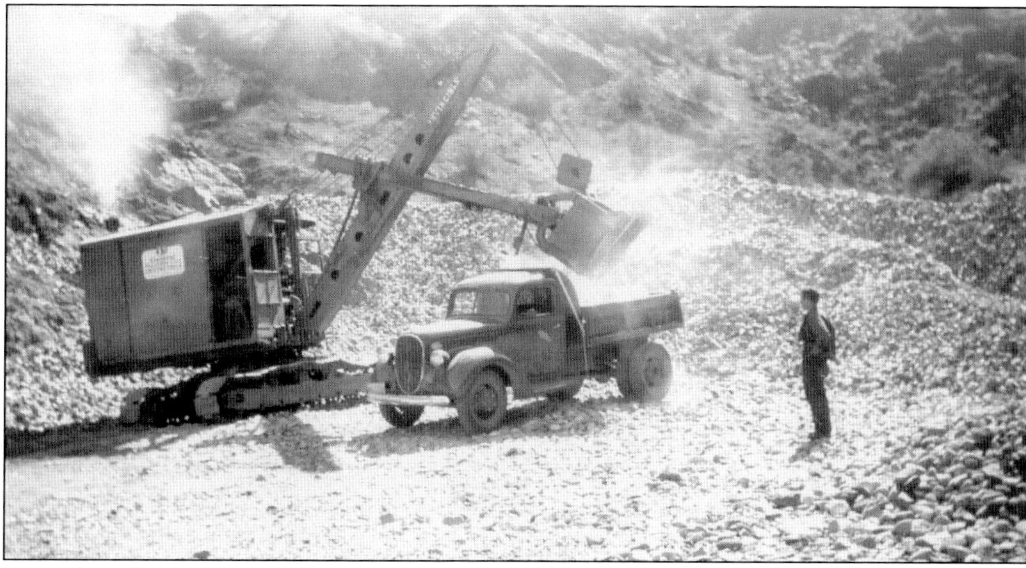

Parker Dam hosted Camp BR-17 from November 1935 to January 1936, and BR-18 from November 1935 to April 1936. They cleared 574 acres of brush and trees for the future dam reservoir and did road maintenance. From September 1941 to approximately July 1942, Camp FWS-1 was located at Parker Dam. Much of its work projects were related to the war effort, such as building Army guard stations and buildings. It also constructed a boathouse and fences along with the Bill Williams Truck Trail seen here in 1942. (NARA-RMR.)

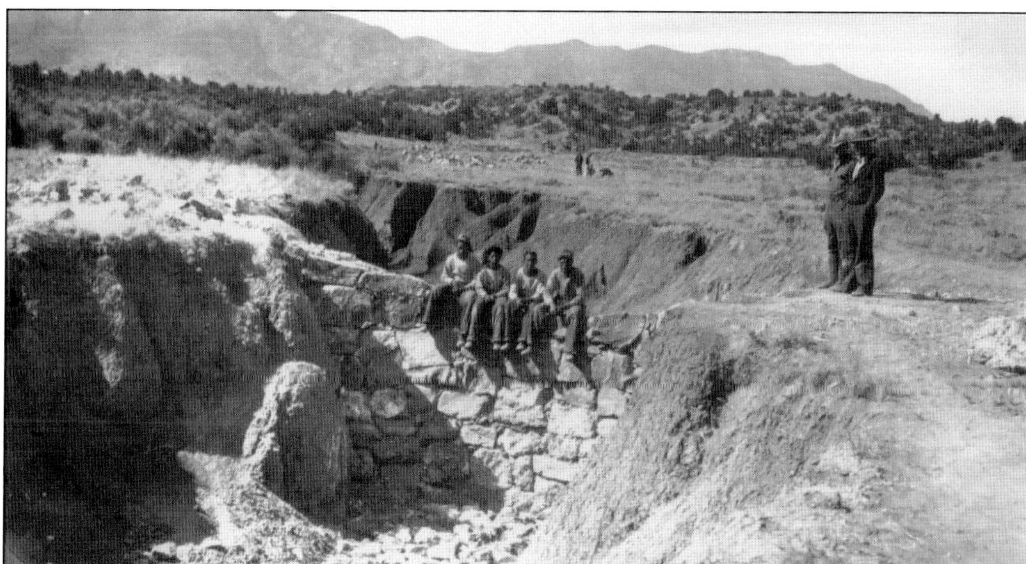

Prescott National Forest enrollees did considerable erosion-control work, as shown in this 1934 photograph of work done by a crew from F-39, Verde No. 1. Other work in the forest included eradicating prairie dogs, improving timber stands, and developing springs. Enrollees constructed roads, truck trails, trails, telephone lines, fences, corrals, levees, bridges, and stock tanks (such as Pine Flat and Cedar Canyon). Considerable resources were put into building the road between Crown King and the Black Canyon Highway. (Photograph by W.M. Beveridge; USFS, SWR.)

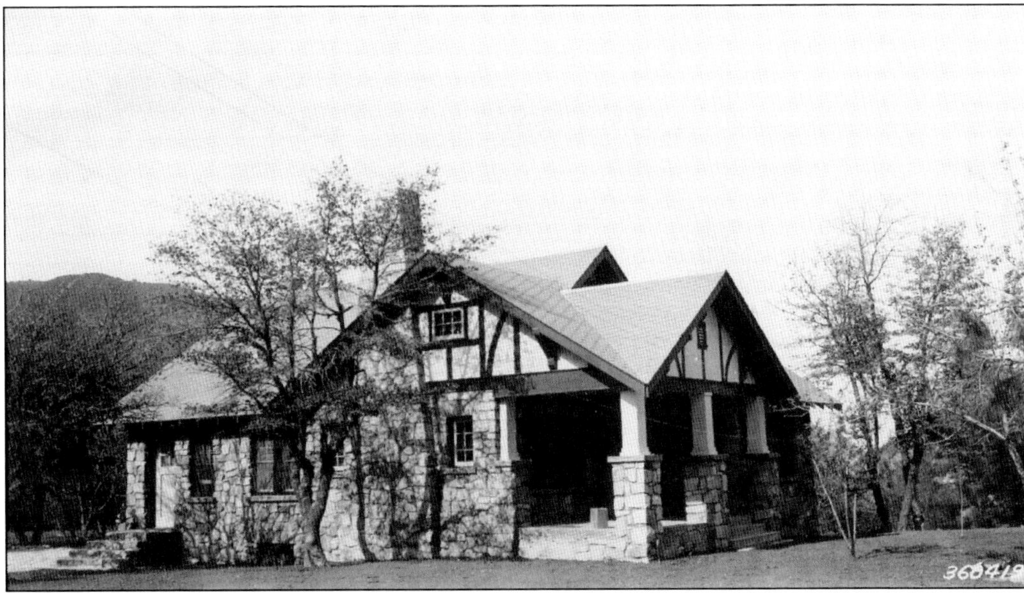

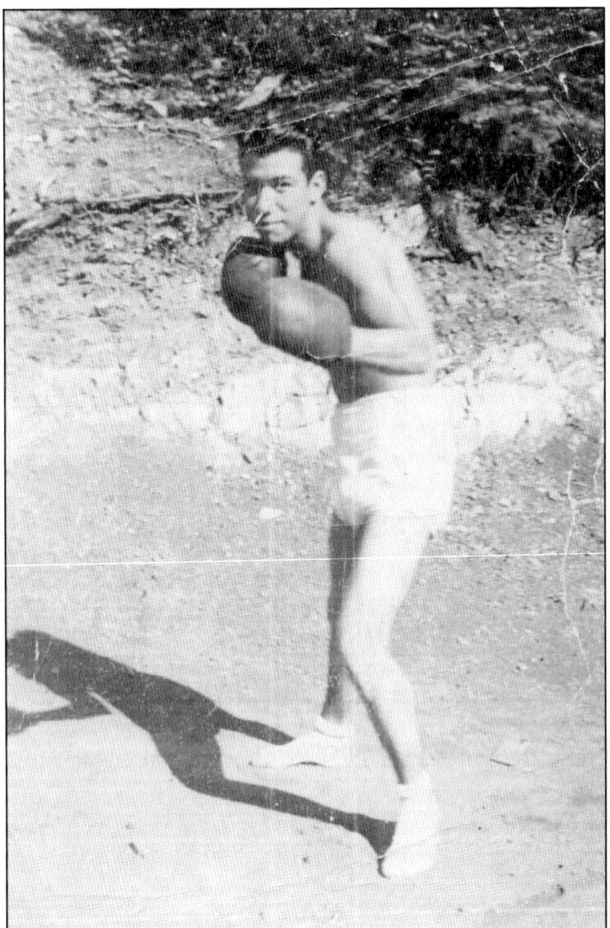

At Crown King, the CCC constructed a ranger station (shown here in 1936), a combination barn and garage, a well, and a new water system. They also constructed the Sycamore Ranger Station and fire lookout towers at Mount Union, Mingus Mountain, and Towers Mountain. (Photograph by R. King; USFS, SWR.)

Enrollee Tomas H. Vega, Camp F-19, poses in 1940. In a 2013 interview, Vega expressed optimism about this camp, as opposed to his earlier service at Camp DG-109, Arlington, where he says Hispanics were frequently abused. In Prescott, he experienced little discrimination. Here he learned to box and make jewelry, something he had wanted to do for some time. He recalled that F-19 had some crack boxers and a champion softball team. Another positive experience was listening to the WPA chorus and orchestra serenading the enrollees. (THV.)

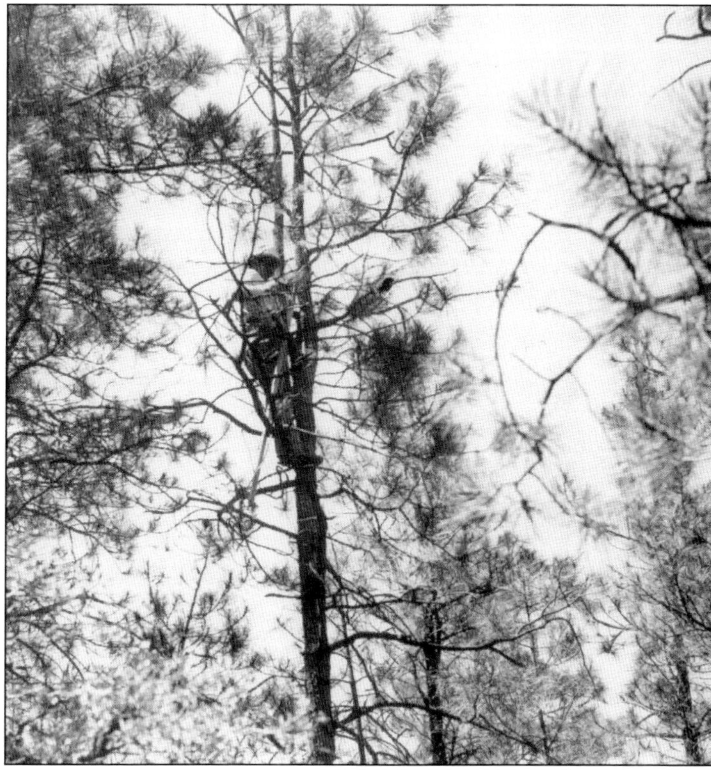

Matsucoccus vexillorum, a type of twig blight, was spreading dramatically by 1933. By 1936, Prescott National Forest frequently had as many as 600 men climbing trees, as much as 100 feet above the ground, to trim the infected branches. Enrollee Randall Legler stated the twig blight work was "hated" by enrollees and many disciplinary problems resulted. Tragically, in 1937, enrollee Porter H. Gilliam died as a result of a fall from a tree. By 1938, scientists had stated the blight was not as serious as first thought, and most twig blight eradication ended. (TNF.)

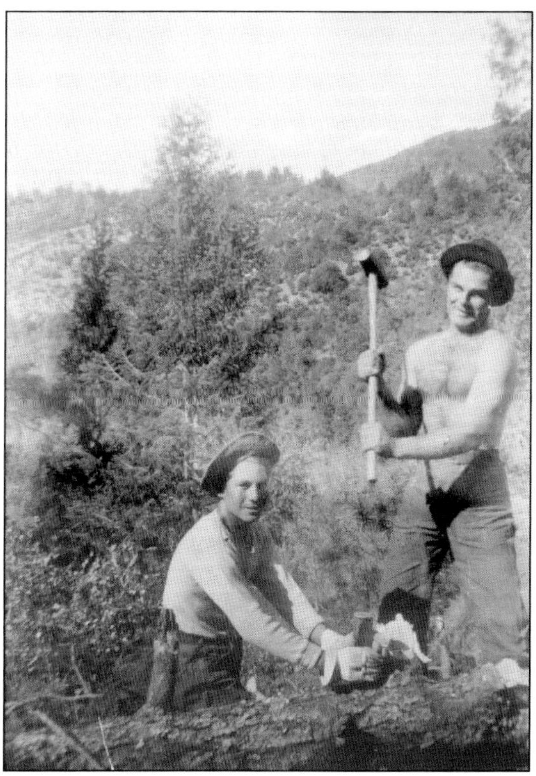

Enrollees Felix Hellman (with hammer, right) and Joe Baca (with wedge, left) clear land for the Granite Basin Dam in 1940. Camp F-19 enrollee Tomas H. Vega recalled clearing land for the dam and the national forest ski area, cleaning up around the Iron Springs Campground, developing springs, trimming small pine trees, and fighting forest fires. Enrollee Randall Legler stated that during fire season a 25-man crew was on standby around the clock, with trucks gassed up and loaded with equipment. Nationwide, the amount of land burned in wild fires dropped dramatically due to the CCC presence. (THV.)

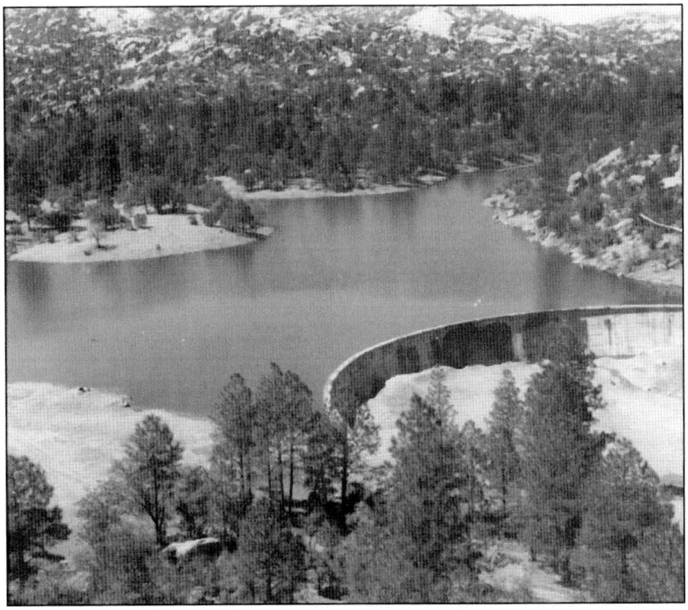

The Granite Basin Dam (shown here in 1940) was dedicated in 1940. It measured 420 feet long and 27 feet high, and the lake area behind it was 10.5 acres. Enrollees also built the nearby camping and picnic facilities. Special Investigator M.J. Bowen called it the "best project in the nation." The local paper, the *Prescott Evening Courier*, as well as the Prescott Chamber of Commerce—including their secretary Grace Sparkes—supported the CCC in Yavapai County. (Photograph by C.W. McKenzie; USFS, SWR.)

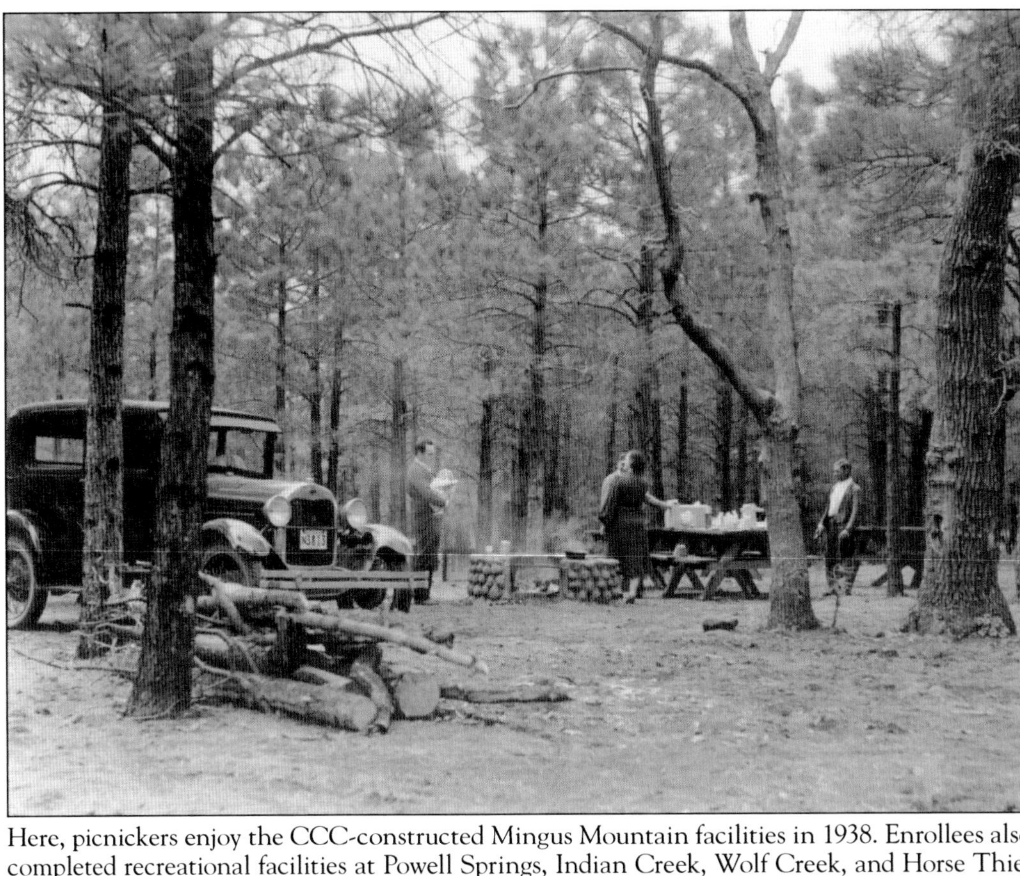

Here, picnickers enjoy the CCC-constructed Mingus Mountain facilities in 1938. Enrollees also completed recreational facilities at Powell Springs, Indian Creek, Wolf Creek, and Horse Thief Basin. In the Indian Creek area, they did considerable work building ski runs, a toboggan run, and a parking lot. (Photograph by Chas. C. Cunningham; USFS, SWR.)

Seven

Native Americans
Civilian Conservation Corps Indian Division (CCC-ID)

Shortly after the CCC legislation was signed into law in March 1933, recruitment of American Indians was authorized (Executive Order 6160). The administration, finance, operations, and reporting of the CCC-ID were handled by the Bureau of Indian Affairs (BIA) and individual Indian reservation superintendents. Superintendents, and occasionally tribal councils, selected individual work projects. American Indian enrollees could be married and there was an age limit. A few females were recruited, and frequently the enrollment period was flexible. Native American enrollees generally did not experience barracks-style living, as they either lived at home or in fly camps.

One notable Native American enrollee was Ira Hamilton Hayes, an Akimel O'odham (Pima) Indian born in 1923 at Sacaton on the Gila River Indian Reservation. He served in the CCC in 1942 and then joined the Marine Corps. Hayes was one of the servicemen who raised the American flag over Iwo Jima during World War II, and he is buried with full military honors at Arlington National Cemetery.

Arizona benefited greatly from the work of the CCC-ID, with 19,520 Indians participating—more than all the other junior and veteran enrollees in the state. The value of permanent work on Arizona Indian reservations exceeded $10,857,110, with the Navajo, Tohono O'odham, Fort Apache, and San Carlos reservations receiving the bulk of the work. CCC-ID work also included the Colorado River Tribes, Havasupai, Hualapai, Hopi, Phoenix Indian School, and Pima.

The CCC was a blessing on the reservations. Unemployment was much higher here than in the white population. Frequently drought had taken its toll, and many reservation lands were heavily eroded from overgrazing. On the Navajo Reservation, some new enrollees were so weak from lack of food that they were given light duty until they were strong enough to do the normal work. Ultimately, many American Indians benefited by learning new skills. Although CCC work no doubt took many enrollees away from a traditional life, it did make many more self-supporting.

It is regrettable that many of the CCC-ID records are no longer in the National Archives or in the hands of the individual reservations. Consequently, this portrait of CCC-ID work is necessarily incomplete.

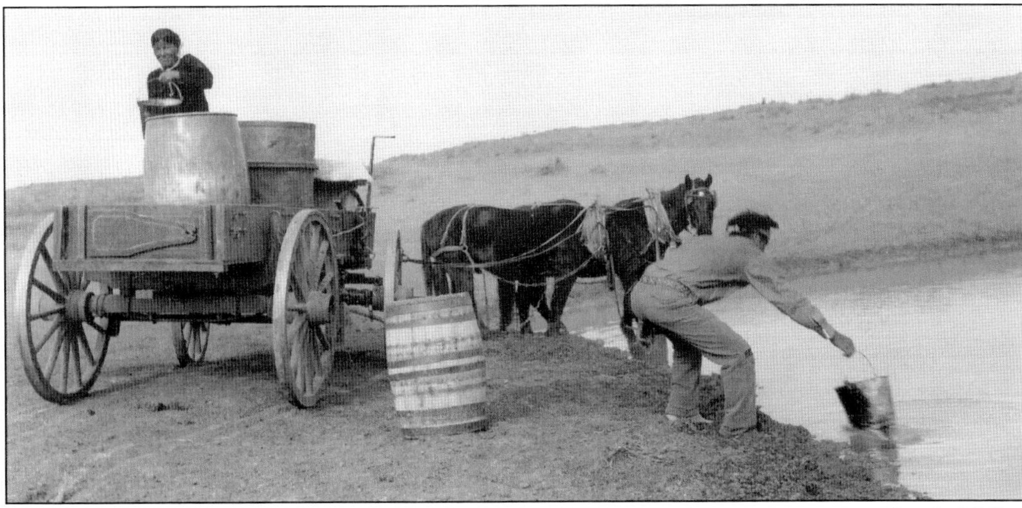

Navajos fill up water containers in 1934 at a CCC-constructed reservoir in the Chinle Valley. Navajo work included building hundreds of stock reservoirs and wells such as Cliff Dwellers. They constructed windmills at Kayenta and Dennehotso, eradicated wild horses, and planted trees at Keams Canyon. Navajo enrollees fought fires and participated in rescue work during the blizzards of 1936–1937. Construction of truck and livestock trails, telephone lines, and fences were also common work projects. (NARA-PR.)

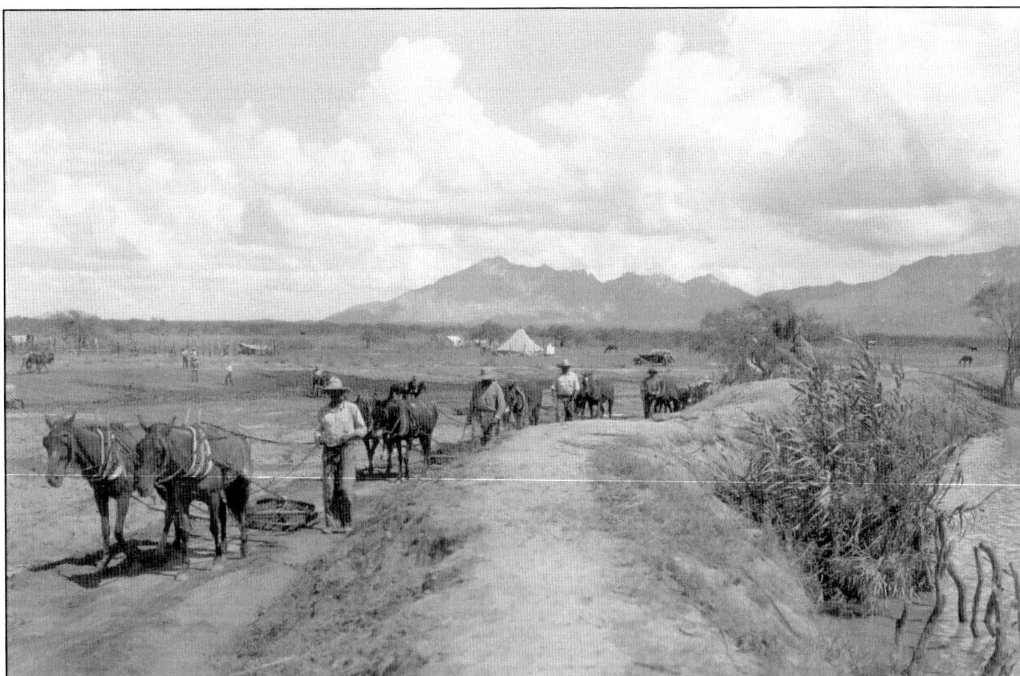

Work on reservations included repair to old *charcos* (ephemeral tanks) such as this one in 1933–1934. The San Carlos Indian Reservation sponsored family camps, which included classes such as sewing for women. Other San Carlos work included building fences, roads, and trails, and stringing telephone lines. Many stock tanks were completed, such as those at Cienaga Corral, Juniper, Rocky Creek, and Freezeout. (NARA-PR.)

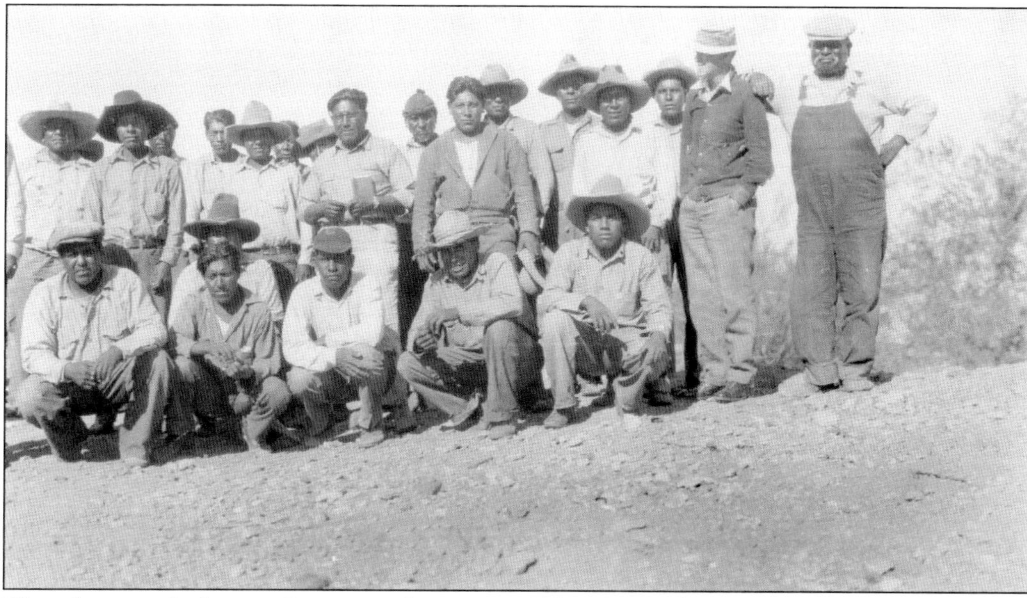

This photograph shows a Papago work crew in 1933–1934 on the Papago Indian Reservation in southern Arizona, now the Tohono O'odham Indian Reservation. The Office of Indian Affairs local agents supervised the work projects here, consulting with the tribal and village authorities on what projects to undertake. The impact of the CCC on the Papago (now Tohono O'odham) was considerable, increasing their interaction with the world outside the reservation. (NARA-PR.)

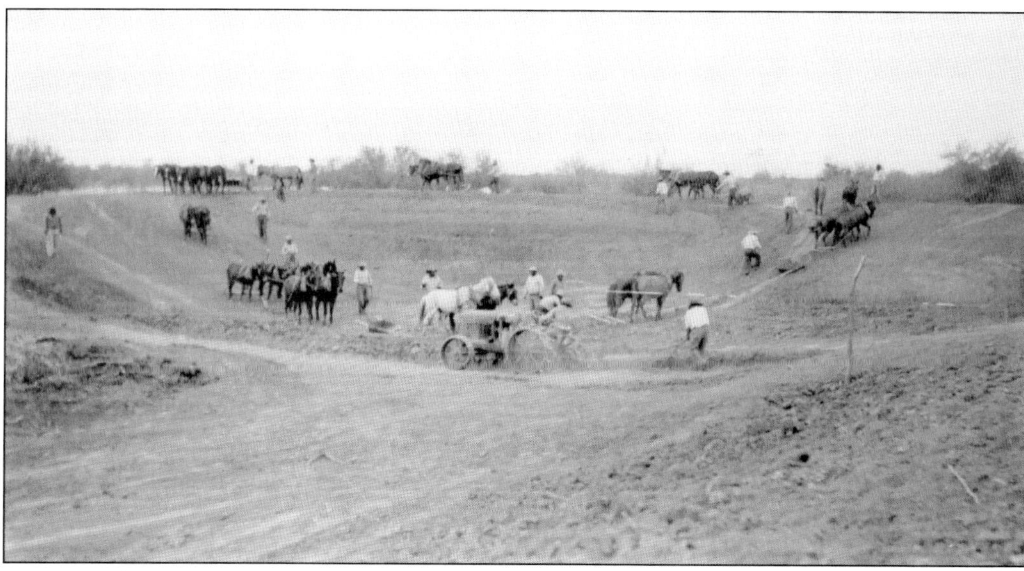

Here, enrollees are building a charco near Aguirre Well on the Papago Indian Reservation in 1933–1934. The men did much erosion-control work on the reservation, along with fighting fires, building fences, stringing telephone lines, controlling weeds, revegetating the land, and eradicating wild horses. They also constructed roads and truck trails into areas previously only accessible by horseback. Papago enrollees in 1933 built a trail and fire lookout station on Baboquivari Peak. (NARA-PR.)

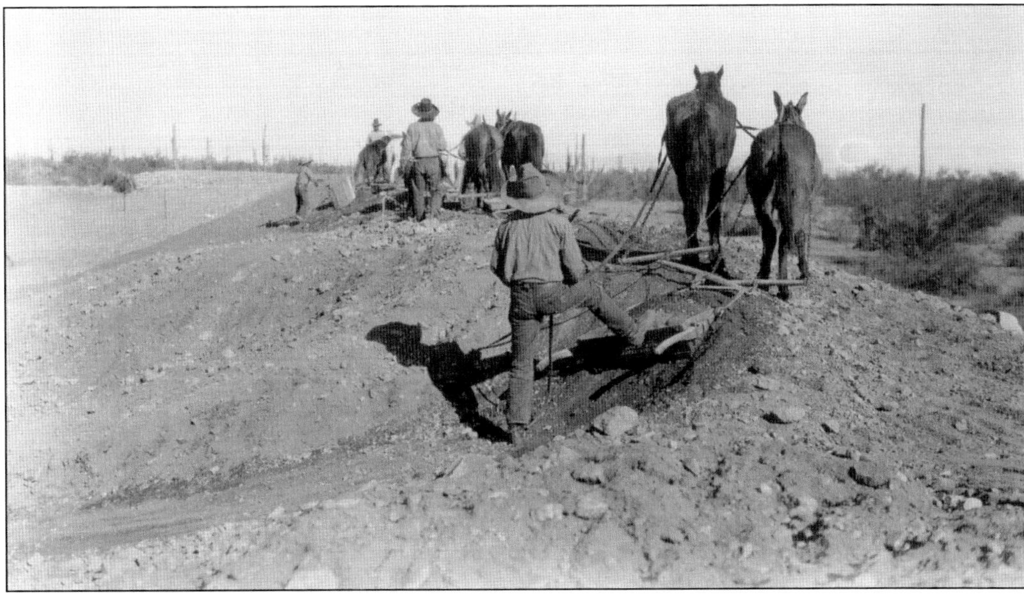

In these photographs from 1933 to 1934, Papago enrollees are working on the Papago Indian Reservation, now the Tohono O'odham Indian Reservation, in southern Arizona. Above, a team of horses and workers are building an earthen dam and charco four miles west of Anegam. Below, enrollees are constructing a spillway five miles west of Quajote. Water is a precious commodity in the desert, and water-storage and water-control features are an important part of life here. Throughout the reservation, the enrollees dug reservoirs and dams and constructed brush dams, charcos, and stock tanks to improve the range and arrest erosion. (NARA-PR.)

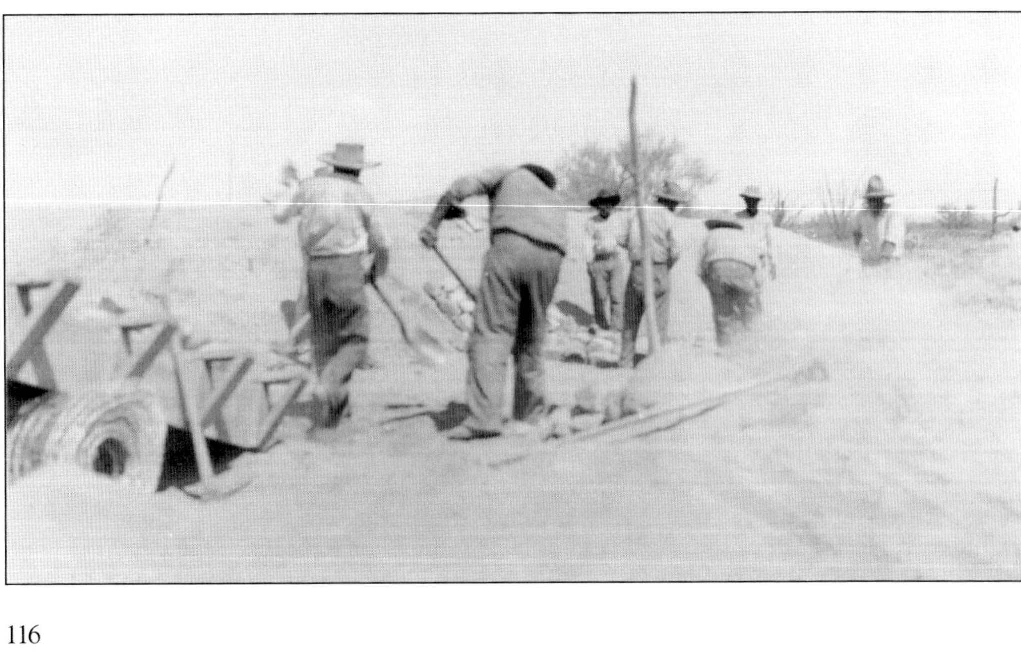

Eight

End of the CCC
An Enduring Legacy

The CCC was the most popular New Deal program, according to a 1938 Gallup poll giving it an 80 percent approval rating. However, when the United States entered the war in 1941, any program not essential to the war effort was evaluated and frequently altered or abandoned. President Roosevelt wanted to preserve the CCC, but Congress had the final say. The CCC was disbanded on July 1, 1942. Even before the congressional debates on the program's future, the number of CCC camps was decreasing dramatically. Between May 31, 1941, and May 31, 1942, Arizona camps dropped from 27 to just five.

During the CCC period, Arizona hosted 98 individual companies. On December 31, 1935, Arizona reached its highest number of camps with 55. The heyday for Arizona was January 31, 1935, to December 31, 1937, when the state averaged 42 camps. Nearly all of the companies were juniors, with the exception of three veterans' companies and one African American company, 2871C. Almost all companies serving in Arizona were from the Eighth Corps, with the exception of just 18 from other Corps areas.

National Forest–sponsored camps totaled 42 percent of Arizona camps, with National Park Service and state park camps totaling 25 percent. Division of Grazing camps encompassed about 17 percent, Soil Conservation Service camps were 12 percent, and Bureau of Reclamation camps made up about 4 percent. There were three Fish and Wildlife Service camps and one military camp.

The work completed on a statewide level is staggering. As much as 50 years' worth of work throughout public lands was accomplished in less than 10 years (see appendix I for details). These activities helped halt economic collapse, saving many young men from lives as drifters or criminals. Because the enrollees' families received $25 of their pay each month, many families were saved from hunger and homelessness. The CCC helped save the state's farming, ranching, and timber industries, with many of the roads, buildings, and structures the men built still in use. The CCC provided the men who served with an education, social skills, and job skills, which they used in fighting World War II, building this country, and raising future generations.

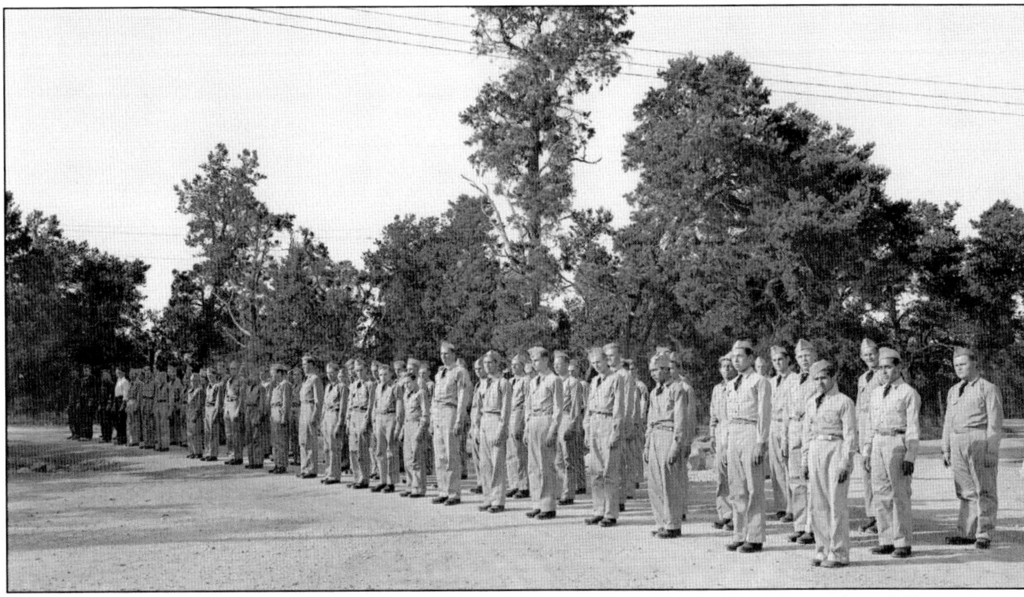

Enrollees were not subject to strict military discipline, but they were required to follow certain uniform and behavioral standards and to stand weekly barracks inspections. Because of war in Europe in 1940, enrollees learned defense training and close order drill. In September 1940, the United States adopted a nationwide compulsory military draft. By late 1941, some CCC companies were working on military projects on military reservations. The CCC dress uniform, shown here at Grand Canyon's Camp NP-2 in 1941, was required attire for the evening meal. (GCNP.)

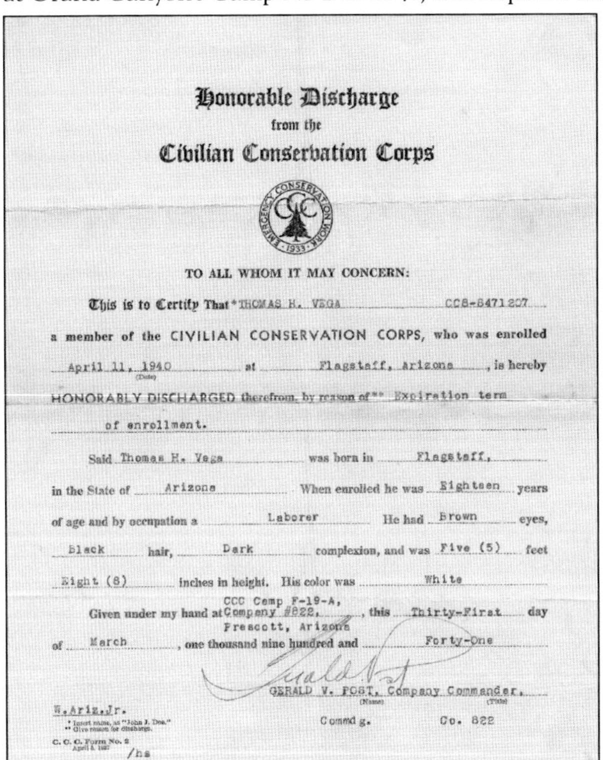

Honorable Discharge
from the
Civilian Conservation Corps

TO ALL WHOM IT MAY CONCERN:

This is to Certify That *THOMAS H. VEGA CC8-8471207
a member of the CIVILIAN CONSERVATION CORPS, who was enrolled April 11, 1940 (Date) at Flagstaff, Arizona, is hereby HONORABLY DISCHARGED therefrom, by reason of ** Expiration term of enrollment.

Said Thomas H. Vega was born in Flagstaff, in the State of Arizona When enrolled he was Eighteen years of age and by occupation a Laborer He had Brown eyes, Black hair, Dark complexion, and was Five (5) feet Eight (8) inches in height. His color was White

Given under my hand at CCC Camp F-19-A, Company #822, Prescott, Arizona, this Thirty-First day of March, one thousand nine hundred and Forty-One

GERALD V. POST, Company Commander,
(Name) (Title)
Commd g. Co. 822

W.Ariz.Jr.
* Insert name, as "John J. Doe."
** Give reason for discharge.
C. C. C. Form No. 2
April 5, 1937
/hs

When an enrollee's period of enrollment expired, his good behavior was noted with an honorable discharge such as this one given to Tomas H. Vega in 1941. An enrollee could be honorably discharged before his scheduled discharge date to accept employment, marry, or attend school. He could also receive an honorable discharge if his family required him at home. Dishonorable discharges were given for desertion, being AWOL, refusal to work, violations of regulations, and the like. (THV.)

Elson Alvarez served in the CCC for five and a half years, first as an enrollee and then as a local experienced man (LEM). He worked as a surveyor at Camps SCS-19, St. David, and SCS-26, Patagonia, in southern Arizona. Elson taught photography to fellow enrollees and took photographs and a video documenting the CCC life, leaving us with an important record. He joined the US Army and served as a photo-lab technician in the Army Air Corps from 1945 to 1946. (EA.)

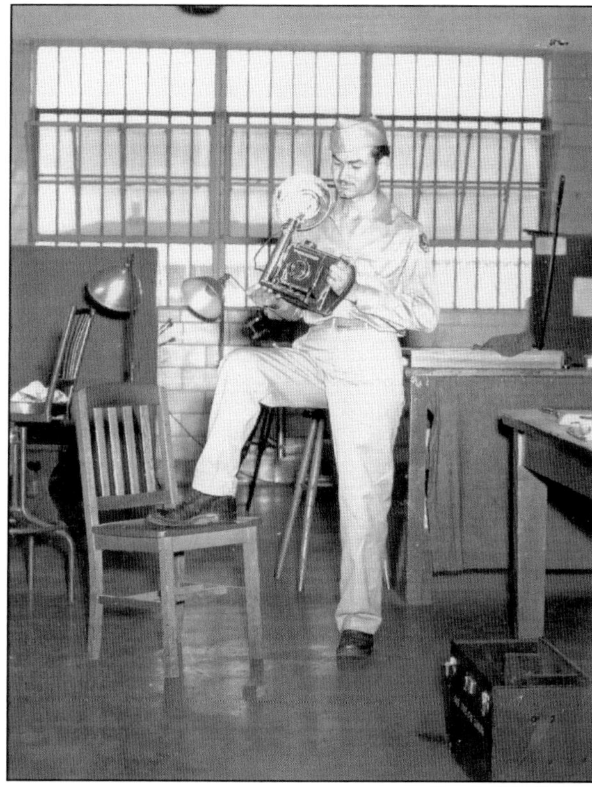

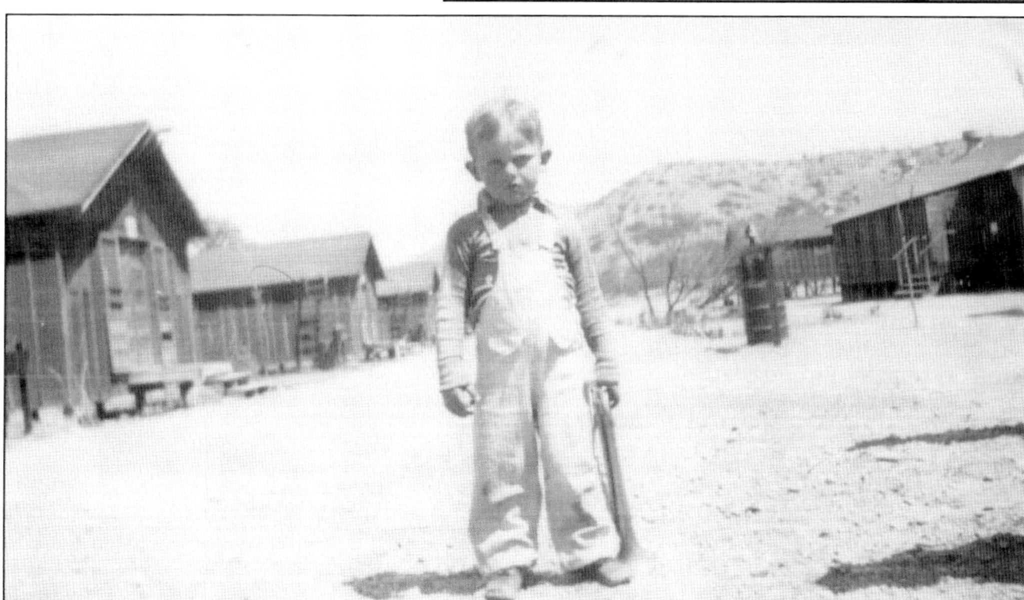

Capt. Ernest H. Bruss served as camp commander in many southern Arizona camps. His wife, young son, and young daughter lived with him in the camps. Here, his son Ernie Jr. poses with his bugle at Camp SCS-19-N, Duncan, Arizona/Virden, New Mexico. The enduring legacy of the CCC includes the children and future generations of its personnel, who benefitted from the education and principles learned by their family members while serving in the CCC. (EB.)

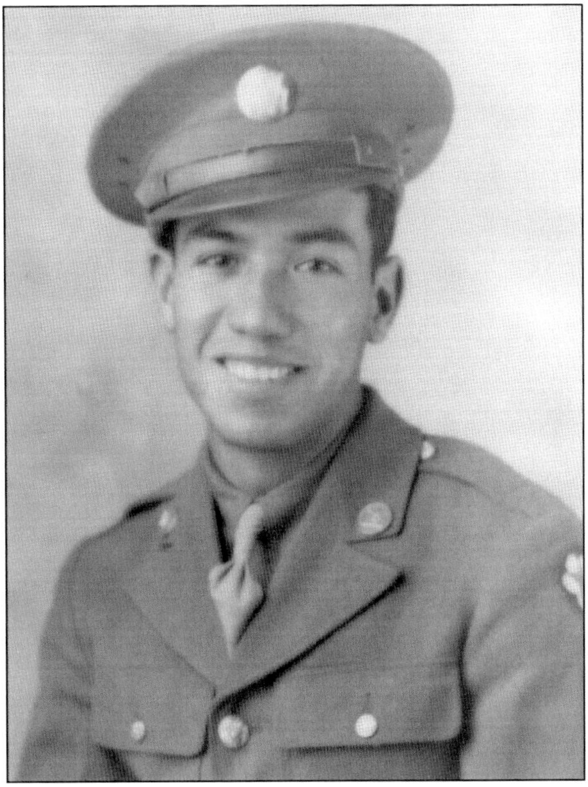

Once the country went to war, many enrollees were drafted or volunteered for the military. Enrollees were physically fit and had already learned basic military discipline and procedures, how to adapt to camp life, and safe work procedures and basic cleanliness, so they were ready for military life. Many enrollees had already learned skills the military needed, such as cooking, radio operation, truck driving, road and bridge construction, and explosives work. Tomas H. Vega, pictured in 1942, served honorably throughout the war in the 49th Engineers Combat Battalion and the 359th Engineer General Servie Regiment. (THV.)

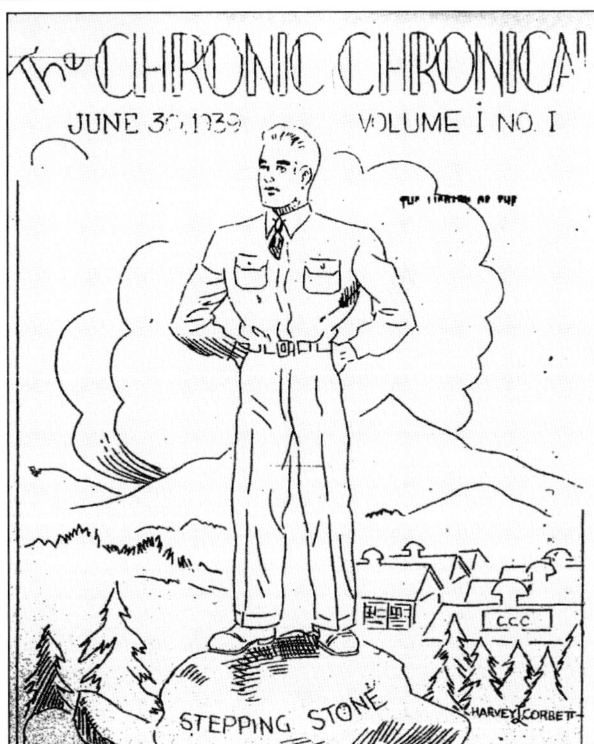

Service in the CCC was frequently a stepping-stone toward achievements later in life, as depicted in this camp newspaper illustration by enrollee and surveyor Harvey Corbett from Camp SCS-19, St. David. The work projects taught the enrollees valuable job, teamwork, and leadership skills. The educational program taught them academic subjects, such as reading and mathematics, as well as job skills, such as typing and blacksmithing. Living with other enrollees under the guidance of the US Army taught them social skills and discipline. The proficiencies and principles developed in the CCC were vital to the enrollees' future successes. (AC.)

Appendix I

Arizona CCC Statistics, April 1933 to June 30, 1942

Men Employed	
Total of Arizona Men Given Employment	41,362
Arizona Juniors and Veterans	17,407
Arizona Indians	19,520
Arizona Officers and Supervisors	4,435
Total of Individuals from All States Who Worked in Arizona	52,905
Camps	
Average Number of Camps per Year	31
Financial	
Total Obligations in Arizona (estimated)	$58,814,534
Allotments to Dependents by Enrollees (estimated)	$3,710,532
Work Accomplished	
Trees Planted	9,246,506
Fire Lookout Towers Constructed	45
Fire Pre-suppression, Prevention, and Fighting (man-days)	124,567
Fences Constructed (miles)	7,030
Buildings Constructed	1,439
Telephone Lines (miles)	3,559
Truck, Foot, and Horse Trails Constructed (miles)	7,071
Springs Improved; Water Holes and Small Reservoirs Constructed	1,563
Erosion-Control Check Dams Constructed	512,093
Predatory Animals Eliminated	184,239
Education, Guide, and Contact Station Work (man-days)	33,190
Campgrounds and Picnic Grounds Developed (acres)	1,559
Emergency Work (man-days)	48,186

Appendix II

Arizona CCC Camps

Caution is advised: In some cases a camp was known by more than one name. For example, Congress Junction was also called Kirkland and Date Creek. From time to time, the beginning date for a camp varied by as much as three days from one government report to another. A = Army; BR = Bureau of Reclamation; CP = County Park; DF = Department of Forestry; DG = Division of Grazing; DSES = Division of Soil Erosion Service; DSP = Department of State Parks; F = National Forest; FWS = Fish & Wildlife Service; G = Department of Grazing; MA = Municipal Area; NM = National Monument; NP = National Park; SCS = Soil Conservation Service; SES = Soil Erosion Service; SP = State Park

Camp	Company	Beginning	Ending
A-1 Fort Huachuca	2871C	8-27-35	1-15-36
BR-13 Yuma	835	11-6-35	5-5-36?
	835	11-2-36	5-6-37?
	2860	10-14-37	
	794	11-19-38	10-5-39?
	2833	10-11-39	5-7-42
BR-14 Papago Park	805	10-31-35	6-4-36?
	2864	10-12-36	6-2-37
BR-17 Parker Dam	1849	11-6-35	1-12-36

BR-18 Upper Parker Dam	2833	11-6-35	4-20-36
BR-19 Tempe	2544	10-24-35	3-38
	2849	1-12-36	3-31-38
BR-74 Yuma	847	11-1-37	6-5-38?
	3832	10-18-39	6-30-41
	3832	10-18-40	7-1-41
DF-30 Tucson	1838	11-9-34	5-15-35?
DF-41 Safford	1839	11-3-34	5-17-35?
DF-42 Tucson	1838	7-13-34	11-9-34?
DF-74 Safford	1839	7-30-34	11-3-34?
DG-8 Yava	2541	10-24-35	1-5-36
	1849	1-13-36	5-2-37
DG-44 Pipe Spring	2557	10-30-35	10-5-39
DG-45 St. George, UT	2558	10-27-35	8-21-39
DG-46 Round Valley	2865	8-21-35	6-30-38?
	340	7-12-38	6-5-39
DG-47 Congress Junction	2854	8-17-35	5-5-36
	852	10-16-36	5-2-37
DG-48 Winkelman	2859	8-20-35	4-15-37
DG-49 Eloy	2540	10-24-35	1-11-36
DG-50 Slick Rock	2850	8-20-35	8-23-37
DG-61 Teague Springs	2854	11-4-36	10-27-39
DG-66 Duncan	2850	8-23-37	6-23-38
DG-109 Buckeye	847	10-7-38	8-10-40
DG-133, G-133 Kingman	340	6-5-39	6-25-41?
	4812	6-25-41	5-13-42
F-3 Blue	842	6-11-33	5-8-34
	842	10-27-34	5-19-35
	842	11-1-35	5-23-36
	842	11-26-36	6-2-37
	842	10-10-37	6-1-38
	842	10-25-38	5-21-39
	842	10-21-39	5-19-40
	842	10-25-40	5-25-41
	842	10-25-41	1-42
F-4 Springerville	847	5-27-33	10-14-33
F-5 Schultz Pass	821	5-28-33	11-2-33
	821	5-1-34	10-29-34
	821	5-19-35	11-7-35
	821	5-1-36	10-19-36
	821	5-15-37	10-16-37
	821	5-22-38	6-29-38?
	311	7-12-38	10-22-38
	311	5-20-39	10-28-39
F-6 Double Springs	863	6-2-33	11-1-33
	863	5-1-34	10-29-34
	863	5-14-35	11-1-35
	863	6-1-36	10-16-36
F-9 Wood Springs	860	6-3-33	11-1-33
F-10 Portal/Cave Creek	865	6-1-33	4-29-34?
	2870	10-6-38	3-42
F-11 Sonoita	852	6-1-33	11-19-33
F-12 Douglas/Rucker Canyon	1826V	7-11-33	4-30-34
	830	10-27-34	5-16-35?
	2870	5-15-37	10-6-38
F-13 Fort Huachuca/ Sunnyside	861	6-3-33	4-13-34
	1841	7-17-34	10-21-35
F-14 Safford	805	5-25-33	11-1-33
	805	5-15-34	10-31-34
F-15 Pima	1830V	7-12-33	5-9-34
F-16 Globe/Pinal Mountain	806	5-23-33	5-21-35?
	2849	7-20-35	1-12-36
	2855	6-5-37	5-22-38

	2855	10-15-38	5-27-39
	2855	10-13-39	5-17-40
	2855	10-12-40	7-41
	807	11-17-41	3-42
F-18 Groom Creek	820	5-28-33	12-1-33
	820	5-1-34	11-5-34
	820	5-15-35	10-22-35
	2870	5-16-36	10-29-36
	2847	5-16-37	9-30-37
	3320?	5-22-38?	10-25-38?
F-19 Thumb Butte	1823V	7-12-33	12-1-33
	822	5-1-34	10-29-34
	822	5-19-35	11-3-35
	822	5-22-37	10-31-37
F-19 Fairgrounds (Prescott)	835	5-5-36	11-2-36
	822	10-31-37	6-24-41
	1826V	6-28-41	7-24-42?
F-20 Walnut Creek	822	5-29-33	12-1-33
F-21 Winslow	823	5-29-33	11-2-33
F-22 McNary/Los Burros	898	6-3-33	11-15-33
	823	5-3-34	11-5-34
	823		5-18-35
	862	5-8-36	10-16-36
	862	5-16-37	10-19-38
F-23 Payson/Indian Garden	807	5-24-33	11-1-33
	807	5-1-34	10-29-34
	807	5-16-35	10-25-35
	807	5-15-36	10-30-36
	807	5-29-37	10-8-37
F-24 Young	864	6-13-33	11-2-33
F-25 Tonto Basin (Sunflower)	1812	10-22-33	6-14-34?
	841	11-17-34	6-13-35
F-27 Bellemont	851	5-25-33	10-31-33
F-28 Williams	848	5-26-33	10-31-33
	1826V	4-30-34	10-27-34
	1838	5-16-35	8-16-35?
	2833	4-30-36	10-22-36
	2848?	7-23-37	10-23-37
	3346	5-26-38	10-22-38
	3348	5-14-39	10-21-39
	3348	5-5-40	10-12-40
F-29 Globe/A Cross Ranch	864	11-1-33	5-15-34?
	898	11-2-34	5-9-35
	807	10-23-35	5-15-36
	807	10-30-36	5-29-37
	2881	7-19-37	5-21-38
F-30 Tucson/Madera Canyon	848	10-31-33	5-14-34?
	1826V	5-21-35	5-16-37
	2848	10-23-37	5-28-38
F-32 Clear Creek/Sedona	860	11-1-33	5-1-34
	860	11-5-34	5-15-35
	821	11-7-35	5-1-36
	821	10-19-36	5-15-37
	821	10-16-37	5-22-38
	311	10-22-38	5-20-39
	311	10-28-39	6-30-40
	311	11-30-40	4-16-41
	822	1-4-42	5-21-42
F-33 Mayer	822	12-1-33	5-1-34
	822	10-29-34	5-19-35
	822	11-3-35	5-22-37
	3320	10-25-38	6-30-39
	3320	11-11-39	6-29-40
	3320	11-15-40	6-21-41

F-34 Cave Creek/Ashdale	851	10-31-33	4-30-34?
	851	11-3-34	5-16-35?
	807	10-8-37	5-18-40
	807	11-3-40	5-23-41
F-35 Clarkdale/Clear Creek	821	11-2-33	5-1-34
	821	10-29-34	5-19-35
	863	10-16-37	5-28-38
	863	10-22-38	5-27-39
	863	10-28-39	5-11-40
	863	11-17-40	5-17-41
F-36 Miami	823	11-4-33	5-3-34
	823	10-25-34	5-17-35
F-38 Tonto Basin	807	11-1-33	5-1-34
	807	10-29-34	5-16-35
F-39 Verde No. 1	820	12-1-33	5-1-34
	820	11-5-34	5-15-35
	1840	7-24-37	5-22-38
F-41 Noon Creek	805	11-1-33	5-15-34
	3346	10-22-38	6-27-39
	2848	10-14-39	6-28-40
	2848	10-19-40	6-22-41
F-42 Tucson	832	11-17-33	5-31-34?
F-45 Miami	898	11-15-33	4-30-34?
	805	11-1-34	5-27-35
F-46 Stockton Pass	2855	8-20-35	5-16-36
	2855	10-29-36	6-5-37
	862	10-16-37	12-19-37
F-47 Turkey Creek	2870	8-21-35	5-16-36
	2870	10-29-36	5-15-37
F-48 Eagle Creek	2857	8-20-35	12-15-37
F-51 Beaver Creek	863	11-1-33	5-1-34
	863	10-29-34	5-14-35
	863	11-1-35	6-1-36
	863	10-16-36	5-19-37
F-53 Hereford	827	11-3-33	5-30-34
F-54 Springerville/ Buffalo Crossing	842	5-8-34	10-27-34
	842	5-19-35	11-1-35
	842	5-23-36	10-26-36
	842	6-2-37	10-10-37
	842	6-1-38	10-25-38
	842	5-21-39	10-21-39
	842	5-19-40	10-25-40
	842	5-25-41	10-25-41
F-55 Alpine	1830V	5-10-34	10-10-35
	862	5-22-35	10-25-34
F-62 Lynx Creek	860	5-1-34	11-5-34
	860	5-19-35	10-21-35
	2855	5-16-36	10-29-36
	2861	5-16-37	10-23-37
F-63 Flux Canyon	852	11-24-33	10-7-34?
	862	10-17-34	5-22-35
F-64 Peña Blanca	2847	12-7-35	5-16-37
	3348	10-19-38	5-14-39
	3348	10-21-39	5-5-40
	4812	10-16-40	6-24-41
F-65 Juan Miller	862	10-23-35	5-8-36
	862	10-21-36	5-16-37
F-74 Safford/Columbine	805	5-28-35	10-31-35?
	2855	5-22-38	10-15-38
	2855	5-27-39	10-13-39
	2855	5-17-40	10-12-40
F-75 Pivot Rock	863	5-19-37	10-16-37
	863	5-28-38	10-22-38

	863	5-27-39	11-28-39
	863	5-11-40	11-1-40
	863	5-17-41	11-1-41
	822	5-21-42	7-23-42?
F-76 Greer	2848	5-28-38	
	2848	5-27-39	10-14-39
	2848	6-28-40	10-19-40
F-77 East Verde	807	5-18-40	11-3-40
	807	5-23-41	11-7-41
F-78 Chevalon	3346	6-27-39	3-41?
	3804	4-30-41	11-41
F-79 Walnut Creek	3320	6-30-39	11-11-39
	3320	6-29-40	11-15-40
F-80 Flagstaff	311	6-30-40	11-30-40
	311	4-16-41	6-24-41?
	822	6-24-41	1-4-42
FWS-1 Parker Dam	3840	9-14-41	7-42?
G-109 Arlington	847	11-17-41	5-42
G-135 Short Creek	1820	4-16-40	7-1-41
G-136 C A Bar Ranch	1814	10-4-39	8-10-40
G-137 Solomonsville	2854	10-27-39	5-42
G-138 Ajo	1820	11-14-39	4-17-40
G-170 Fredonia	847	8-10-40	11-13-41
G-173 Antelope Valley	1814	8-10-40	11-6-41
NM-1 Petrified Forest NM	831	7-3-34	5-6-36?
	805	10-11-36	7-30-38?
NM-2 & NP-9 Chiricahua NM/NP	828	6-7-34	6-25-40
NM-2 & NP-8 Petrified Forest NM/NP	3342	8-2-38	6-21-41?
	1837	6-22-41	3-7-42
NM-5 & NP-12 Flagstaff Area National Monuments	3345	8-2-38	4-30-41?
	3838	5-10-41	3-21-42
NP-1 Grand Canyon NP North Rim	818	5-30-33	10-17-33
	818	5-16-34	10-22-34
	818	6-8-35	9-28-35
	818	5-18-36	10-15-36
	2833	6-17-37	10-17-37
	2833	5-21-38	10-28-38
NP-2 Grand Canyon NP South Rim	819	5-29-33	7-21-42
NP-3 Grand Canyon NP Phantom Ranch	818	10-15-33	5-15-34
	818	10-22-34	6-8-35
	818	9-28-35	5-18-36
NP-4 Grand Canyon NP South Rim	847	10-18-34	10-31-37
	4814	10-16-40	6-30-41
NP-5 Grand Canyon NP Desert View	2543	10-25-35	1-36
	2833	1-36?	5-26-36
	2833	10-24-36	6-17-37
	2833	10-17-37	5-20-38
NP-6 Grand Canyon NP North Rim	3318	7-14-38	10-28-38
	3318	5-28-39	10-21-39
	3318	6-3-40	10-12-40
SCS-1/DSES-1 Duncan	1840	7-11-34	7-24-37
SCS-2/DSES-2 Pima	852	10-7-34	10-15-36
SCS-3/SES-3 Safford	848	10-7-34	8-24-37
SCS-4 U Diamond Ranch	2858	7-22-35	6-13-36
SCS-5 CA Ranch	2863	7-28-35	10-28-36

SCS-7 Joy Valley	2848	8-6-35	7-8-37
SCS-8 Thatcher	2860	7-22-35	1-11-36
SCS-9 Teague Springs	2861	7-22-35	10-20-36
SCS-10 Black Rock (Fort Thomas)	2856	7-22-35	6-30-38
SCS-11 Sanchez	2867	7-23-35	10-11-36
SCS-12 Buckeye	2869	8-20-35	1-11-36
SCS-13 Apache Pass	2894	8-20-35	7-8-37
SCS-14 San Simon	2881	8-20-35	7-19-37
SCS-15 Rillito	2852	8-5-35	3-31-37
SCS-18 Naco	3839	8-24-35	7-12-37
SCS-19 St. David	3840	8-13-35	10-1-39
SCS-20 Apache Junction	2864	8-5-35	10-12-36
SCS-21 Randolph Park	2858	6-14-36	
SCS-22 Cave Creek	2863	10-28-36	10-6-38
SCS-23 Slick Rock	848	8-24-37	
	368	7-19-38	10-6-39
SCS-24 Rucker Canyon	2863	10-6-38	7-20-34
	2863	1-13-41	5-16-41
SCS-25 Solomon	368	10-6-39	10-40
	4813	10-13-40	6-42?
SCS-26 Patagonia	3840	10-1-39	9-13-41
SCS-27 John A. Thompson Ranch	2863	7-20-40	1-31-41
	863	5-17-41	3-42?
SP-1 & MA-1 Randolph Park	1809	10-17-33	7-1-34
	858	10-31-34	6-13-35
	3318	11-1-38	5-28-39
	3318	10-23-39	6-17-40
SP-3 & MA-2 South Mountain Park	831	11-22-33	7-3-34
	874	10-26-34	6-4-35?
	2545	10-24-35	
	818	10-17-36	
	1826V	6-30-38	6-28-41
SP-4 South Mountain Park	830	11-2-33	6-10-34
	864	10-8-34	5-9-35
	2542	10-24-35	1-10-36?
	2860	1-11-36	10-14-37
SP-5 Papago Park	874	10-17-33	7-3-34
	1826V	10-26-34	5-21-35
SP-6/DSP-6 (DSP-1) & CP-1 Tucson Mtn. Park/ Manville Wells	828	11-17-33	6-6-34?
	1837	8-1-34	7-1-35
	2853	7-21-35	5-6-36?
	2861	10-20-36	5-16-37
	1826V	5-16-37	6-30-38
	2833	11-1-38	6-2-39?
	1837	10-21-39	5-19-40
	1837	11-3-40	6-22-41
SP-7 Rodeo Park	858	10-15-33	5-8-34
SP-8 & CP-2 Hualapai Mtn. Park	830	6-10-34	10-26-34
	1837	7-1-35	10-20-39
	1837	5-19-40	11-3-40
SP-9 Hualapai Mountain Park	874	7-3-34	10-25-34
SP-10 Colossal Cave	858	5-9-34	10-31-34
	2851	8-20-35	9-30-37
SP-11 Saguaro NF	2862	7-20-35	5-1-38

Sources: US War Department, Location and Strength of CCC Companies, 1933–1942, NARAMD RG 35 530/65/22/04/05 E-108; US BLM (Grazing Service), CCC, Camp Histories, 1933–1945, NARACO RG 49 Entry 5 Box 22; L.A. Gleyre & C.N. Alleger, *History of the Civilian Conservation Corps in Colorado*, 1936; Audretsch, *Shaping the Park and Saving the Boys*; Audretsch, *We Still Walk in Their Footprint.*

Bibliography

Audretsch, Robert W. *Shaping the Park and Saving the Boys: The Civilian Conservation Corps at Grand Canyon, 1933–1942*. Indianapolis, IN: Dog Ear Publishing, 2011.

———. *We Still Walk in Their Footprint: The Civilian Conservation Corps in Northern Arizona, 1933–1942*. Indianapolis, IN: Dog Ear Publishing, 2013.

Civilian Conservation Corps camp newspapers. www.crl.edu

Cohen, Stan. *The Tree Army: A Pictorial History of the Civilian Conservation Corps, 1933–1942*. Missoula, MT: Pictorial Histories Publishing Co., 1980.

Collins, William S. *The New Deal in Arizona*. Phoenix, AZ: Arizona State Parks Board, 1999.

Hunt, Sharon E. *Vail and Colossal Cave Mountain Park*. Charleston, SC: Arcadia Publishing, 2007.

Melzer, Richard. *Coming of Age in the Great Depression: The Civilian Conservation Corps Experience in New Mexico, 1933–1942*. Las Cruces, NM: Yucca Tree Press, 2000.

Moore, Robert J. *The Civilian Conservation Corps in Arizona's Rim Country: Working in the Woods*. Reno, NV: University of Nevada Press, 2006.

Nolte, M. Chester, ed. *Civilian Conservation Corps: The Way We Remember It, 1933–1942*. Paducah, KY: Turner Publishing Company, 1990.

Official Annual, 1936, Tucson District. 8th Corps Area, Civilian Conservation Corps. Baton Rouge, LA: Direct Advertising Co., 1936.

Otis, Alison T., et al. *The Forest Service and the Civilian Conservation Corps: 1933–42*. Washington, DC: US Dept. of Agriculture, Forest Service, [1986]. www.nps.gov

Paige, John C. *The Civilian Conservation Corps and the National Park Service, 1933–1942: An Administrative History*. National Park Service, US Department of the Interior, 1985. www.nps.gov

Pfaff, Christine E. *Bureau of Reclamation's Civilian Conservation Corps Legacy*. Denver, CO: US Bureau of Reclamation, US Department of the Interior, 2010.

Purvis, Louis Lester. *The Ace in the Hole: A Brief History of Company 818 of the Civilian Conservation Corps*. Columbus, GA: Brentwood Christian Press, 1989.

Salmond, John A. *The Civilian Conservation Corps, 1933–1942: A New Deal Case Study*. Durham, NC: Duke University Press, 1967.

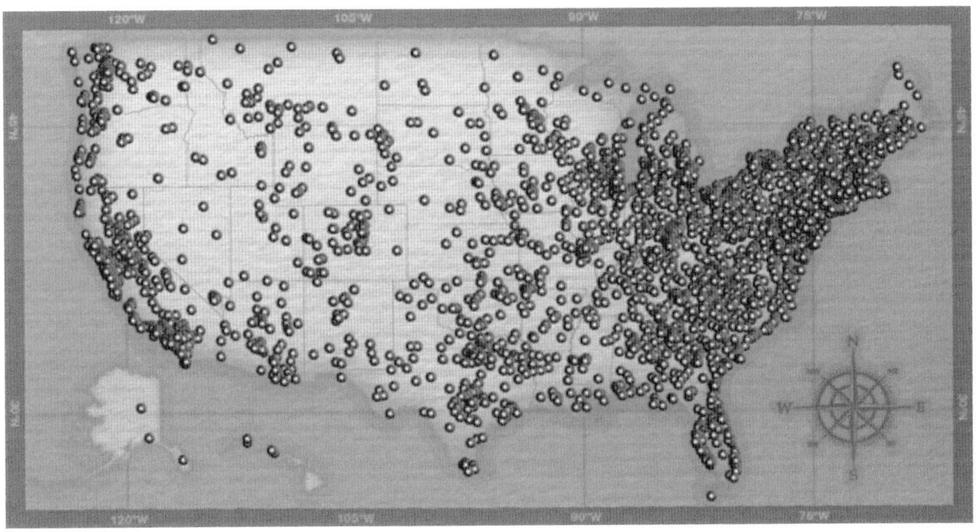